Race and Art Education

Art Education in Practice Series   Marilyn G. Stewart   Editor

Artmaking, Play, and Meaning Making
Assessment in Art Education
Community Art in Action
Differentiated Instruction in Art
Engaging Visual Culture
Rethinking Curriculum in Art
Roots of Art Education Practice
Teaching Meaning in Art Making
Therapeutic Approaches in Art Education
Thinking through Aesthetics
Using the Art Museum

Amelia M. Kraehe and Joni B. Acuff

Race and Art Education

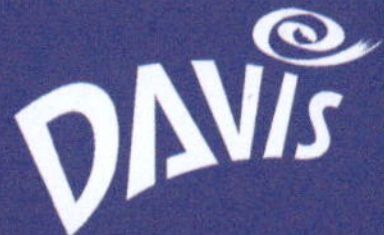

Davis Publications, Inc.   Worcester, Massachusetts   DavisArt.com

Series Preface

Follow an art teacher around for a day—and then stand amazed. At any given moment, the art teacher has a ready knowledge of materials available for making and responding to art; lesson plans with objectives for student learning; resources for extending art learning to other subjects; and the capabilities, interests, and needs of the students in the artroom. Often shifting several times a day from working with preschoolers to those in elementary, middle, and high school, the art teacher decides what to teach, how to teach it, whether students have learned it, and what to do next. The need for rapid decision making in the artroom is relentless.

The art teacher's day continues after school with student learning assessments, curriculum planning, organization of materials, and activities within the school community. Although most teachers want to stay current with new findings and developments in their field, finding time regularly to keep up with the literature is a challenge. *Art Education in Practice* provides the art teacher, museum educator, student, scholar, and layperson with an overview of significant topics in art education theory and practice. The series is designed to meet the needs of art educators who want to think critically about the issues, rationales, and practical implications of accepting curricular proposals, with input from a variety of scholarly and political perspectives.

The series emphasizes informed practice. Each book focuses on a timely, relevant topic from art education literature and advocacy statements, and connects the ideas to the classroom. The goal of the series is to complement the professional libraries of practitioners in the field of art education and, in turn, enhance the art-related lives of their students.

Editor's Introduction

Settling down to write this introduction in mid-February 2021, I did what I do every day as I ease into work—I perused the morning paper and did a quick scan of Facebook.

The paper reported a horrific "Zoom-bombing" that took place during a state university's student Black Caucus meeting. According to the story, several individuals viciously disrupted the meeting, exposing themselves to the student group while screaming racial and homophobic slurs and using white supremacist and anti-Semitic language and symbols.

While disgusting and unsettling, the news of this Zoom attack is consistent with other stories of racial violence coming into our lives daily from all over the world—ongoing signs that hatred festering just beneath the surface of our so-called civil societies has been emboldened and unleashed.

I moved on to Facebook where I was struck by a post in an art teacher group:

> I am teaching about the Harlem Renaissance. I want to be accurate and teach my students about anti-racism. I admit that I am from a small town…and I am naïve about the issues facing my fellow Americans, and I want to be part of the solution and not the problem. Any advice on how to teach my students? I am most likely missing a lot of information, but I would like to start somewhere.

> How can I teach my students about anti-racism through art?

Yes, this seems to be my world these days. In the space of a few minutes, I encounter, first, a report of despicable actions by people stuck in centuries-old racist assumptions and hatred fueled by fear. Immediately following, I read a sincere request from a teacher who sees a need to address racism with her students. She recognizes her lack of knowledge and reaches out virtually to colleagues for assistance. In my role of editor of the *Art Education in Practice* series and, more to the point, this book on race and art education, I am especially aware of the persistence of these two phenomena—recurrent stories of racial violence coming in from all parts of the world, alongside repeated calls for action to put an end to racism. It's not that there have not been public calls for action in the past. Over the years they have tended to ebb and flow with media coverage of race-related incidents. Since the summer of 2020, however, they have reached a higher and steadier pitch.

I suspect that it was the events of that summer that moved the teacher on Facebook in her desire to be "part of the solution and not the problem" and to "start somewhere."

Beginning in late May 2020, millions of people worldwide watched and rewatched the murder of George Floyd. Video showing the horrifying 9 minutes and 29 seconds it took for the 46-year-old Black man to die, helpless, with his neck under the knee of Minneapolis police officer Derek Chauvin, spawned a wave of protests, demonstrations, and rallies against racial injustice and police brutality around the globe. For some, painfully aware of centuries-old wounds, this kind of violence against Black people was all too routine. For others with varying levels of racial literacy, the sight of Chauvin's cool, unfeeling gaze as his knee literally pressed the life from Floyd's body, was finally, it seemed, enough. Silence, complacency, and, thus, continued complicity were no longer options.

Since then, mainstream media coverage of race and racially charged aggression has remained at high volume, along with a steady stream of reported violence. Talk shows, magazine articles, and a new influx of books have addressed race and anti-racism at a far higher rate than in the past. Expressions such as systemic and institutional racism, privilege, white privilege, whiteness, racial justice, restorative justice, and reparations moved from narrower circles of discourse into broader mainstream conversations. The language is new to some but exhaustingly familiar to others.

In the midst of all of this, voices—Black, Brown, White—emerge from many places. Some might resemble the art teacher on Facebook—with a low level of racial literacy but an interest in allyship. Others have been at the heart of it for decades. Of those, some may be hopeful, anticipating fresh conversations and, finally, real action, while others feel no reason to believe that this time the conversation will be any different or go any further. There may be others who, over the years, have actively educated themselves and addressed issues of race through listening, reading, talking, and, in some cases, teaching, but within the context of newer conversations, recognize gaps in their understanding. I count myself among this group. As a White college professor, I strive to provide a safe, inclusive space for my students to engage with issues of race, class, gender, and ethnicity, primarily through the artists I introduce and the discussions prompted by their work. I have been sensitive to challenges that confront the few Black and

Brown students in my classes and have sought ways to celebrate diversity and promote empathy. Increasingly, however, I realize that I have been holding back, keeping myself—and my students—at a safe distance from the deeply honest work that needs to be done. Reading the various drafts of this book has been an important catalyst for more introspection. The recent conversations I've held privately with myself and also within a broader public inevitably lead to one conclusion: There will be no genuine movement without a lot of work—individually and collectively.

From what I have witnessed over the years, art educators do not shy away from issues of social justice, long recognizing art's potential to raise awareness of important human concerns. Art teachers are keenly aware of the art room as a space where difficult conversations can happen and minds can be opened. In my own work with teachers to create curriculum around issues of gender and sexual identity, in particular, I have been moved by so many art teachers who have found ways to go really deep with themselves and their students to sort through personal beliefs, assumptions, and actions. I believe that a similar inclination motivates art educators when it comes to discussions of race and racism.

Amelia (Amy) Kraehe and Joni Acuff make it clear that we all start at different points on the path of anti-racist pedagogy, with different histories and varying degrees of understanding. The authors offer an empathic, firm hand as they present the history of racial inequity and the complexities of race in culture. This book takes a close look at how visual representations in art and popular culture impact beliefs, values, and behaviors. At its core, though, this is a workbook, scaffolded to guide readers in a process of knowing themselves while envisioning ways to involve their students. In the process of taking readers through the compelling content and reflections, the authors insist that once on the path, there's no getting it "wrong." The whole book is about becoming—trying and retrying. I have a vision of how it will look in the hands of the educators who seek it out, return to it often, marking it up with comments in the margins and sticky notes on its pages. Kraehe and Acuff encourage readers to use it in this way. What becomes increasingly clear as one moves through its pages is that the work we readers do here is of the greatest consequence.

Marilyn G. Stewart

Author Biographies

Amelia M. Kraehe, Ph.D., is Associate Vice President for Equity in the Arts; Co-founder and Co-director of Racial Justice Studio; and Associate Professor of Art and Visual Culture Education at The University of Arizona. She is recognized for her research on arts equity as well as her publications, workshops, podcasts, and public lectures that illuminate the role race, racism, and anti-racism play in art and museum education, visual culture, curriculum, pedagogy, and the professional development of art educators. Amy, as she is called, has received numerous honors and awards for her leadership and scholarly contributions to the field of art education. Her writing, teaching, and curriculum development draw from a rich interdisciplinary background in studio art and art education, urban education, and cultural studies in education, along with a breadth of professional experiences. She taught in public school, museum, and community settings prior to teaching in higher education. Her other books include *The Palgrave Handbook of Race and the Arts in Education* and *Pedagogies in the Flesh: Case Studies on the Embodiment of Sociocultural Differences in Education*.

Joni Boyd Acuff, Ph.D., is Associate Professor of Arts Administration, Education, and Policy at The Ohio State University. Acuff utilizes frameworks such as Critical Race Theory, Critical Multiculturalism, Black Feminist Theory, and Afrofuturism to develop and disseminate pedagogical and curriculum strategies that activate critical race knowledge in art education. Acuff has taught undergraduate and graduate courses such as Critical Analysis of Multicultural Art Education, Social and Cultural Theory in Art and Art Education, Critical Pedagogies of Critical Multiculturalism in Teaching Visual Culture, and Art Education for Children with Special Needs. Acuff has art and art education teaching experience in both traditional and non-traditional classrooms and has taught throughout diverse demographic settings. She has worked extensively with classroom art teachers and art museum educators across the United States, facilitating in-service training, leading professional development workshops, and presenting lectures about anti-racism, Afrofuturism, and abolitionist teaching practices in the art classroom.

Acknowledgments

Books can take years to write. This holds true for *Race and Art Education*, a project we began in 2018. Many people have supported its development along the way, and we wish to express our deepest gratitude. Thank you to *Art Education in Practice* series editor Marilyn Stewart and the dedicated and talented team at Davis Publications who believed in and championed this project from start to finish. In particular, we wish to express gratitude and admiration for Missy Nicholson, Emily Henderson-Sperber, and Julia Wade. The dedication that was demonstrated to complete this project was phenomenal. A special thank you to Amber Coleman for sharing our work with her undergraduate students and providing thoughtful comments on early drafts. We are grateful to Rachel Zollinger for assisting with the final stages of the book. We also thank external reviewers Alina Campana and Kim Cosier for their incisive feedback and encouragement.

We are indebted to the many art education students we have taught over the years, especially those who graciously lent their work to this project. To the brilliant artists whose artworks appear throughout the book, there are few words that describe our humbled spirits. We appreciate your generosity. Many thanks to the scholars, artists, and educators we cited throughout the book, as the research, words, and teachings of these people have guided and deepened our thinking and practice over the years. We want to acknowledge the teachers, mentors, and friends who were supportive of our journey in anti-racist teaching. Especially, a tremendous thank you to the Coalition for Racial Equity in the Arts and Education (crea+e). Their unwavering support and love supplied throughout this project energized us to bring the book to fruition. Thank you to our forebearers, the critical practitioners who blazed the trail that allowed this work to come into being. Finally, a hearty thank you to our family members for their sacrifices made and grace given to support this project. Much love, appreciation, and thanks to you all.

Funding and support for this book was provided by The University of Arizona.

Publisher: Julian Wade
Series Editor: Marilyn Stewart
Senior Editor: Missy Hall Nicholson
Editor: Emily Henderson-Sperber
Design: Tyler Kemp-Benedict and Douglass Scott
Art Director: Julia Wade
Proofreader: Piper Morris
Indexing: Ruth Okin

Library of Congress Control Number: 2020951245
ISBN: 978-1-64164-042-8 (print book)
978-1-64164-429-7 (ebook)

10 9 8 7 6 5 4 3
Printed in the United States of America.

Front cover image: Kerry James Marshall, *Untitled*, 2009. Acrylic
on PVC panel, 61 1/8" x 72 7/8" x 3 7/8" (155.25 x 182.8 x 9.8 cm).
© Kerry James Marshall. Courtesy of the artist and Jack Shainman
Gallery, New York.

To all the educators, artists, and visionaries who "go for broke."[1]

Contents

1 James Baldwin, "A Talk to Teachers," in *The Price of the Ticket: Collected Nonfiction, 1948–1985*, 1st ed. (New York: St. Martin's/Marek, 1985), 81.

Chapter 1

Understanding Race and Racism in Art Education

A Journey

Joni *I am from Starkville, Mississippi…a place with no art museums but lots of racists. I was never interested in the visual arts as a teen, or younger, so I can't say that I made any conscious connections between the arts and race. It wasn't until I was 19 and a sophomore in college that I saw art, physically and metaphorically.*

Amy *Hmm…what do you mean by that—physically and metaphorically?*

Joni *Well, my experience and, thus, my perspective was twofold. First, I went on my first museum visit to see art on a megabus trip from Penn State to New York City. The mall of museums was overwhelming and White.*

Amy *Did you perceive those two things as related?*

Joni *I thought, "Is this something that only White folks do? Hmm…who is art for?" Second, when I started creating my own art just weeks later in my university classes, my instinct was to use the process to examine, question, and heal from the racist violence that had been happening at Penn State while I was there in 2001. I saw art as a means for an intervention.*

Amy *That sounds like a paradox.*

Joni *I know! How can art be both white property and my personal tool for destabilizing racial power? These contradictory experiences are at the foundation of my years of research around the relationship between art and race.*

Amy *Like you, Joni, my relationship with art really crystallized in college. After growing up in the suburbs of Atlanta, I attended a small women's college just outside of Boston. The student body was predominantly White and affluent. I was able to take art classes. There were no barriers or prerequisites. Before long, I was hooked. After a few courses, I declared my major as studio art. That meant I would have to take some art history classes.*

Joni *Were those the standard sort of Survey I and Survey II courses?*

Amy *Yes. They covered the world of art from antiquity to the European Renaissance, and from there to the mid-20th century. I would sit in the lecture hall with the large screens that projected images side by side. My professors were world-renowned art historians. From behind the podium, their pale faces glowed from a single overhead spotlight. I viewed them as authorities.*

They were the keepers of art knowledge. I wrote down everything they said.

I had a racial awakening in that same auditorium. It was when a visiting scholar stood behind the lectern. She delivered two or three lectures on the intellectual life, art, and architecture of ancient Timbuktu in west Africa. It was remarkable.

Joni Why do you say that?

Amy First of all, it was the only time I learned of great art made by Africans. Of course the professors and the textbook discussed Egypt. But they cast Egyptians as though they were not Africans. It was as though Egypt were cut off from the rest of the continent, a dismemberment of sorts. I now know this is a characteristic of Western art history's worldview. It's a story of art that has been constructed and repeated over time. Most often Egypt is noted for its contributions to European art. Hardly ever is Egyptian culture addressed on its own terms or as part of the rich and diverse artistic achievements of Africa. That stood out to me so clearly at the time, but I didn't have the language then to describe it. It registered in my body and my spirit. I now would call it racial trickery.

Joni As you recall this experience, I am coming to the realization that this is the very reason why I hated art history courses. I was so emotionally disconnected from the material. The professors sure were the "keepers of art knowledge," and the narrative they orchestrated with the art made me feel and believe that I had no place within it. I often wondered why I was even there.

Amy There was another more obvious reason this moment became a racial awakening. The visiting scholar who stood behind the lectern was a Black woman, full-figured just like my mother. What's funny is that I was shocked—by her physical presence as the authority figure and by my surprise in seeing her there. She was both familiar to me and yet strange in this setting. My eyes were wide open that day. She was the embodiment of knowledge, and she commanded the attention and respect of the room. I became aware of how pervasive and unspoken whiteness is in art and my own art education. This was a flashpoint in my learning—totally unexpected and profoundly affective. When learning like that happens, a person becomes more perceptive and critical of norms that mask injustice. I know I was changed by it.

Over the last half century, art education has seen many changes. Art teachers now talk about multiculturalism, popular culture, gender representation, inclusion, and socially engaged art practice along with more traditional themes of self-expression, perspective drawing, elements of art, and principles of design. Our curriculum conversations are multidimensional. No longer focused on gimmicky one-and-done lesson plans, art educators today learn theories and methods that enable them to *teach art as if the world mattered.*[1] Art lessons are about "big ideas" that endure over time and have deep resonance with life beyond the classroom or studio.[2] Many of these developments in art education have been accompanied, if not inspired, by an increased awareness of specific ways in which sociocultural differences influence learning, and the broader social, cultural, economic, and political contexts that make art a dynamic field of practice.

Despite these changes, there remains a third rail for many art educators—topics that are too emotionally and politically charged to go near. Having been engaged in art and art education for more than 50 years combined, we believe that third rail is race—or more precisely, racism. We have written this book so that we might share with others the research, frameworks, stories, examples, vocabulary, and strategies that we ourselves have found most fruitful. It reflects our quest to understand how race and racial hierarchies operate in art and art education. The book also reflects our teaching and professional development work in support of art educators in schools, museums, and universities. The book is filled with ideas and activities from our classes, workshops, and presentations.

Each chapter addresses race head-on, providing readers the tools needed to step closer and take on the third rail by overcoming the habit of avoidance that makes us all unwitting accomplices to racism. At the end of the journey, you will understand what race is and how it functions. It will be easier to recognize racism in art education, and you will be better prepared to deliberate and take action to remedy racial inequities in and through your own art education practice.

We believe in the pedagogical power of dialogue. We also recognize that dialogue is not easy, predictable, or always fruitful. Throughout our careers as art educators and in the writing of this book, we, Joni and Amelia (Amy), have relied on dialogue to move us forward. Our conversations are not solely about communicating our ideas. The conversation is how we work out our ideas. The experience of telling our stories enables us to figure out what we think, to test and discard ideas that are no longer viable, and to formulate new stories that make us more resilient, hopeful, and brave. The dialogue that runs through this chapter mirrors this philosophy and practice. You will learn about us, our backgrounds, and the methods we suggest using when reading this book.

Rules of Engagement

We suggest thinking about this book as an opportunity and provocation to dialogue. So, how do we prepare for such an experience, particularly if this is the first foray into racial dialogue? Some rules for engagement can help set the stage for a successful journey. The following are practices we employ in our classrooms and workshops that have proven helpful. You can, of course, add your own. We offer these suggestions as a starting point:

1. Be Curious.

Race is an old idea. It has roots that date back more than a millennium. Yet many readers of this book are newcomers to talking about race. Maybe you have never discussed racism in an open, straightforward manner, or perhaps you grew up in a family that treated racism as a basic fact of everyday life. Each of us sits somewhere along this spectrum of racial experience, and our understanding of race and racism is tethered to that location.

We have written this book for all readers who desire to know more, to help them extend beyond the tethers. At the same time, we understand that new knowledge can be frightening when it troubles previous conceptions. You might even feel uncomfortable at times as you move through the pages ahead. This means you are doing it right! After all, learning requires that we step out of our routine ways of thinking, doing, and feeling. So remain eager to learn by arming yourself with an attitude of curiosity. This is the best way we know to grow.

2. Be Humble.

We all come from a particular place and time. These leave indelible impressions on us and make us who we are. Thus, no two people have the exact same experience and no individual can perceive the world as it is from every possible angle. As much as our backgrounds provide us with knowledge and know-how to navigate the world, they also limit what we can perceive. By reading and listening to the stories of others, we can learn to perceive more than would be possible on our own. But this requires that we be receptive rather than reactive.

Have you ever tried to communicate something sensitive—maybe it was something that happened to you or a feeling you had—with someone who acted as though they were listening, but you could tell they were just being polite and waiting their turn to interject, to explain away your concerns, or to fix everything for you? This reactive posture can be a hindrance to understanding race and addressing racism. It reminds us of "mansplaining," an expression that arose from a patterned behavior women experience. When attempting to speak, often a woman will be interrupted or receive unsolicited explanations from a man. This phenomenon is rooted in a power dynamic whereby the man projects authority and superiority of knowledge over the woman, even when she is speaking about her own experience or expertise. It is a learned form of dominance in a patriarchal society where men's voices are valued more than women's.

Whitesplaining is similar to mansplaining. It is when the experiences, stories, and perspectives of racially marginalized people are discounted, overly simplified, or explained away by members of the dominant racial group. We have found that when learning about race and racism, listening is important but humility is even more so. A humble attitude can help overcome learned habits, like mansplaining and whitesplaining, that can prevent us from receiving and benefiting from the wisdom of others.

3. Be Real.

Are you familiar with the saying "Keeping it real"? It is a colloquial phrase that refers to intentional acts of raw honesty and genuineness. It speaks to the importance of authenticity, regardless of social and/or emotional consequences. In order to benefit from this book, it is important to "keep it real" with yourself. In a dialogue, it is critical that participants be willing to recognize and admit their own flaws, biases, and possible prejudices. Whether intentional or not, everyone has biases. This is a fact of being human.

Enter this book as the person you *are*, not the person you *want* to be. Dig deep into your mind and heart with sincerity and answer the tough questions honestly. Consider the information without defense. No one is standing behind you, watching, ready to judge. It is just you and your own personal work as an educator. With such authentic engagement with the content, you are giving yourself a better opportunity to grow and become the person you intend to be.

4. Be Vulnerable.

Any kind of personal examinations that center on race can be a scary task. Feelings of fear, guilt, resentment, and despair are actually common responses to a growing understanding of the construction of race. However, this response too often leads to racial inertia, a tendency to sit safely on the sidelines doing little and remaining unmoved as others engage vulnerably in the discomforting yet ultimately rewarding work of racial dialogue. To move forward, it is important to resist the urge to opt out. Instead, acknowledge your feelings when they arise; they offer points of departure for personal learning and transforming relationships with students and colleagues.

To benefit from participation in a racial dialogue requires that we be vulnerable. This means submitting to the emotional roller-coaster that goes hand in hand with deconstructing a racialized identity. Nevertheless, just like at the amusement park, when the roller-coaster stops, your feet are always planted firmly back on the ground. Respect this process, regardless of how bumpy or uncomfortable it may become.

Avoiding Common Pitfalls

Many readers may be new to thinking and talking about race. We find that there are five common pitfalls to be mindful of and we revisit these throughout the book:

1. De-centering Race

When talking about social justice, equality, or equity, it has become commonplace to conflate concepts like race, culture, ethnicity, diversity, and multiculturalism. Although these concepts have connections to one another and can be entangled in many ways, each actually has its own definition and conceptual frameworks that can be used to guide justice-oriented practices in art education. While reading this book, it will be helpful to remember that we center race and racism, not because they matter more than other social systems but because they all too often are avoided, minimized, and misunderstood in art education and in art teacher education. We take up Critical Race Theory (CRT) as an overarching theoretical frame for the book. A framework is a set of ideas that enables a person to perceive, articulate, and reflect on a phenomenon. CRT is a powerful framework for understanding, critiquing, and responding to racism as an endemic feature of modern life in the U.S. and beyond.[3] Our approach to race in art education is multidisciplinary and grounded in cultural studies, psychology, sociology, history, art, and education research.

2. Vocabulary and Definitions

At various points throughout this book, we use the words *whiteness* and *White people*. It might be tempting to think of whiteness and White people as one and the same thing, but they are not. Nor are they synonyms. Chapter 2 discusses these terms and their definitions in detail. Nevertheless, we caution readers not to conflate White people and whiteness.

3. Naming

In some communities, the subject matter of race and racism would be perceived as controversial. Even uttering the word *race* is, for many people, taboo. Yet it is impossible to identify, much less address, a thing that cannot be named. Wanting to be polite and being quick to take offense are stumbling blocks to engaging in racial dialogue.

4. Getting Stuck

Various psychologists have established frameworks for understanding the different phases involved in the development of racial identities.[4] During these phases, there may be feelings of guilt, anger, frustration, or even denial. It is important to avoid sitting with these feelings for too long. What you find out about your privileges and/or disadvantages during the phases of racial identity development may run counter to your desired beliefs or ideas about yourself. However, as you read through this book and come upon possibly identity jolting information, remember that "guilt" or "anger" is just a feeling that is fleeting; it is not a place to live. Getting "stuck" is a stumbling block that could sabotage your personal and professional growth. Keep moving forward.

5. Complacency

Becoming too self-content with where you are in your journey toward a critical understanding of race is perhaps the greatest pitfall. Reading this book is not so much an achievement as it is a starting point. The knowledge and know-how that fill its pages require practice. We encourage readers to try out the strategies, iconography, vocabulary, and concepts in the classroom as soon as possible. Don't wait until you have read the whole book to talk with colleagues and friends about what you are reading. Above all, take action! Use the tools provided here to identify where and how you can make positive change. And when you do get comfortable with the material, continue with quarterly check-ins with the book to assess your own progress and to guard against the tenacity of old habits.

Although we have noted these pitfalls as most common, we encourage you to stay alert and note additional stumbling blocks that may inhibit you from integrating some of the information offered in this book. Reflect on feelings of resistance; note moments where you may not feel you are as engaged as you may want to be in the material. What is happening mentally and emotionally? While this book serves as an educational resource for art teaching and learning, it is also a resource for critical self-reflection as well as self-actualization.

How to Use This Book

We think of the art classroom as a racial ecology that mirrors many of the same racial inequalities found in society. It also consists of opportunities to advance racial and social justice. This book aims to help art educators acquire theoretical concepts, factual information, and critical capacities to understand the ways race and racism influence their classrooms, students, teaching, and the broader worlds they inhabit. Chapter 2 introduces readers to how race was (and still is) socially constructed by human beings to serve political and economic purposes and how racism was (and still is) embedded within a wide array of vital social institutions. Chapter 3 examines race in visual culture, pointing out the use of racial codes in visual representations that circulate in art and popular culture. Chapter 4 focuses on how race and racism impact the lives of students on a daily basis and affect learning. Chapter 5 looks at how race tacitly shapes art teachers' biographies and professional practice, and presents an abolitionist approach to anti-racist practice in art education. Chapter 6 closes the book with a discussion of four guiding principles for anti-racist art pedagogy as well as supporting learning activities for students that are inspired and informed by contemporary artists whose creative practices challenge racism in art and visual culture. A visual racial literacy glossary is provided at the end of the book.

 Race and Art Education by Amelia M. Kraehe and Joni B. Acuff

We encourage you to approach the book with intention. Be an active reader: highlight words and phrases to reflect on, take notes and ask questions in the margins, dog-ear the pages where you sense your comfort being disturbed. In our experience, these are "sweet spots," places that might warrant a second or third reading. We recommend that you read *all of* the sidebars, as they are an integral part of the journey contained within the book's pages. Consider assigning the text for a book club meeting for you and fellow art teachers, or suggest it to an administrator as a text that could guide a professional development seminar. Ultimately, it is also our hope that you will use this text to reimagine art education as a practice that contributes to the creation of a more just world.

Notes

1   Paul E. Bolin, "Teaching Art as if the World Mattered," *Art Education 52*, no. 4 (1999): 4-5, doi: 10.1080/00043125.1999.11650862.

2   Tom Anderson and Melody K Milbrandt, *Art for Life: Authentic Instruction in Art* (Boston: McGraw-Hill, 2004); Marilyn G. Stewart and Sydney R. Walker, *Rethinking Curriculum in Art* (Worcester, MA: Davis Publications, 2005).

3   Amelia M. Kraehe, Rubén Gaztambide-Fernández, and B. Stephen Carpenter, II (eds.), *The Palgrave Handbook of Race and the Arts in Education* (Cham, Switzerland: Springer, 2018).

4   William E. Cross, Jr., "The Negro to Black Conversion Experience: Toward a Psychology of Black Liberation," *Black World 20*, no. 9 (1971): 13-27; William E. Cross, Jr., Thomas A. Parham, and Janet E. Helms, "The Stages of Black Identity Development: Nigrescence Models," in R. Jones, ed., *Black Psychology*, 3rd ed., (San Francisco: Cobb and Henry, 1991): 319-338; Janet E. Helms, ed., *Black and White Racial Identity: Theory, Research and Practice* (Westport, CT: Greenwood Press, 1990); and Beverly D. Tatum, *Why Are All the Black Kids Sitting Together in the Cafeteria? And Other Conversations about Race* (New York: Basic Books, 1997).

Chapter 2

Race: It's Not so Black and White

> "Many individuals have been taught that in polite society, it is not okay to acknowledge difference."
>
> —Najuana Lee[1]

If you have been to a grocery store, shopping center, place of worship, school, park, or any public space where children are present, at some point, you have likely witnessed an adult whisper to a curious child, "Shh…don't say that out loud," or "That's not nice," or "It's not polite to ask that," as the child inquisitively questions a stranger's physical appearance that is either dissimilar to their own or different from what they deem "normal."

Questions about gender, sexual orientation, religion, ability, and race seem to come up for kids at the most inconvenient times for adults. But among that list of identity markers, race is often avoided, even in settings where education is the goal. In schools, teachers of all races exhibit fear and avoidance when curious learners ask unassuming questions about race or racialized experiences.[2] To overcome this tendency, we need to face that fear head on, starting with the basics—what is race?

What Is Race?

This book adopts a standpoint that race is a fiction. If you are a sighted person, you might be thinking, "Hold on. I'm not making any-

thing up. Race is as obvious as the color of my skin. I can see it with my own eyes."

We concede that it is likely people always have observed the natural range of human complexions. People come in a variety of colors, with different hair textures and facial characteristics. These observable qualities that result from evolutionary processes are known as *phenotypes*. Such phenotypical attributes may seem to be self-evident—clear and apparent to anyone looking. But this is not so. Seeing is not simply an anatomical function of the eyes. It is also a cultural practice, one that we as art and visual culture educators take very seriously.

In this chapter, we focus on these key concepts:
- Race as a social construction
- White supremacy
- Racial prejudice
- Institutionalized racism

Learning to See Race

By and large, everyone is influenced by socialization within the family, community, media, and educational institutions. From a young age, people learn from others how to perceive and make sense of the world around them. Directly and indirectly, we all are taught to notice some things while also being taught to misrecognize others. What those are largely depends on the social spheres one inhabits. Race is one of the things that one learns to notice, yet racism is commonly misrecognized.

Metaphors for Unlearning Race

There are three metaphors we want to introduce to help elaborate and illustrate the core idea that although race is an illusion, racism is not. We start by exploring the **myth of race**.

What's in a Name?

Racial categories have shifted over time. They often become codified by the U.S. Census, which is updated by the U.S. government once every 10 years. Check out this interactive infographic to see how racial categories have evolved over 200 years: www.census.gov/data-tools/demo/race/MREAD_1790_2010.html.

Study how race has shifted over the years from 1790 to 2010 using the infographic. What do you notice? What seems odd? What seems familiar? Respond by making your own visual representation of racial construction. Consider how racial construction has been incomplete, adaptive, and remade over time.

Myths are widely held and enacted beliefs and ideas that are false. Examining the myths associated with race will help readers move away from the misconception that race is somehow rooted in biology or nature. This cultural myth is powerful, yet it is untrue. Race is not a product of nature or some divine order of the cosmos. Still, many people believe race is biologically real. Because we recognize the tenacity of myths, we take the time in this chapter to carefully lay out how race is socially constructed by human beings to serve social, political, and economic aims.

The second metaphor we discuss is the **alchemy of racism**. Alchemy is the process of turning base metals into gold. Just as race is a baseless myth, it nonetheless has been given social value and, thus, is made to have real-world consequences. These consequences have had a lingering effect on the way society and its educational and cultural institutions are organized to promote racial inequality. This is the reality of racism. It exists independent of any human actors intentionally or knowingly engaging in racist behavior.

The final metaphor we offer in this chapter is the **three-legged stool of racial inequality**. This metaphor describes the interdependence of three areas of U.S. society—employment, housing, and education—that were designed long ago to produce racialized differences in people's lived experiences and life outcomes from one generation to the next. Artists and art educators are generally well acquainted with the three-legged stool. There are probably tens of thousands of them in art classrooms and studios across the country. Not only is the three-legged stool familiar, it is so ubiquitous that it largely goes unseen—it is normal-ized. Much like racial inequality, the stool is a perennial presence—durable over time and adaptable to changing conditions, so much so that it is taken for granted and regarded not as a choice someone made but as a given that cannot be changed. Resisting normalization of racial inequality is important for art educators because the perpetuation of racism, both in art education and the larger world, depends fore-most on people not being able to see, at least not right away, the manner and mechanisms by which it is structured and given form. Who better to intervene in habits of seeing and not seeing than art educators?

Social Foundations for Art Education

We believe it is essential to understand each of these metaphors. Admittedly, the ideas embedded within them are complex and

likely will be new to many art educators. One might be tempted to skip this chapter, but we discourage that. It lays out important foundations for all art educators, whether they teach or plan to teach in racially diverse settings or more homogeneous ones. These are social foundations of art education for anyone interested in knowing how to teach art with diversity, equity, and inclusion in mind. Indeed, ignoring the history that gave birth to present-day racism is to become an accomplice, contributing to the maintenance of hierarchies of racial difference through art curricula, teaching methods, and assess-ment tools. It would be inaccurate to equate (racial) ignorance, or not-knowing, with (racial) innocence. Ambivalence and refusal to look at difficult histories that so deeply affect how different communities experience life in the United States is an act of *ignore-ance* and a bar-rier to just and equitable art education.[3]

Reflecting on our own personal and profes-sional development, we recognize that the information in this chapter represents critical racial knowledge that we learned over decades and with the support of peers who were on a parallel journey of actively seeking to under-stand how race and racism affected our lives as art teachers and our students' learning.

Illusions of Difference

Some readers may struggle to understand the illusion of race and its material effects. Instead, issues of oppression, marginalization, and prejudice may be seated more in class, gender, religion, ethnicity, or nationality. If this is the case for you, how does the "illusion" of difference (in your context) materialize in real ways?

In what ways are people classified, and how do those classifications align with things like governmental power, political influence, economic growth, etc.? How were you introduced to the power of "difference" and the implications of said differences?

We have taken care to scaffold this historical backdrop to provide entry points for newcomers to critical racial thinking, while also giving readers with prior knowledge of racial histories in the United States and elsewhere a framework and resources to go further in their learning. To support readers in applying the ideas presented here to their own professional development and teaching, we have included question prompts, activities, inspirational and informational quotes, and other artifacts in the sidebars. In the same way we have grown in our understanding of racism and our antiracist teaching practices by revisiting the lessons of history, readers also may benefit from rereading this chapter after having moved through the book.

Biological Mythbusting: Race Is a Social Construction

Time and again, historians and social scientists have debunked the assertion that genetically distinct races exist. Geneticists have joined the chorus of earlier voices to substantiate this truth—that race has no basis in biology and cannot be found in nature. Race is fundamentally an idea born of the human imagination and put into practice by people. There is no evidence within human DNA to support the belief in the existence of different "races" of humans. To the contrary, human difference expresses itself most at the level of the individual. This means that there is more biologically based diversity to be found within racial groups than there is between racial groups. In other words, race has *social significance*. It is a categorizing scheme that may provide people with a sense of belonging, but it is *scientifically meaningless.*

Social Construction of Race

You might be asking yourself, "What is race if it is not part of our human biological makeup?" **Race** is a **social construction**—a set of beliefs, ideas, and assumptions people share about reality. Historian Nell Painter traces the modern construction of race through its more than 2,000-year development in Western civilization.[4] In the 18th century, writers and thinkers in Europe created ways of talking about whiteness that were new. Specifically, Germans conceived of the idea of "Caucasian" beauty. This aesthetic theory associated fairer skin with the color white, and the color white with the beautiful and the good. The superiority of whiteness made it possible for disparate and often warring ethnic groups in Europe— "Saxons," "Anglo-Saxons," and "Teutons"—to adopt the image of themselves as a "White" people and, thus, a superior kind of being—the quintessential human.

To say that race is socially constructed is to acknowledge that the making of race requires (1) education into a worldview or shared way of perceiving reality; (2) a system for representing and communicating that reality through signs and symbols, such as words, images, and gestures; and (3) the creation and enactment of laws, institutional policies, and norms of behavior to regulate and reinforce that worldview.

"Whiteness is a racial discourse, whereas the category 'white people' represents a socially constructed identity, usually based on skin colour."[5]

—Zeus Leonardo, *Race, Whiteness and Education,* 2009

"White-*ness,* in this sense, refers to a set of assumptions, beliefs, and practices that place the interests and perspectives of White people at the center of what is considered normal and everyday. Critical scholarship on Whiteness is not an assault on White people themselves; it is an assault on the socially constructed and constantly reinforced power of White identifications, norms, and interests."[6]

—David Gilborn, "Intersectionality, Critical Race Theory and the Primacy of Racism: Race, Class, Gender and Dis/ability in Education," 2018

Racial Constructions Are Incomplete and Adaptive

The ability to perceive and make sense of the world racially must be taught and learned. Usually that learning occurs in childhood, when adult ways of looking at the world begin to focus children's innate ways of seeing the world outside of themselves.

For example, I, Amy, grew up in a biracial household. Racial categories were not a conscious part of how I understood myself. I remember as a third-grader in Georgia, sitting at my desk with a sharpened yellow #2 pencil in hand and the standardized Iowa Test of Basic Skills in front of me. My first task was to make sure all my personal identifying information had been entered correctly by the teacher on my scantron form. My eyes moved quickly across my name but came to an abrupt stop over the bubbles for race. I recall vividly my puzzlement over the options: *White. Black. Hispanic. Other.* The bubble that had been pre-filled for me was Black. That moment was formative. It impressed upon me how others perceived me. I like to say that is when I became Black. Thirty-five years later I was in a fender-bender in Texas. The police officer listened to my story of the incident and the story of the other driver. He handed me a small carbon copy paper with his handwritten police report. I read it and was instantly confused by his description of me. *Brown hair. Brown eyes. Female. White.* How is it that the same person, the same body, can be racialized so differently?

The answer lies with history, which shows that the idea of race has changed many times. It has been adapted to different local and global contexts, and it shifts from one era to another. The meaning of race is not stable or fixed in biology but rather at different moments is reshaped by human beings to exploit a variety of circumstances. This versatility has a few implications. First is that race and racial identities, in particular, are incomplete. They can fluctuate depending on the social context. Second, for ideas about race to have staying power, they must serve a significant social function. We describe race as a myth because, much like other myths, it serves the function of validating the worldview, desires, and beliefs of the most influential members of society while also serving a large swath of the general public who feel invested in and derive benefits from believing in the reality the myth offers. These social functions help explain why the idea of race and racial hierarchy has persisted for as long as it has. There is another side to race making, however. By accepting that race is a social construction, we also can appreciate its vulnerability, as people resist assimilation to oppressive racial ideas and identities and assert new ways of thinking, living, and being. Race is incomplete and open to adaptation in different global locations and with the passage of time.[8] This versatility means that constant maintenance is required to keep the myth of race alive and relevant.

Root Problems

In 2020, schools adapted to the crisis brought about by the COVID-19 pandemic by transitioning from brick-and-mortar buildings and in-person learning to online environments. Young children and teens were dependent upon the resources in their households and the ability of adults in their homes to provide instructional support. This transition did not equalize the benefits of school for students but instead exacerbated inequalities. According to Richard Rothstein, an economist who has studied educational inequality for decades, the educational "achievement gap mostly results from social-class based advantages that some children bring to school and that others lack, as well as disadvantages stemming from racial discrimination that only some children have to face. The coronavirus, unfortunately, will only exacerbate the effects of these advantages."[9]

Do you agree or disagree? Did the pandemic lessen institutionalized racism or worsen it? Show how and why by drawing or diagramming with images and words.

Middle Passage

The enslavement and forced migration to the New World began in 1525 and ended more than 300 years later in 1866. Not only were Africans held in bondage but so too were Irish and Native Americans. Using archives of shipping records, historians' best estimates are that 12.5 million Africans were transported across the Atlantic to the Americas and the Caribbean, of which only 10.7 million survived the treacherous Middle Passage. Of those, 388,000 Africans were brought to North America. Enslaved Africans were by law the property of Whites, to be bought and sold in a racial system of slavery. They and their U.S.-born children could expect to live out their lives in bondage characterized by unpaid labor, oversight, torture, rape, and the forced separation of families, tactics used by slave owners to

2.1 Stowage of the British slave ship *Brookes* under the regulated slave trade act of 1788. Public domain.

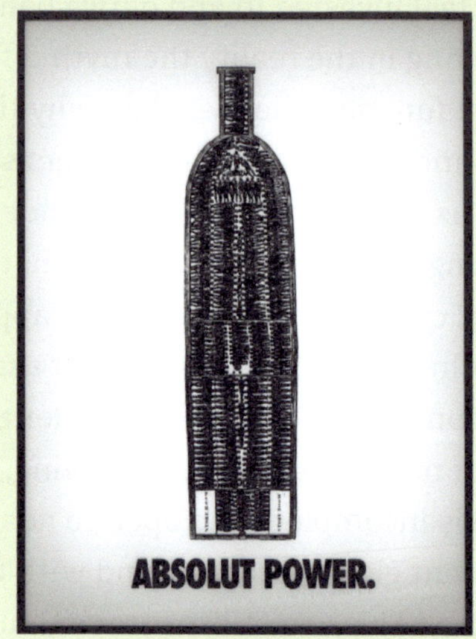

2.2 Hank Willis Thomas, *Absolut Power*, 2003. Inkjet print on canvas, 40" x 30" (101.6 x 76.2 cm). © Hank Willis Thomas. Courtesy of the artist and Jack Shainman Gallery, NY.

quell slave resistance. Images were central to planning and executing the kidnapping and enslavement of Africans. Today we can refer to these visualizations created at the time of the Middle Passage to understand the enslavers' ways of seeing non-White bodies.

Artists who depict the Middle Passage help us learn about how art contributes to how we understand race and how race contributes to the different ways in which an artist approaches subject matter.

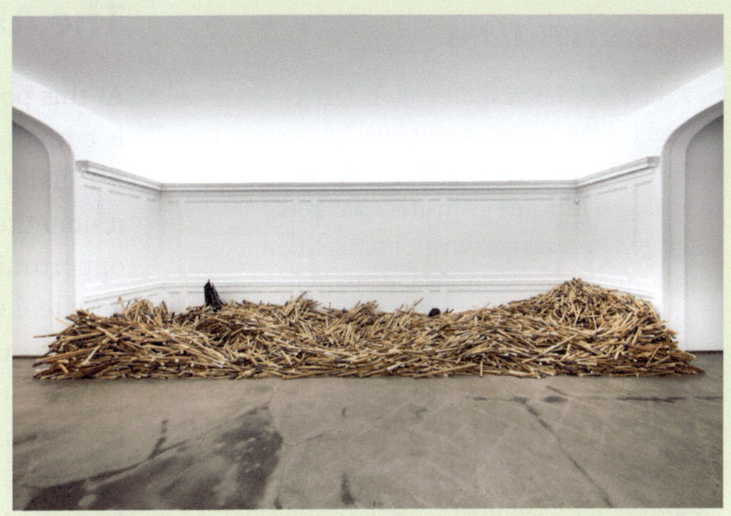

2.3 Radcliffe Bailey, *Windward Coast*, 2009. Piano keys, plaster bust, and glitter, dimensions variable. © Radcliffe Bailey. Courtesy of the artist and Jack Shainman Gallery, NY.

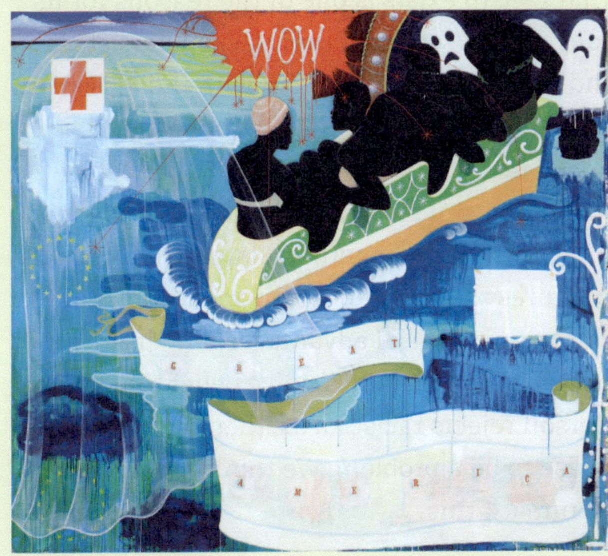

2.4 Kerry James Marshall, *Great America*, 1994. Acrylic and collage on canvas, 103" x 114" (261.62 x 289.56 cm). © Kerry James Marshall. Courtesy of the artist and Jack Shainman Gallery, NY.

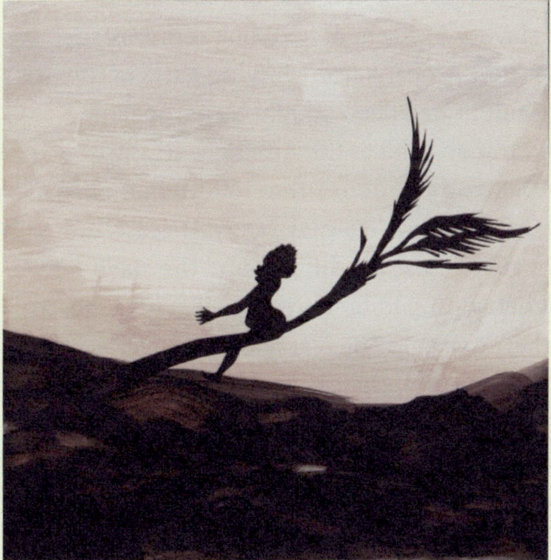

2.5 Kara Walker, *Middle Passages (3)*, 2004. Gouache, cut paper, and collage on board, 1 of 5 works, 15" x 15" (38.1 x 38.1 cm). © Kara Walker, courtesy of Sikkema Jenkins & Co., NY.

Rhetorical Fictions

In 2016, Black Texas mother Roni Dean-Burren posted a video about how her son's McGraw Hill Education textbook referred to enslaved Africans as migrant workers. On page 126, a section about immigration called Africans brought to work on American plantations "workers" rather than slaves. It spoke about the 1500–1800 slave trade in terms of immigration, which sounds like an option, instead of forced migration.

These rhetorical maneuvers are an example of the dominant group's ability to create an alternative narrative that removes accountability for the history of slavery and Black Americans' continued state of oppression in the U.S. The erasure of slavery in a school textbook removes the fact that Africans from varying parts of the continent had been bought by Europeans and transported to the Americas in ships with living conditions that left them malnourished and diseased. Many Africans did not survive the conditions, and the slave owners dumped their dead bodies into the Atlantic Ocean. The disregard of slaves' state of powerlessness and helplessness as they entered America places the onus of their continued oppression on them for not being able to gain wealth and sufficient education, instead of considering the historical relevance of centuries of physical, mental, emotional, and economic abuse.

The Alchemy of Racism

At this point, you may be thinking, "If race is a myth, isn't racism as well?" Race may be a socially constructed biological myth, but it nonetheless impacts and shapes people's opportunities, experiences, and privileges in very real ways. To understand this, we have to engage our imaginations to put the present in conversation with the past and connect our individual experiences to the actions of others.

Historically, race has informed the unequal distribution of power, material wealth, benefits and burdens, rights and duties.[10] Denial that racism exists is one of the reasons for its longevity. A second reason racism persists is individualism. The problem with individualism is that it is a way of thinking that attributes social inequality and other ills to the behaviors and attitudes of individuals acting independently of one another. Blaming individuals obscures the power of social institutions in maintaining racial advantages and disadvantages. It also leads to a naive belief that if each person rejects racist ideas, then racism will cease to be a problem. We think it is important to unpack this.

Individual Racism or Institutionalized Racism: What's the Difference?

From school and popular media, we learn to associate racism with imagery and symbolism of bad people doing bad things. For example, for many people, racism looks like White slave masters and overseers whipping enslaved Africans as they labor in crop fields for the economic gain of Whites only. Racism looks like White men cloaked in all white regalia with hoods burning crosses, forming lynch mobs, and hunting non-White bodies to torture and murder.

However, this narrow focus on bad individuals doing bad things masks **institutionalized racism**—the ways in which racism manifests in the day-to-day operations and outcomes of institutions. When we speak of institutions, we are not talking about buildings. Rather, institutions are those fairly durable organizational systems that enable a society to function. They comprise people and the policies and practices they enact every day.

For example, during the COVID-19 pandemic in 2020, many school campuses and buildings were closed to formal gatherings, but the institution of school did not cease to exist. Instead, it took a new form, adapted as it was by teachers, students, parents, and administrative leaders who moved school online to conform with distancing protocols. School in the virtual realm became accessible only to those with digital technologies available in their homes and with prior experience or assistance to be able to navigate online platforms.

The government, economy, schools, family, religion, law, medicine, and the media are some examples of institutions, and by and large, they touch the lives of everyone in a society. They are established by previous generations and developed over a very long time. These previous generations were people who engaged in racial thinking, and that thinking informed the creation, aims, and functioning of social institutions. Throughout most of U.S. history, racial thinking has been suffused with **white supremacy**, particularly among those groups of people who held power, wealth, and positions of influence. White supremacy is a system of human hierarchy based on (1) a belief in an innate moral, intellectual, and cultural superiority of persons perceived to be White and (2) a set of tacit norms and explicit rules that prove mostly beneficial for White-identified people.

The institutions we have inherited from past generations—including our own parents, grandparents, and other people we know inti-

Check Yourself

White American scholar Peggy McIntosh speaks about how she understood the impact of gender-based privilege. Applying this critical lens to race, McIntosh began to see how racial oppression of others afforded her certain invisible privileges. In her writing, she names numerous daily effects of having white privilege, essentially "unpacking her invisible knapsack of privilege." Below are sample statements from her text:

- I can if I wish arrange to be in the company of people of my race most of the time.

- I can avoid spending time with people whom I was trained to mistrust and who have learned to mistrust my kind or me.

- If I should need to move, I can be pretty sure of renting or purchasing housing in an area which I can afford and in which I would want to live.

- I can be pretty sure that my neighbors in such a location will be neutral or pleasant to me.

- I can go shopping alone most of the time, pretty well assured that I will not be followed or harassed.

- I can turn on the television or open to the front page of the paper and see people of my race widely represented.

- When I am told about our national heritage or about "civilization," I am shown that people of my color made it what it is.

- I can be sure that my children will be given curricular materials that testify to the existence of their race.[11]

   To extend your knowledge further, check out the website www.Yourprivilegeisshowing.com. It offers an interactive social justice training experience that becomes a game of self-reflection as it relates to many contexts of difference, including race. Lillian Medville, the developer of the website and game, offers a TedxTalk about the impetus for the project. The talk can be viewed at tedxbeaconstreet.com/videos/your-privilege-is-showing/.

mately—are relics of a white supremacist past. Without conscious and persistent anti-racist intervention, U.S. institutions can and probably will continue to produce many of the racial hierarchies and privileges of white supremacy upon which they were designed and built at their beginning.

Racial Privilege: Who Gets to Ignore Race?

When teaching about race, racism, and racial equity in art education, we always situate our discussions historically. White students will often ask, "I didn't own any slaves; what does this have to do with me?" This is a really important question! It gets at the heart of institutionalized racism and the unbroken link of colonialism and slavery to the present day.

The enslavement of Africans and their descendants coupled with the taking of Indigenous lands fueled the growth of the modern capitalist economy. Those people whose language, land, and labor were stolen by White settlers were never remunerated. Their descendants have never been compensated. As a consequence, people living in the United States today have inherited the racial imbalances of the past. One such imbalance is **white racial privilege**—the unearned and often invisible

Our Racial Inheritance

Black American journalist Isabel Wilkerson, author of *Caste: The Origins of Our Discontents*, helps us to see that history offers a critical and necessary lens for understanding our present situation. She likens colonization, slavery, and Indigenous displacement to a house that we all have inherited, when she writes:

> We in this country are like homeowners who inherited a house …. Many people may rightly say: "I had nothing to do with how this all started. I have nothing to do with the sins of the past. My ancestors never attacked Indigenous people, never owned slaves." And yes. Not one of us was here when this house was built. Our immediate ancestors may have had nothing to do with it, but here we are, the current occupants of a property with stress cracks and bowed walls and fissures in the foundation. We are the heirs to whatever is right or wrong with it. We did not erect the uneven pillars or joists, but they are ours to deal with now. And any further deterioration is, in fact, on our hands.[12]

economic and psychological advantage that attaches to people who are perceived as White and, to some degree, people who engage in cultural practices that are associated with whiteness. White racial privilege is not something that an individual necessarily asks for or is even aware of. It is the complex of economic, social, and symbolic resources owing to race ideology that are embedded within laws, social institutions, and culture more broadly. A person does not need to espouse racist views or hurl racist insults to benefit from the unearned advantages of racial privilege or for others to be harmed by it.[13]

Displacement and slavery institutionalized racism, as so-called White people controlled the majority of social institutions and developed society's laws, rules, and order. Thus, racism is embedded in most societal and behavioral norms still today. Things like language, educational and public policies, laws, institutional practices, and cultural representations play key roles in the enactment and legitimation of white racial privilege in the U.S. These are all systems that effectively oppress non-White people. Even school textbooks, children's films, and literature books utilize language and discourses that marginalize non-White groups and reproduce racial domination through language.

Racism can occur without human intent. For example, racial inequality is institutionalized even through seemingly well-meaning educational policies like the *No Child Left Behind* Act of 2001 and *Every Student Succeeds* Act of 2015. The practices of narrowing the curriculum and mandating high-stakes testing encouraged by these policies perpetuate and even exacerbate racial inequality in schools across America. The ideas and beliefs that frame these policies are situated in white dominance, and the consequence is a continuation of educational disparity since the onset of compulsory school in the early 1800s. So while people may work to be anti-racist on an individual level, there are institutional structures in place that maintain white supremacy.

Am I Experiencing Racism or Racial Prejudice?

Racism is a system of inclusion and exclusion, privilege and disadvantage, domination and subordination based on racial categories. Its forms and targets can shift, depending on relationships or hierarchies of power in a given context, to create and reinforce unequal economic, political, and social power. Racism results in the oppression of groups and individuals who find themselves on the downside of the power relationship. Thus, institutionalized racism is a self-sustaining system that results in white racial privilege and non-White

Who Is Affirmed?

Affirmative action is one of the most contested policies with relation to race and access. Affirmative action refers to a set of procedures that aim to counter discrimination against minoritized applicants seeking educational or employment opportunities. It is a set of procedures that aim to counter discrimination against minoritized groups when seeking educational or employment opportunities. It is often challenged on the basis that it is "reverse racism." Critics claim that it discriminates against White applicants. However, a 1995 study conducted by the Department of Labor reveals that affirmative action, from its inception, has actually benefited White women more than it has non-White applicants overall. Black American civil rights advocate and leading Critical Race Theory scholar Kimberlé Crenshaw writes, "The primary beneficiaries of affirmative action have been Euro-American women."[14] Nevertheless, the distorted narrative is that non-Whites, particularly Black people, are favored and thus unfairly take jobs and seats in college classrooms that would otherwise be given to more qualified, deserving, and capable Whites.

Mark Kantrowitz, a White American, nationally recognized expert on student financial aid, scholarships, and student loans, analyzes and reports on financial aid data, obtained from the National Postsecondary Student Aid Study, that reveals that disproportionate access to financial resources continue, even with affirmative action policies in play.[15]

White students still make up almost three-quarters of all private external scholarship recipients in four-year bachelor's programs, almost two-thirds of all institutional grants and scholarship recipients, and over three-quarters of all merit-based grants and scholarships, although White people only make up about 62 percent of the college student population and about half of all people under 19. White students are more likely than black, Latino, and Asian students to receive scholarships.[16]

This is why affirmative action is relevant and still necessary. This example is further evidence that affirms the concept that racism is systemic and, therefore, cannot be combated by one person's actions or a single policy.

peoples' oppression. White racial privilege can be present even when there may be other non-privileged aspects of one's location within social hierarchies. For example, a White woman may receive the benefits of racial privilege and at the same time experience gender oppression because of the institutional status of women. Whether or not they want or are aware of the racial privilege of whiteness, such is the default inheritance in a racial system in which White people are the dominant group.

Racism, as we use the term in this book, is different from racial prejudice. **Racial prejudice** refers to preconceptions and biases about people on the basis of their perceived racial identity. Every person has biases. They often operate beneath conscious awareness, yet they direct our actions. (This is explored in greater depth in Chapter 5.) Prejudice and racism are not interchangeable. A key difference between them is power. To put it simply:

racial prejudice + power = racism.

In our teaching about race, someone inevitably will raise the question, "So what about reverse racism?" The social and economic impact of racial prejudice against White people is non-existent since non-White people collectively have little to no economic, political, and social power to leverage. When non-White people show prejudice against White people, for example, by using a racial epithet or slur (e.g., honky, cracker, peckerwood), it does not diminish the institutional status of whiteness and advantages that attach to people who are perceived to be White. Presently, non-White people do not have the power to define White people's reality in that way.

However, the opposite can happen. White people may be discriminated against in certain circumstances because of the racial prejudice of others, but the prejudice of non-White people does not result in a White person's loss of any racial privilege. The historical naming and identifying of non-White people in derogatory terms (e.g., nigger, lazy, spik, kike, dune coon, chink) are lodged in the collective consciousness of society and can have real effects, such as a lack of access to equitable education, healthy food and water, affordable health care, and even personhood. White people can be called by a racial slur, but that act does not operate at the level of racism because, by and large, White people as a group still occupy the top rungs of economic, political, and social power.

How Did We Get Here?: The Three-Legged Stool

The number three plays a special role in art and design: The *rule of thirds* used by painters and photographers to create a pleasing composition. The *rule of threes* in interior design to achieve a

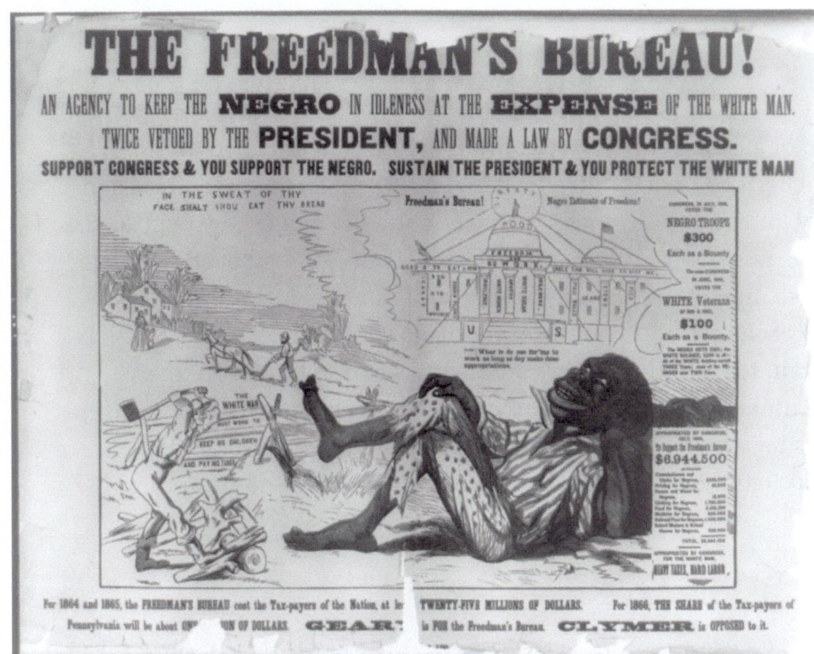

2.6 An 1866 political poster demonizing a Black American freed man as being "idle" while the White man works hard to plow the field. "The poster takes aim at the expense and perceived wastefulness of the Freedmen's Bureau, which was established to protect the newly freed slave population." Photograph. Retrieved from the Library of Congress.

balanced arrangement within a room's decor. The *three touchpoints* needed at the base of a freestanding sculpture to achieve stability.

We also can think of racial equality—or inequality as it were—as a built form, one that resembles a three-legged stool. The three legs work together to form the pillars or foundation to stabilize what sits on top. We find this metaphor especially meaningful for art and art education. After all, stools are ubiquitous in artists studios and art classrooms. We sit on them. They become part of still-lifes. Indeed, stools are so commonplace they receive little notice, that is, until a leg begins to wobble. Just as artists work with threes to add strength and dynamism to build forms, it is impossible for a stool with three legs to wobble.

We want to give some attention to "three legs" that uphold the stool of racial inequality in the U.S. Easy to overlook, these structural underpinnings buttress the alchemical transformation of racial mythology into concrete forms of institutionalized racism.

Leg I: Employment and Economic Exploitation

To understand how employment factors into racial inequality, we need to go back in time and look at what comprised the U.S. economy at its foundation. In doing so, we

Whose American Dream?

The American dream is "that dream of a land in which life should be better and richer and fuller for everyone, with opportunity for each according to ability or achievement.... It is not a dream of motor cars and high wages merely, but a dream of social order in which each man and each woman shall be able to attain to the fullest stature of which they are innately capable, and be recognized by others for what they are, regardless of the fortuitous circumstances of birth or position."[17]

What other dreams are attached to the "idea" of America? Complete a research assignment that asks students to investigate how "the American dream" is understood by individuals from varying backgrounds. For example, does race or class make a difference in how the American dream is conceptualized, experienced, or coveted? Create an artistic response—drawing, collage, arts-based investigation, installation, or performance—to this prompt.

can more clearly see the structures upon which the modern-day economic system is built. To begin, the first enslaved African was brought to what is now the U.S. mainland in 1619. The land itself was the traditional territory of various Indigenous groups. European colonial settlers arrived (invaded might be a more accurate term), occupied the land, and eventually enacted genocidal policies and practices against Native peoples. Along with taking the land and its resources for themselves, the settlers exploited enslaved Africans and Indigenous people through unpaid, forced labor. Slavery was cheaper than paying indentured servants who were mostly poor Europeans. These two moves produced enormous wealth for the settlers that transferred to future generations of White descendants.

In 1865, slavery was lawfully "abolished" and thus deemed illegal. Although physical bondage was no longer legal, economic enslavement did not necessarily end, nor was the economic playing field leveled in any way. Newly freed people had little money or resources for sustainable, independent living. This forced many of them to seek employment on the farms they had previously worked on for free, thus, having little or no choice but to continue relationships with the same White people who had owned them. They had to adjust to a new labor system, one that included laws that prevented them from gaining too much prosperity. For example, the ex-enslaved could be self-employed or be hired by any employer willing to hire them; however, contract enforcement laws

Americana Reinterpreted

Kadir Nelson is a Black American artist best known for his magazine and book illustrations. In his contemporary work titled *Black Gothic*, Nelson channels *American Gothic*, the 1930 painting by Grant Wood. Wood's painting depicted a White farmer holding a pitchfork with his daughter by his side. The work intended to evoke 20th century Americana. According to a 2013 Entry Guide at the Art Institute of Chicago, "Wood intended [*American Gothic*] to be a positive statement about rural American values, an image of reassurance at a time of great dislocation and disillusionment. The man and woman, in their solid and well-crafted world, with all their strengths and weaknesses, represent survivors."[18]

In that same vein, Nelson's *Black Gothic* depicts a Black American, multigenerational family in front of their brick home in the Midwestern United States. The boy in the image holds an American flag, while "the mother and grandmother look on, preparing the family for obstacles," according to Nelson. While we know that Black Americans disproportionately

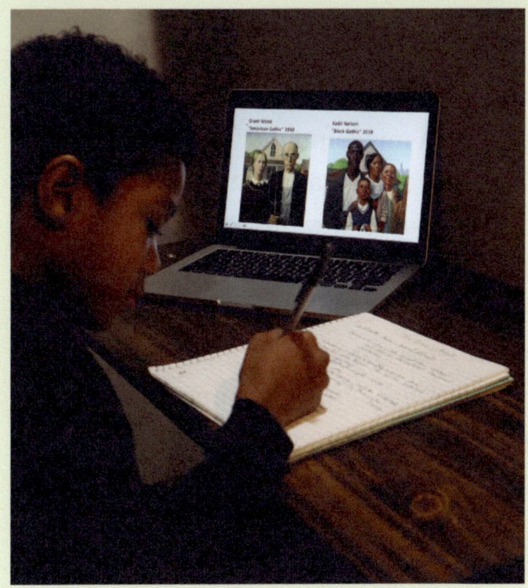

2.7 Comparing Grant Wood's *American Gothic* (1930) and Kadir Nelson's *Black Gothic* (2017).

suffer the most from economic poverty, Nelson's 21st century reinterpretation of Wood's work brings forth a stark counter narrative that offers a positive message about the upward mobility of the Black American family and their neighborhoods. Nelson's work illustrates a story of survival and hope.

imposed criminal sanctions for breach of contract. Additionally, **vagrancy laws** made it a crime to be unemployed if one was otherwise unable to financially support themselves. (See image 2.6.)

Although they might seem neutral and fair on their face, these newly devised criminal laws were incredibly easy to violate, especially by recently freed people wandering about in search of displaced family members. Any person who appeared to White authorities to be homeless or unemployed was jailed and charged with a misdemeanor. These laws were a new method of bondage put in place by the White ruling class. They effectively reinstituted slavery in all but name only.

The **convict-lease system** is another method by which slavery was reimposed upon the freed Black people. It permitted the state or county government to "lease" people convicted of a crime. This meant their labor was made available to private firms and companies at low cost.[19] A market exchange was created for convict labor, in which entrepreneurs bought and sold convict leases. For decades after slavery was legally abolished, White people continued to gain economic wealth and advantage from a criminal justice system that fed cheap convict labor into the economy. This was an economic system designed to maintain the power and wealth accumulated by White people who owned property. Where in earlier centuries European settlers and their White descendants had benefited from slave labor and the right to own human beings as property, emancipation brought not so much freedom to pursue the so-called **American dream** as it spurred new laws that enabled the old racial caste system to endure under a new guise.

Leg II: Housing

A second leg that holds up the stool of racial inequality is housing. Beginning as early as the 1930s, unfair housing practices resulted in a wealth gap that has persisted well into the 21st century.[20] The federal government, specifically the Federal Housing Administration (FHA), pursued policies that worked to segregate cities in ways that had not previously been done. Policies that intended to segregate public housing were developed by housing officials on the local level. For example, from World War II to 1955, the public housing authority in New York City used disqualifying factors (e.g., irregular employment history, single-parent family, out-of-wedlock birth, poor housekeeping habits, mental illness, lack of furniture, and others) that they thought would make Black families ineligible for obtaining public housing in certain locations.[21] To be clear, Black people were not more likely to engage in these behaviors; it was just more likely that they were accused of them as reasons for refusing to grant them access.

At every turn, non-White mortgage applicants looking to purchase homes in neighborhoods where mostly White families lived were met with roadblocks. The FHA made a deal with suburban neighborhood developers to subsidize their development of homes if they

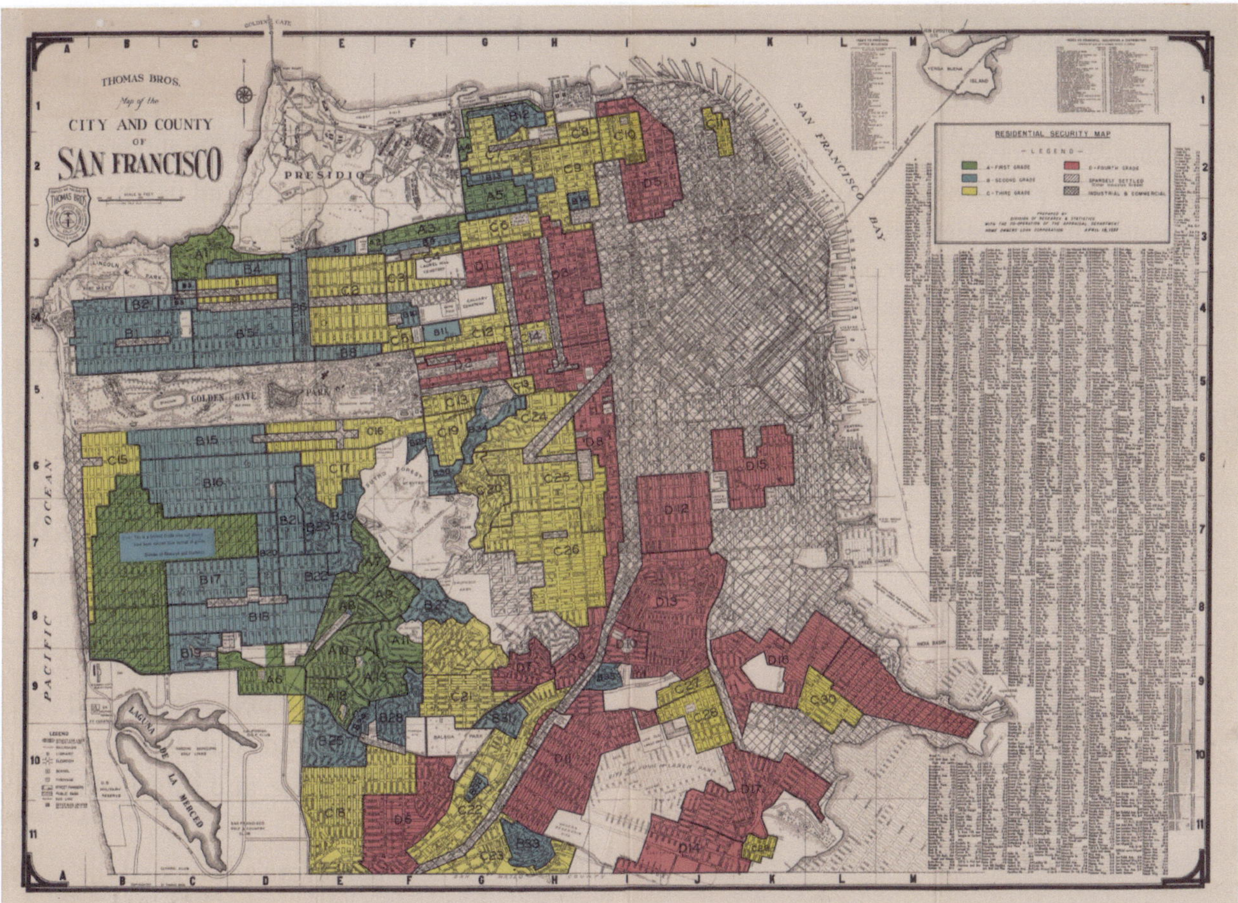

2.8 Redlining map, San Francisco, California, USA, 1937. From the Federal Housing Authority Manual: "Red areas...are characterized by detrimental influences in a pronounced degree, undesirable population or infiltration of it.... Some mortgage lenders may refuse to make loans in these neighborhoods and others will lend only on a conservative basis."

offered racially exclusive deeds that prohibited the resale of the homes to Black people.[22] Banks and credit unions often offered White people loans that ensured long-term fixed rates with low monthly payments, yet offered non-White applicants balloon or subprime mortgage loans with high interest rates. The consequence of this was that non-White people paid more for housing than White people. This housing discrimination was pervasive throughout the banking and home loan industry. And so each month non-White homeowners had less money after paying their housing costs than White people had. This is important to highlight because historically homeownership has been the greatest source of wealth

Crossing the Line

In 2016, White American art educator Diane Kuthy published an instructional resource that discussed redlining in the journal *Art Education*. In her paper, titled "Redlining and Greenlining: Olivia Robinson Investigates Root Causes of Racial Inequity," Kuthy introduces White American artist Olivia Robinson's art-based research that tracked and analyzed the legacy of redlining and other discriminatory housing practices in Baltimore, Maryland. Kuthy provides a biography of Robinson, information about the Baltimore uprising, an introduction to redlining, visual culture materials that provide historical context, web-based resources for further exploration of Baltimore and the context of 2015, and finally, discussion questions that are aligned with the National Visual Arts Standards.[23]

accumulation and upward mobility for U.S. families. Where one lives matters a great deal, but where one's parents and grandparents lived might just matter more when it comes to the resources one is able to pass on to future generations.

The neighborhoods that were relegated to non-White people were often zoned for undesirable uses like waste disposal and toxic industrial plants. Non-White neighborhoods that were rezoned for industrial use turned into slums. These minority-occupied neighborhoods would be **redlined**.

In the 1930s, neighborhoods across all regions of the U.S. were graded and color coded in an effort to identify which were "best" (green), "still desirable" (blue), "definitely declining" (yellow), or "hazardous" (red). (See image 2.8.) The codes took into account the racial demographics of its inhabitants. Neighborhoods that were predominantly made up of Black Americans, as well as Catholics, Jews, and immigrants from Asia and southern Europe, were deemed undesirable, and thus coded red.

The government surveyors who coded the neighborhoods saw people who were not Northern European White as a detraction from the value of the area.[24] Therefore, they literally color-coded city and county maps to communicate these interpretations of land value. The redlined areas were undesirable for investment, and the local lenders discounted them as credit risks. To protect predominantly Northern European White neighborhoods, the FHA maintained that in order to retain market stability, homes should continue to be inhabited by those in the same social and racial class.

A change in occupancy destabilized the market and home values.[25] The FHA's assertions encouraged banks to deny prospective homebuyers loans for redlined neighborhoods, and further, homeowners in redlined neighborhoods were denied equity loans for home improvements. With these challenges, there was no way for people in redlined neighborhoods to invest in their property or build assets for their families and businesses. As a consequence of redlining, certain groups of people were, and continue to be, locked into concentrated areas of poverty. Redlining buttressed the segregated structure of American cities.[26] Moreover, it has led to over-policing in certain communities.

Even when developers attempted to build integrated housing, the FHA's influence was too overbearing for them to be successful. Fortunately, the Federal Housing Act of 1968 slowed down the discriminatory practices by declaring specific race-based actions unlawful. However, it was too little too late; the damage had been done. The Act did not undo the segregation that had already been orchestrated; it only addressed future discriminatory, racist practices. While redlining was banned in 1968, its impact can be seen even now. The areas of lowest opportunity in the U.S. today are those that were redlined decades ago.

Housing segregation has directly impacted the development of wealth for White families. Homes that White people purchased for a few thousand dollars in the mid 1900s are now worth hundreds of thousands of dollars. The equity appreciation over time enabled White homeowners to pass down their high-value assets to heirs, which continues to benefit each subsequent generation decades later. Today, the U.S. Federal Reserve Bank reports that White families in general have nearly 10 times the net worth of Black families and more than 8 times that of Hispanic families. This enormous wealth gap is almost entirely attributable to the unconstitutional, yet institutionalized racist housing policies and practices of the mid-20th century, as home ownership is the number-one means for acquiring wealth.[27] The institutionalized racism that produced neighborhood segregation is intertwined with school segregation.

Leg III: Education

Just as the first two legs of inequality— employment and housing—are interrelated, so, too, is the third leg, education. It was (and still is) common for White people and non-White people to live in different neighborhoods and areas of town. Because they generally did not live in the same neighborhoods, schools and school districts reflected similar demographic segregation. Up until the mid-1950s, it was legal for states and municipalities to require that White students attend separate schools from non-White students. Racial segregation was also embedded in many mundane areas of life for White people and non-White people.

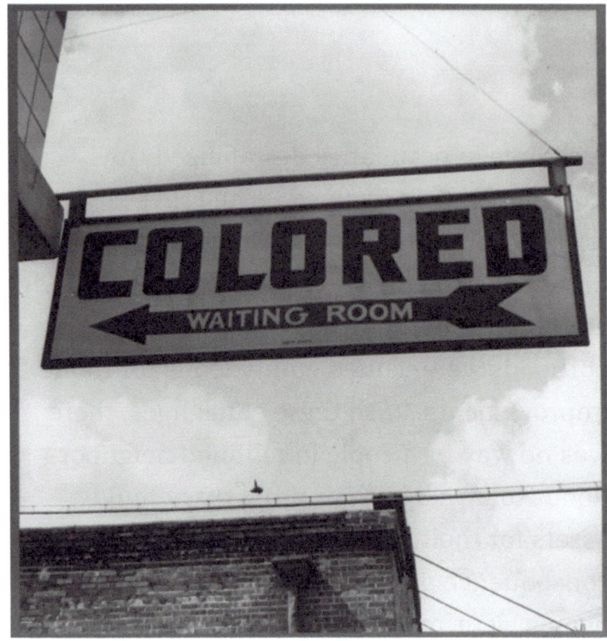

2.9 Esther Bubley, *A Greyhound bus trip from Louisville, Kentucky, to Memphis, Tennessee, and the terminals. Sign at bus station. Rome, Georgia*, 1943. Library of Congress.

From separate bathrooms and water fountains to different public buses and public swimming pools, segregation was pervasive. (See image 2.9.) So, for decades after the end of slavery, separate schooling remained commonplace, even though it was painfully obvious that the schools White people attended had superior facilities to those that non-White people attended. Schools for non-White children lacked essentials like desks, books, running water, electricity, and working bathrooms. Access to these basic resources further impacted the economic disparity among certain communities.

"The America I Knew"

Norman Rockwell is a White American author, painter, and illustrator who was born in New York City in 1894. He achieved global notoriety for his iconic paintings, including, *The Problem We All Live With*, which is a visual representation of the story of Ruby Bridges. Bridges was a young Black girl who was photographed being guarded by U.S. Marshals as she walked into her newly desegregated school in New Orleans. This image visually memorializes the 1954 *Brown vs. Board of Education* ruling that asserted separate schooling is not equal and thus is unconstitutional. The ruling forced racial integration in public schools in the U.S. However, schools in the state of Louisiana did not abide by this ruling immediately. It wasn't until the 1960s that the state began to submit to the court's initial judgements.

Rockwell's illustration appeared in the January 1964 issue of *Look* magazine and was met with both support and contention. Rockwell said, "Without thinking too much about it in specific terms, I was showing the America I knew and observed to others who might not have noticed."[28]

It was not until 1954 that the U.S. Supreme Court case *Brown vs. Board of Education* made state-sponsored school segregation illegal. (See "Did You Know," page 36.) School desegregation was met with excitement and joy from most non-White families. They were encouraged and more positive about their children's future knowing that all students, regardless of race, would benefit from top-notch educational resources and facilities. However, desegregation was met with anger, hate, and violence from many White parents and even some non-White parents. Some White families did not want to share with non-White children the educational privileges they enjoyed, arguing that non-White children were not worthy to be in the same space as their academically superior White children. In some instances, non-White parents also demonstrated frustration and anger about desegregation. Primarily, Black parents communicated a sense of deep community loss, as Black teachers in Black schools emphasized not only academic subject matter but nurtured self-worth and self-validation in the Black children, hoping to counter the negative, destructive imagery and messages emanating from dominant culture. Desegregation also resulted in the dramatic loss of the Black teaching workforce, as *Brown vs. Board* only required schools to integrate the children, not the teachers. Black teachers, oftentimes holding master's degrees, were either let go or made to be classroom assistants to the White teachers with lesser professional education and experience. Consequently, public schools were systematically drained of the cultural knowledge, community ties, and commitment to racial equity that characterize excellent teaching of Black American children.[29] The effects of housing segregation on the public school system can still be seen today, as research shows that schools are more racially and economically segregated than before *Brown vs. Board of Education*.[30]

Before Moving Ahead

This chapter is just the beginning for the journey ahead. It provided a definition of race, some essential concepts and vocabularies for talking about racism, and social foundations for understanding the racialized world as a shared inheritance and racial justice as a shared responsibility. As a reflection of larger society, the arts are susceptible to reproducing racial hierarchies in ways that, consciously or unconsciously, maintain or exacerbate racial inequality. In the chapters that follow, readers are presented with critical racial knowledge and activities specific to art and visual culture education. The content builds so as to enable art teachers to understand and implement anti-racist art pedagogy within classrooms and communities. Remember to return to this chapter whenever a refresher of "the basics" is needed.

Notes

1   NaJuana Lee, "Culturally Responsive Teaching for 21st-Century Art Education: Examining Race in a Studio Art Experience," *Art Education* 65, no. 5 (2012): 48–53.

2   Linda Markowitz and Laurel Puchner, "Racial diversity in schools: A necessary evil?" *Multicultural Perspectives* 16, no. 2 (2014): 72-78; Mica Pollock, *Colormute: Race Talk Dilemmas in an American School* (Princeton, NJ: Princeton University Press, 2004).

3   Barbara Applebaum, *Being White, Being Good: White Complicity, White Moral Responsibility, and Social Justice Pedagogy* (Lanham, MD: Lexington Books, 2010).

4   Nell Painter, *The History of White People* (New York, NY: W. W. Norton, 2010).

5   Zeus Leonardo, *Race, Whiteness, and Education* (New York: Routledge, 2009): 169.

6   David Gilborn, "Intersectionality, Critical Race Theory and the Primacy of Racism: Race, Class, Gender and Dis/ability in Education," in Tania Das Gupta, Carl E. James, Chris Andersen, Grace Edward Galabuzi, Roger C.A. Maaka (eds.) *Race and Racialization: Essential Readings*, 2nd edition (Canadian Scholars, 2018).

7   Ta-Nehisi Coates, *Between the World and Me* (New York, NY: Spiegel & Grau, 2015).

8   Patrick Wolfe, *Traces of History: Elementary Structures of Race* (London, UK: Verso, 2016).

9   Richard Rothstein, "The Coronavirus Will Explode Achievement Gaps in Education," *Shelterforce*, April 13, 2020, para. 4, https://shelterforce.org/2020/04/13/

the-coronavirus-will-explode-achievement-gaps-in-education/.

10 Charles W. Mills, *The Racial Contract* (New York: Cornell University Press, 1997).

11 Peggy McIntosh, "White Privilege: Unpacking the Invisible Knapsack," 1989/2010, 2, https://nationalseedproject.org/images/documents/Knapsack_plus_Notes-Peggy_McIntosh.pdf.

12 Isabel Wilkerson, "America's Enduring Caste System," *The New York Times*, July 1, 2020, para. 7, https://www.nytimes.com/2020/07/01/magazine/isabel-wilkerson-caste.html.

13 Sven Beckert and Seth Rockman, eds., *Slavery's Capitalism: A New History of American Economic Development* (Philadelphia: University of Pennsylvania Press, 2016).

14 Kimberlé W. Crenshaw, "Framing Affirmative Action," *Michigan Law Review First Impressions* 105 (2006): 129, https://repository.law.umich.edu/mlr_fi/vol105/iss1/4/.

15 Mark Kantrowitz, "The Distribution of Grants and Scholarships by Race," September 2, 2011, https://www.racialequitytools.org/resourcefiles/Distributionracescholarships.pdf.

16 Vann R. Newkirk II, "The Myth of Reverse Racism: The Idea of White Victimhood Is Increasingly Central to the Debate over Affirmative Action," *The Atlantic*, August 5, 2017, https://www.theatlantic.com/education/archive/2017/08/myth-of-reverse-racism/535689/.

17 James Truslow Adams, *The Epic of America* (Little Brown & Company, 1931): 214–15.

18 Art Institute Chicago, *Essential Guide, Entry* (2013): 56, assessed September 19, 2018, http://www.artic.edu/aic/collections/artwork/6565.

19 PBS.org, "Convict Leasing: Slavery by Another Name," assessed May 30, 2020, https://www.pbs.org/tpt/slavery-by-another-name/themes/convict-leasing/.

20 Richard Rothstein, *The Color of Law* (New York, NY: Liverwalk Publishing Corporation, 2017).

21 Ibid.

22 Richard Rothstein, *The Color of Law* (New York, NY: Liverwalk Publishing Corporation, 2017).

23 Diane Kuthy, "Redlining and Greenlining: Olivia Robinson Investigates Root Causes of Racial Inequity," *Art Education* 70, no. 1 (2017): 50–57.

24 Bruce Mitchell and Juan Franco, "HOLC 'Redlining' Maps: The Persistent Structure of Segregation and Economic Inequality," National Community Reinvestment Coalition, accessed September 12, 2018, https://ncrc.org/holc/.

25 Federal Housing Administration, *Underwriting Manual* (Washington, DC: US Government Printing Office, 1947).

26 Bruce Mitchell and Juan Franco, "HOLC 'Redlining' Maps: The Persistent Structure of Segregation and Economic Inequality," National Community Reinvestment Coalition, accessed September 12, 2018, https://ncrc.org/holc/.

27 Richard Rothstein, *The Color of Law* (New York, NY: Liverwalk Publishing Corporation, 2017).

28 Norman Rockwell Museum, "Norman Rockwell: A Brief Biography," accessed September 19, 2018, https://www.nrm.org/about/about-2/about-norman-rockwell/.

29 Gloria Ladson-Billings, *The Dreamkeepers: Successful Teachers of African American Children* (San Francisco, CA: Jossey-Bass, 1994/2009); and Vanessa Siddle Walker, *The Lost Education of Horace Tate: Uncovering the Hidden Heroes Who Fought for Justice in Schools* (New York, NY: The New Press, 2018).

30 Gary Orfield and Chungmei Lee, *Racial Transformation and the Changing Nature of Segregation* (Cambridge, MA: The Civil Rights Project at Harvard University, 2006).

Seeing Is Believing
Racism through Technologies of Looking

> *"To see what is in front of one's nose needs a constant struggle."*
>
> —George Orwell

In February 2019, world-renowned designer brand Gucci marketed an $890 black wool turtleneck. The sweater has a long neck that can be pulled up over the wearer's mouth and nose, with an opening that outlines the mouth in fire-engine red. Whether intentional or not, presented online on a White female model, the turtleneck evoked **blackface**, a racist visual practice that has been used to dehumanize Black Americans since the mid-1800s. This practice will be discussed in detail later in this chapter.

The Gucci sweater is a contemporary example of the visual repertoire to which young people are exposed. Images in popular visual culture and digital media often carry subtle and not-so-subtle racial narratives from the past into the present. Yet, the past does not fully determine the future. Recent public debates leading to the removal of Confederate monuments in the U.S. and the global success of the Afrofuturist film *Black Panther* provide evidence of this. Whereas racial myths that support supremacist thinking are perpet-

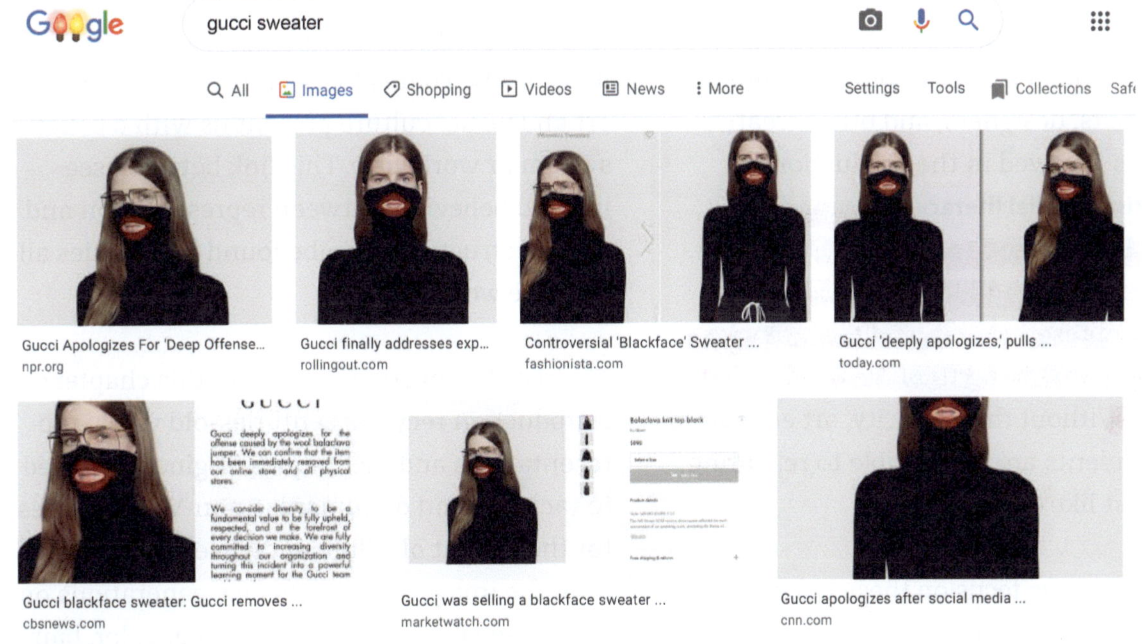

3.1 Google search screen shot.

uated in popular culture, these myths are also contested and the battleground is very often visual culture.

We have asked ourselves, how is it that, with all the artists, designers, and other creative cultural producers working at Gucci, the iconic fashion label created a product that perpetuates anti-Black racism? How did that object and its offensive imagery make it through all the stages of design, prototyping, manufacturing, and marketing without anyone stopping production and distribution? As art educators, we believe Gucci is a microcosm of a broader problem in arts education that stems from a lack of visual racial literacy among artists, designers, and other creative individuals involved in the production of culture. **Visual racial literacy** is a capacity that enables a person to recognize, critically interpret, and respond to visual codes, conventions, representations, and technologies used to prop up the myth of race and racial hierarchy. Without this capacity, art educators and art students are susceptible to repeating history, just like Gucci.

In this chapter, we focus on these key concepts:
- Visual racial literacy
- Race essentialism
- Practices of looking
- Mainstream media
- Popular (visual) culture

When Is Visual Literacy Not Enough?

Art and the broader visual culture are carriers of racial narratives and meanings. They mediate and shape a person's experiences by composing the visual environment that "teaches" certain practices of looking.[1] They convey messages that directly and indirectly invite ways of seeing, feeling, and thinking in a society. That is to say, representations in art and visual culture present us with a belief system or worldview. This link between seeing and believing, between representation and mental structures, can be found in societies all over the world.

The racist imagery described in this chapter's introduction recycles centuries-old visual representations and techniques originally created to racialize and dehumanize non-White bodies for the benefit of White audiences. More than that, the imagery instructs new generations on how to see race. Differences in skin color, hair texture, and body features are visible characteristics of human beings, but their social significance and connection to something called "race" is not obvious. In fact, seeing physical differences as racial or indicative of distinct human types is a learned cultural practice.

The practice of seeing race is not universal. Seeing race requires that one be educated into white supremacist thinking, an ideology or worldview that is culturally specific in its design and advanced over centuries by Europeans and Euro-Americans for the purpose of making the idea of their own superiority seem real and natural. Such an education is not benign or without consequences.

In art education, the concept of visual literacy is often used when referring to the practice and skill of looking at and interpreting visual compositions of all sorts. Even though the visual has always played a central role in the construction of race and racial hierarchy, advocates of visual literacy have given little attention to racism as a visual phenomenon. This has left a gap in the way looking practices are taught in art education. We address this gap by bridging visual literacy and racial literacy. **Racial literacy** is the capacity to recognize, decode, and critically interpret the various forms and methods by which racism is communicated, from overtly vicious to polite expressions.[2] Yes, racism can appear civil or sweetly wrapped with a smile. So how does one become racially literate, able to read, write, speak, listen, *and look* with critical awareness of racial codes and their meanings?

Critical race theorist Lani Guinier says acquiring racial literacy is like learning the "grammar" of race, the system and structures of meaning that make race make sense in different contexts.[3] In our experience, racial literacy is like all other forms of literacy—it develops over time and with practice. Where an individual lies on the spectrum from racially literate to racially illiterate depends on whether the person has historical knowledge and cultural familiarity with racial iconography, dominant racial narratives, and the supremacist logics embedded within visual technologies. Therefore, let us cross the bridge from visual literacy to visual racial literacy by first traveling back in time to places that are perhaps unfamiliar so we can develop the requisite background knowledge to conjugate the visual grammar of race.

Technologies of Looking

Beginning in the European period of Enlightenment, ideas about race were inter-mixed with artistic creation, scientific pursuits, and technological inventions. If we look at historic artifacts, we can learn a great deal about how modern technologies of looking both expressed and invited particular ways of knowing the world. **Technologies of looking** are the modes and processes by which ideas and social relations are made visible. This is important because technologies of looking organize vision and other human senses through the literal and mental images they produce. We begin with the early technologies of race paintings and race photography. Familiarity with these historical artifacts serves as a foundation for visual racial literacy.

Paintings and the Making of a White Utopia

In the 1700s and 1800s, castas paintings were a popular genre in New Spain, an empire that encompassed much of South America, Central America, and North America, including most of the modern-day U.S. west of the Mississippi River and the Floridas.[4] Castas paintings depict family groupings carefully arranged into a taxonomy of races. A *taxonomy* is a system scientists use to classify organisms. Castas paintings invite the viewer to think of human-ity as comprising distinctive types of racial beings. Each type is labeled—*Peninsular, Criollo/Criolla, Mestizo/Mestiza, Indio/India, Negro/Negra,* and others—in a manner that links phenotype to social status.

In addition to dividing humans into types, racial taxonomies are hierarchical. Thus, castas paintings were organized as a hierarchy. Moving left to right and top to bottom, it progresses from lighter-skinned to darker-skinned figures. The viewer quickly grasps that lighter skin represents a higher social status, power, and privilege through its placement on the visual plane. Figures were commonly arranged in a grid format, with each compartment numbered from 1 to 16. The castas painting "teaches" the viewer an association between darker skin and lower position.

Castas paintings invite the viewer to adopt a colonial gaze. More than just a way of seeing, the **gaze** in visual culture is defined as the dynamic or relationship (of power) in which looking and being looked at takes place.[5] It is a social understanding through which individuals' thoughts, emotions, and behaviors are filtered. A shared gaze enables members of a group to make sense of the world and to derive meanings in roughly similar ways.

Racial Caste

In Colonial Spanish America, the caste system of racial hierarchy in society had five main categories.

- **Peninsular**, a person born in Spain to Spanish parents.

- **Criollo/Criolla**, a person of Spanish descent born in New Spain.

- **Mestizo/Mestiza**, a person born in New Spain with one Spanish parent and one indigenous parent (later this comes to be used for any person of European and indigenous ancestry).

- **Indio/India**, a descendant from any indigenous group of the Americas.

- **Negro/Negra**, a person of African descent.

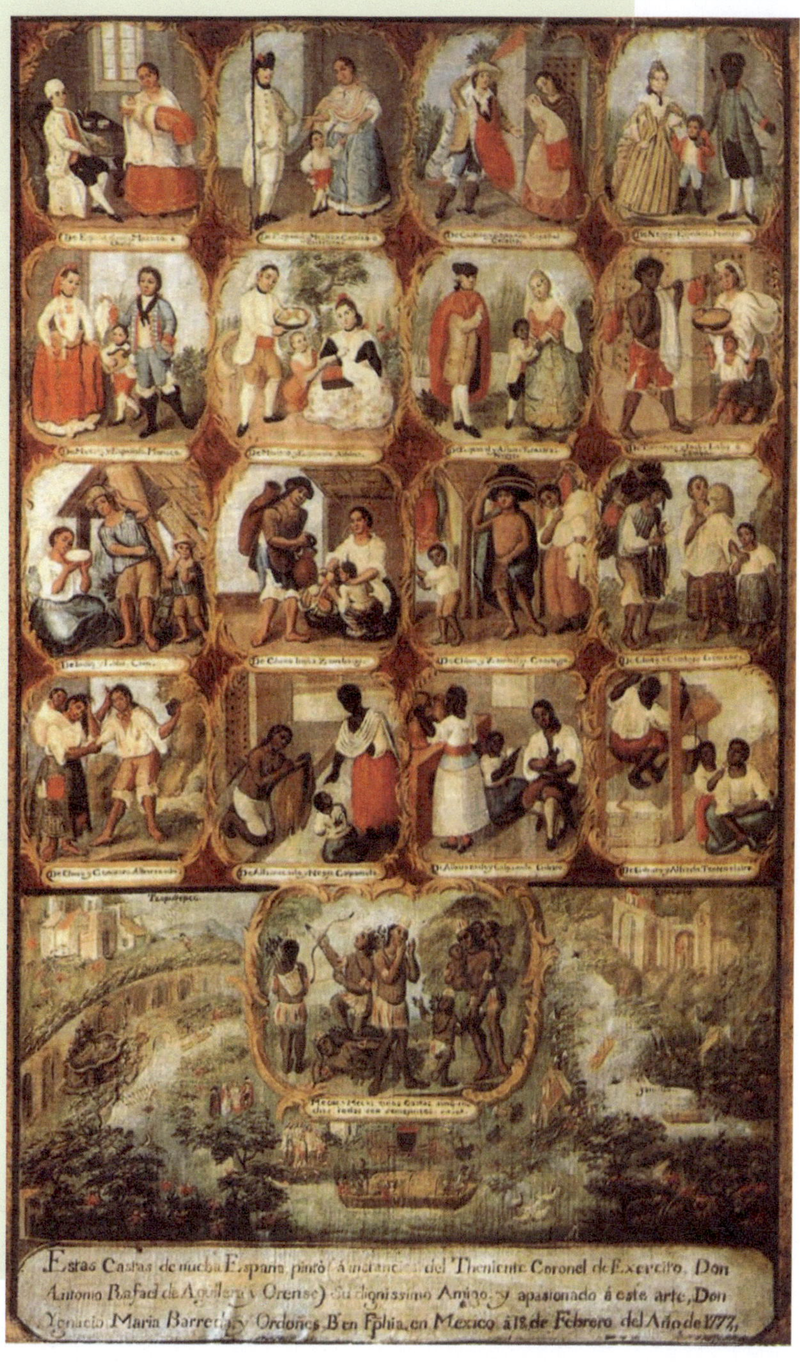

3.2 Ignacio María Barreda, *Las castas mexicanas* [The Mexican castes], 1777. Oil on canvas, 30 1/3" x 19 1/3" (77 x 49 cm). Public domain.

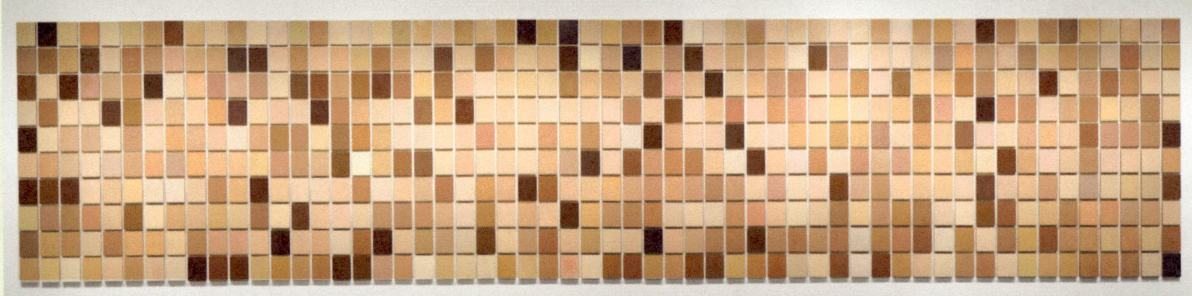

3.3 Byron Kim, *Synecdoche*, 1991–present. Oil and wax on lauan plywood, birch plywood, and plywood, each panel (overall installed dimensions variable) 10" x 8" (25.4 x 20.3 cm). National Gallery of Art, Washington, Richard S. Zeisler Fund. © Byron Kim 2020. Image courtesy of the artist and James Cohan, NY.

Race Portraiture

Contemporary artists recognize the significance of racial ideology and the role it has played in the visual arts. Byron Kim, a Korean American artist, uses abstraction to explore color, power, and representation through race portraiture. Kim bases his portraits on sitters who are his friends, family, strangers, neighbors, and other artists, creating a record of skin color by matching each person's hue in oil and wax on plywood panels. In *Synecdoche* (image 3.3), each person's name is listed beneath the corresponding panel that is 10" x 8", a traditional scale for portraiture. The artwork's title is a figure of speech in which a part is used to stand in for the whole. In what ways does skin color stand in for the whole person?

Peruvian artist Claudia Coco Sánchez explores the colonial fiction of race and its representation through figural portraiture (image 3.4). Referencing 18th century castas paintings, the artist composes family units and captions each portrait with text from an original castas painting that was commissioned by a colonial ruler in Peru seeking to ingratiate himself with the King of Spain. This intertextual strategy allows the artist to reflect on the

The colonial gaze in this early American context extended a white utopian vision of racial order. There is no evidence that the castas paintings reflect the reality that existed in the 18th and 19th centuries. Instead, they were images that projected the desires of the powerful elites at the time. These early race paintings uphold a particular worldview in

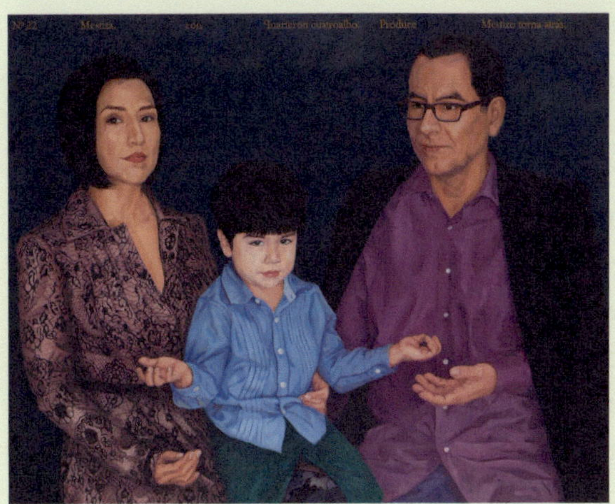

3.4 Claudia Coco Sánchez, *Castes and Bad Breed No. 22*, 2014. Oil on canvas. **Museo de Arte Contemporáneo, Lima. Courtesy of the artist.**

letter written by the Peruvian ruler to accompany a castas painting, in which he showed off the "strange" skin colorations among the offspring in multiracial families, highlighting in particular the so-called "mutations" produced by family mixtures with "Indio" (Indigenous) and "Negro" (Black) people.[6] Sánchez depicts herself and her family in this portrait, showing the intimate and enduring reach of the colonial discourse on race, a fiction that shaped how Peruvian society saw itself and its future.

which whiteness is the purist form of humanity and blackness is its opposite. Not only that, the images naturalized racial hierarchy by associating race with bloodlines or family rela-

tionships. Casting race as a matter of blood or biology, the castas paintings signified the idea that European-born Spanish blood was inherently superior and through interracial procreation would gradually whiten, and ostensibly improve, the New World.[7]

Photography and the Quest to Capture the Human Essence

Cameras and the photographic images they produce are a newer and more widely accessible technology of looking than paintings. The reproducibility of photographic images is part of what makes this mode of perceiving reality so persuasive. In Europe in the mid-1800s, photography was popularized by *daguerreotype*, the first commercially successful photographic process.[8] Named after inventor Louis Jacques Mandé Daguerre, a daguerreotype is a unique image on a highly polished silvered copper plate.

Daguerre was an artist. He marketed his invention to other artists as an expressive tool and to scientists as an instrument for viewing details with precision. Both artists and scientists adopted the idea that a photograph could capture the essence of a subject better than many other popular methods of image-making at the time, such as painting, drawing,

Power in Looking

American Black feminist and cultural critic bell hooks once wrote, "There is power in looking."[9] What might this mean given the history of race photography? What do the images tell us about the eye behind the frame? How is looking learned?

and printmaking. People also understood that photographic technology lent itself to distortion. A photographic image reflects the intentions of the person behind the lens as much as the subjects in front of it. Nonetheless, the precision and affordability of daguerreotype made it attractive to clients who wished to memorialize loved ones by capturing their likeness through portrait photography.

Scientists in Europe and North America saw value in photographic imaging technology. Many of them employed artists to observe and document bio-racial markers—traits such as hair, skin, eyes, noses, and other physical features—through daguerreotype photography. These scientists believed they could "see" the true nature or essence of what they believed to be different races of humans.[10] Key to this project was the cultural belief that objective exterior characteristics could reveal something about a person's natural biological or

psychological interior. This way of thinking is called **essentialism**. It is the idea that objects have stable intrinsic qualities or "essence" that make them what they are. We can see in daguerreotype photography White scientists' essentialist practices of looking and how this leads them to perceive race as biological and thus intrinsic. Hence, racial hierarchies are assumed to be determined by natural order rather than culturally produced by social institutions.

Photography is still used to essentialize people.[11] Digital facial recognition software and artificial intelligence have been used to distinguish criminals' headshot photographs from those of non-criminals. Using photographs to capture facial features, such as the shape of lips, eye spacing, and the distance between nose and mouth, scientists claim to be able to predict whether a person is gay or straight. Scientists also claim that soon intelligence will be measurable using photographic images. In education, some universities are using still images from live online classes to draw conclusions about students' feelings and level of engagement based on their facial expressions.[12] Is it really possible to interpret a person's sexuality, intelligence, or emotional state through a photograph? Do photographs present human subjects as they really are, or do they merely create the appearance of objective truth? What role might cultural assumptions and biases play when taking, looking at, and displaying photographs of others?

Photography Turns a Social Category into Truth

The invention of photography and the popularity of daguerreotype helped fuel racial iconography. In art history, iconography is a visual system for identifying, describing, and interpreting the subject and meaning of images. **Racial iconography** is a visual system developed to give racist ideas an air of truth. The effects of early racial iconography can still be seen today, but to understand their meanings and "visual violence"[13] requires familiarity with their historical origins.

In 1850, Swiss-born Harvard University scientist Louis Agassiz hired artist Joseph Zealy to create daguerreotypes of enslaved people on a plantation in South Carolina for his study of human types. The purpose was to provide objective evidence or "proof" that different races of humans existed. He wanted to show that not only were human races different in outward appearance, but they were also distinct species and unequal by nature. Agassiz's scientific photographs employed techniques of portraiture photography. They showed fully nude subjects in front of a blank backdrop in profile, frontal, and posterior poses.[14] Images 3.5 and 3.6 are daguerreotypes of Renty, an enslaved

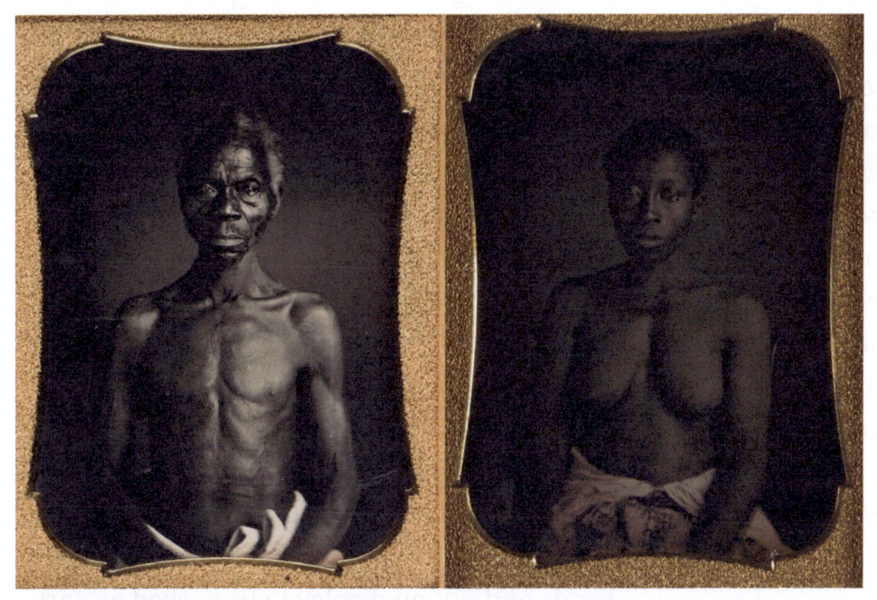

3.5 and 3.6 J. T. Zealy, *Daguerreotypes of Renty and Delia,* 1850. Courtesy of the Peabody Museum of Archaeology and Ethnology, Harvard University, 35-5-10/53037 and 35-5-10/53040.

African from Congo, and Delia, his enslaved U.S.-born daughter. These images are part of a much larger series of photo-portraits Agassiz commissioned.

The marriage of scientific methods and photographic techniques helped globalize the white colonial gaze. In Australia and Asia, for instance, English anthropologists incorporated measurement into their individual nude portraits of indigenous peoples living under British colonial rule. (See image 3.7.) The image-makers placed rulers and grids within the photographic frame alongside the non-White subject to bring greater precision and standardization to images. Measurement lent an aura of objectivity to the side-by-side comparisons of people. Thus, essentialist beliefs about the kinds of human differences that matter most were made to appear real, that is to say, true to the subject of the photograph rather than a product of White racial beliefs and the colonial desire to subjugate non-White peoples around the world.

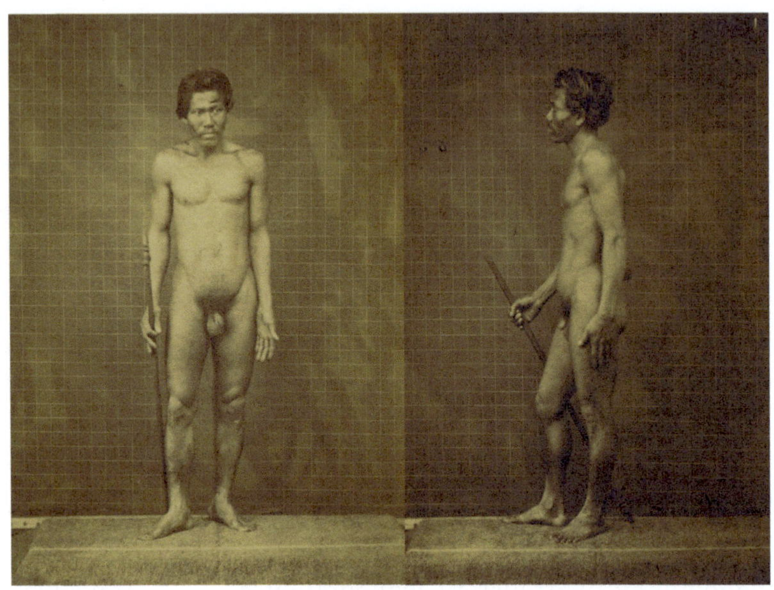

3.7 Ternate, Malagasy male, at 25, full face and profile, full length. Photographed according to Lamprey method. 400_002116 and 400_002117. 1868–69 © Royal Anthropological Institute.

Technologies of Looking Become Popular Entertainment

Before European and Euro-American scientists like Agassiz worked with artists to devise visual methods for explaining their belief in racial categories and their own superiority, some artists used their skills to visually represent perceived racial differences for entertainment purposes. The example of Sarah Baartman is a painful illustration of this. Baartman was a Khoikhoi girl who was removed from her home in South Africa, enslaved, and transported to Europe around 1810. Baartman was dressed in feathers and beads and put on display to be viewed as part of so-called "freak shows."[15] She was promoted

 Race and Art Education by Amelia M. Kraehe and Joni B. Acuff

The Birth of Venus

Let's practice visual racial literacy by critically interpreting the advertisements used to promote exhibitions of Sarah Baartman as "the Hottentot Venus." Hottentot refers to the ethnic group to which Baartman belonged.

- What does Venus refer to? What images and associations come to mind?

- Why do you think the image-makers and Baartman's exploiters would have juxtaposed the words Hottentot and Venus?

- What audience would find these words meaningful and appealing?

- What effect might the combination of words and image have on viewers?

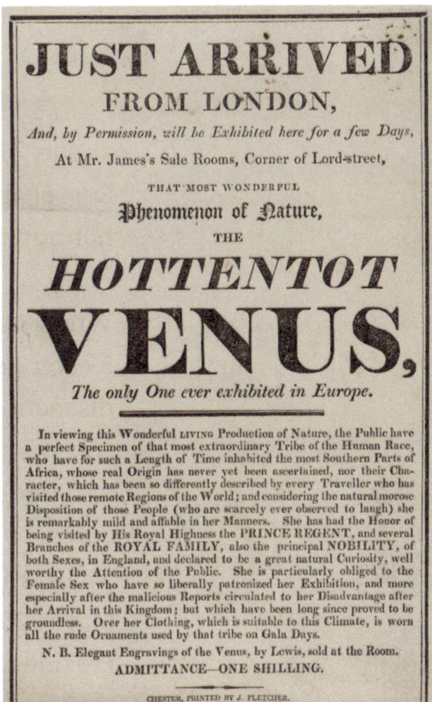

3.8 Wellcome Collection. Attribution 4.0 International (CC BY 4.0).

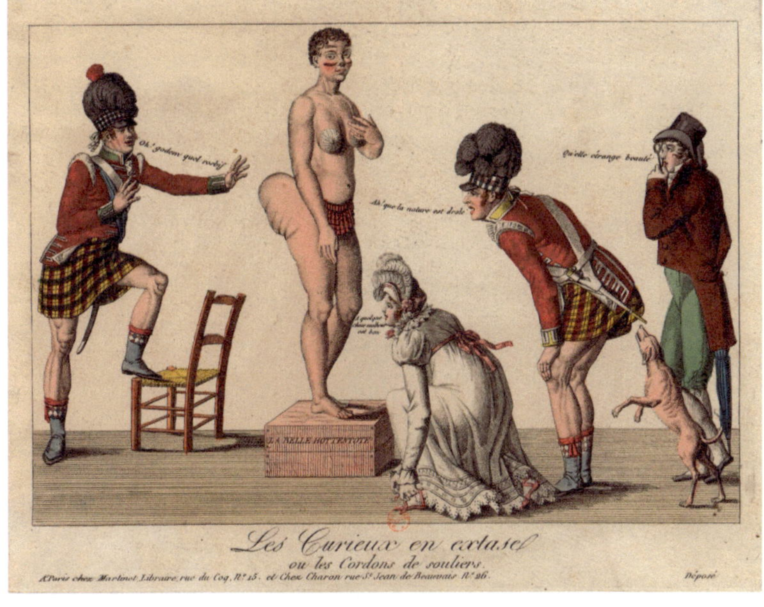

3.9 *Les Curieux en extase*, 19th century French print. Public domain.

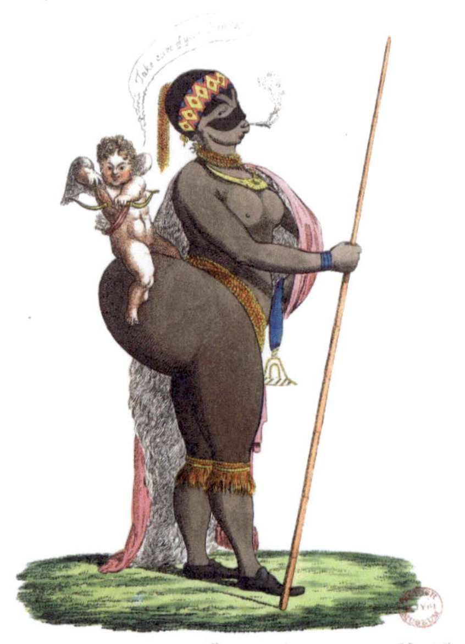

3.10 *Love and Beauty—Sartjee the Hottentot venus*, 1822.
© The Trustees of the British Museum, released as CC BY-NC-SA 4.0

as the "Hottentot Venus." (See images 3.8–3.11.) European onlookers took particular interest in her buttocks.

When Baartman died in 1815 at the age of 39, her genitals and brain were requested for dissection by a European scientist. The request was granted. Her corpse was cast in plaster, and her body was put on display again. Her corpse was circulated throughout European museums for nearly 190 years. It was not until March 2002, at the request of South African President Nelson Mandela, that the French government agreed to repatriate Baartman's remains to South Africa, and she was buried in an Eastern Cape province.

The image of the "hottentot," a term that is now widely considered derogatory, became a dominant racial type that visually encapsulated European myths about the primitive, overly sexual nature of African women.[16]

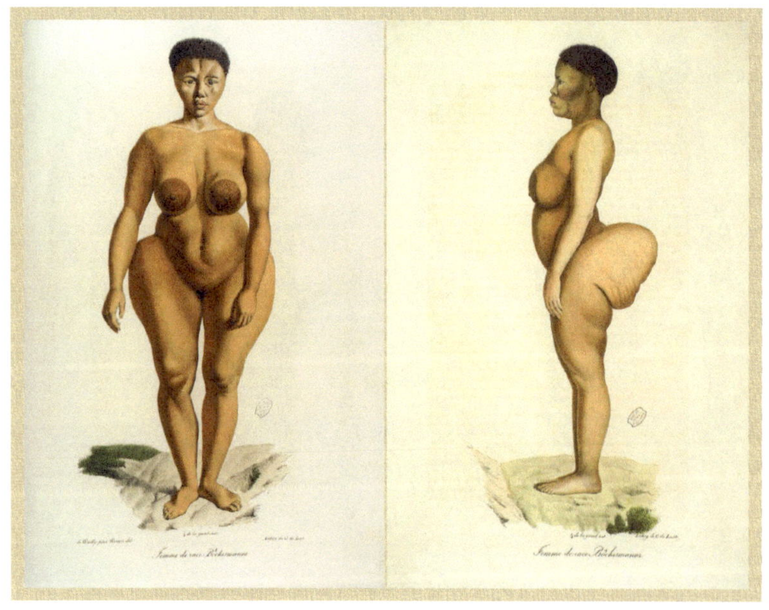

3.11 Wermer, Maréchal, Huet, designers; C. de Lasteyrie, lithograph; Etienne Geoffroy Saint-Hilaire, Frédéric Cuvier, authors of the text, 1815. Uploaded, stitched and restored by Jebulon. Public domain.

Baartman's image was reproduced and circulated widely in cartoons, periodicals, and other popular media. As audiences looked at the images, they could "see" objective evidence that confirmed their own presumptions of superiority as a white race and the supposed inferiority of non-White others.

When Whitestream Becomes Mainstream

Technological advancements enabled a white colonial gaze to be more frequently broadcast to **the masses**. The masses, a concept introduced in the 19th century, refers to a grouping of people and the ways in which that unified grouping can determine what opinions and social practices are "right," what are "wrong," what is "true," what is "false."[17] **Mass media**, then, refers to the types of media that have a centralized distribution source that reaches the large, group audience that is "the masses."

Throughout the 20th century, mass media such as radio, broadcast television, film, magazines, and newspapers were largely controlled and used by commercial advertisers and politicians to generate and distribute messages that reflected and promoted dominant ideologies. These ideologies concerned not only race relations but also industries, education, wars, economics, and politics. By circulating specific messages, sights, and sounds, cultural producers represented aspects of U.S.-American culture as though they were shared interests. The distribution of these "shared interests" through mass media helped spread and popularize certain ideas and beliefs. They were so pervasive that they eventually became "common sense" to the masses. Today, these dominant opinions are considered **mainstream**.

The landscape of mass media has expanded to include digital technologies such as the internet, the World Wide Web, and mobile devices like cell phones and tablets. In 2019, at least 96 percent of the U.S. population owned a smartphone. Simply put, mass media are ubiquitous in the modern world, so much so that when people encounter them in daily life, their content is often consumed unconsciously and internalized with very little awareness or criticality. Dominant racial narratives, imagery, and sentiments come to be popularly held as they seep into everyday life. Mass media can and often has shaped public imagination.

Do You See What I See?

Joseph Kern, a multiethnic art teacher, employs a phoropter—an instrument used during eye examinations to measure refractive error—as a visual metaphor to communicate the complexity of representation and perception. His work also speaks to society's socialization of flawed understandings of the world and people around us.

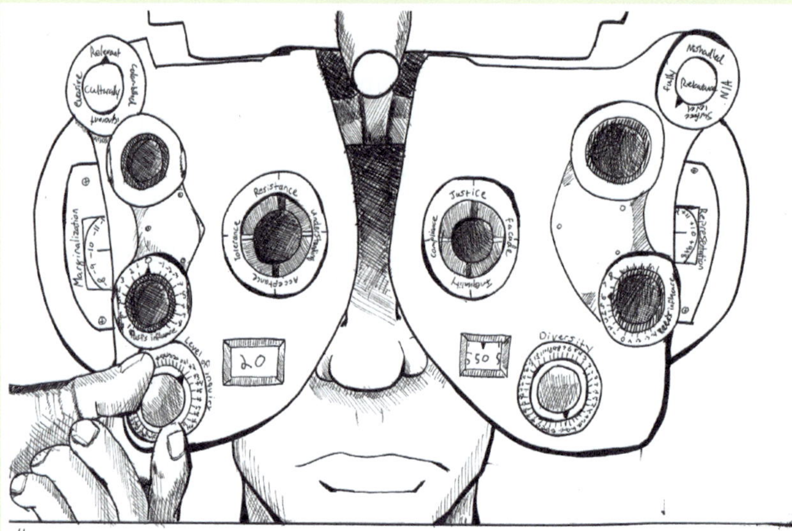

3.12 Joseph Kern, 2017. Pencil and ink drawing. Courtesy of the artist.

In an eye exam, the optometrist changes the phoropter lenses in front of the eye in order to correct vision and find the most effective prescription for the patient. In Kern's drawing, the left side of the phoropter is labeled "Marginalization," and the right "Representation." The lens over the right eye features the words resistance, understanding, acceptance, and tolerance. The lens over the left eye features the words justice, facade, inequality, and compliance. On the left side of the image you can see a hand adjusting the lens to 20, while the lens on the right is still at a 50. Quoting education scholar Chris Emdin, Kern writes, "Our understandings of who was and wasn't a good student were rooted less in our experiences with urban students and more on our perceptions of them, which were largely based on flawed narratives."[18]

Kern's accompanying written response queries, "I have realized many factors are involved in shaping someone's cultural outlook from the obvious to the subconsciously integrated. [I have] re-examine[d] the meanings for my own view multiple times. How can we work towards pre-conceived notions having less pull on our mindset while approaching unfamiliar situations in the classroom?"

Wealth and the Power to Manufacture Visual Environments

In the 1980s, about 50 corporations controlled U.S. **mainstream media**, outlets such as television, newspapers, popular magazines, books, and radio that deliver messages to a large portion of the population. In 2019, five corporations continued to dominate about 90 percent of the mainstream media. These media outlets are owned and operated by wealthy White men who consult with executive boards who are also about 98 percent White and male.[19] It would be more accurate to characterize the "mainstream" media as malestream and whitestream. *Malestream* was coined by feminist philosopher Mary O'Brien to call attention to the way male perspectives are assumed to be shared by women as well.[20] It inspired human rights scholar Claude Denis to adapt the term further, making **whitestream media** a concept that properly recognizes how White men have held nearly exclusive rights over the production, distribution, and even cultural criticism of media.[21] This has resulted in the creation of certain aesthetic preferences and value judgements that show the viewing public who and what is normal, loathsome, desirable, dangerous, trustworthy, and worth looking at. White men who hold media power have been able to place their own subjective views of the world at the forefront. They have created a visual environment within which others must operate.

In addition to White males being the primary distributors of mainstream media, they also write, produce, and direct the overwhelming majority of mainstream American film and television programming and content. For example, in 2018 only 1.3 out of 10 film directors were not White.[23] As a consequence, visual non-White people or the narratives that derive from their experiences and perspectives.[25]

The relative absence of non-White perspectives in media results in cultural scripts and imagery that reflect a white racial imagination and assign distorted and distorting **racial tropes** to non-White people. A trope is any commonly used rhetorical device or visual image created for the audience to easily recognize a concept or character. More specifically, racial tropes are stereotypical representations of people that contribute to the durability of race over time. They consist of characters and storylines that are static and recurring. Historically, the racial characterizations of non-Whites are generally disparaging. Much like Sarah Baartman's image, racial tropes fuel cultural stereotypes in ways that have real consequences for members of racialized groups.

The chart on page 57 shows some of the most common racial tropes in film and media. Tropes are powerful because they flatten differences. They are so often repeated that over time racial tropes calcify in the memory of people who have encountered them and become an implicit part of how they understand themselves and others.[26] Exposure to tropes is a cumulative process. Despite their

representations of U.S.-American culture are often **whitewashed** renderings that are reductive and limited in scope. Ideas and images are considered whitewashed when they are conceptualized without the consideration of inaccuracies, the cultural scripts encoded in tropes come to feel familiar. For children this presents a problem when their development of positive self-concept and identity is undermined by racial tropes viewed in movies, on television, and now in video games, and become the means by which they make sense of themselves and their place in the world.

The categories of male and female are a part of the dominant trope construction. They function to simplify race and gender at the same time. In so doing, non-conforming

Trope Characterizations

	Male	Female
Black/ African American	Uncle Tom, scary, violent, dangerous, comic relief, drug dealer, gangbanger	Mammy, matriarch, angry Black woman, Sapphire/independent Black woman, Jezebel, welfare queen
Native American	savage, dirty, alcoholic	nature worshiper, magical and mystical
Hispanic or Latinx	gangbanger, lazy, drug dealer	hypersexual temptress, short-tempered fireball, sassy, exotic
Asian or Pacific Islander	educated, nerdy, broken English, magical Asian	meek, submissive, thin/small body frame, tiger mom
Arab/ Middle Eastern	terrorists, manipulative, aggressive, wealthy	oppressed, belly dancers, manipulative, weak
Jewish	wealthy but frugal, business owner	wealthy but frugal, overweight and apathetic, asexual
White	protagonist, superhuman, debonair	innocent, vulnerable, savior

people—for example, queer Black women, transgender Asian American women, non-binary Latinx—are rendered invisible in popular culture. When transgender and non-binary people have been introduced in film and media, the characterizations generally are disparaging. Across all racial categories, transgender and non-binary characters are portrayed as mentally ill, sex workers, or peripheral comic relief.[27]

Dominant Popular Culture

Mass media are the technological means by which narratives, images, and ideas are disseminated to large swaths of society, even worldwide, by a relatively small group of cultural producers. **Popular culture**, on the other hand, refers to the practices and ideas that arise within a group. Mass media have been used to amplify the popular culture of the dominant or most influential groups in society. Thus, it becomes easy for leaders of powerful media corporations to suggest that they are merely supplying on the screen, over the sound waves, and in print what the public demands.

Historically, the dominant popular culture that provided much of the content produced,

distributed, and consumed through mass media was created by White people (males mostly) for consumption by other White people. As a result, dominant popular culture representations of Whites were flattering and multidimensional, whereas representations of non-Whites were largely negative and exaggerated in ways that were reductive, flattening the complexity and diversity of non-White individuals. Over time, a catalog of ethnic and racial caricatures emerged that belittled and made fun of non-White "others." For example, Black people were represented with monkey-like characteristics, for instance, big, wide gaping mouths, large ears, oversized hands and feet, and sloping foreheads. Popular culture reflected White society's low regard for people perceived as not White, thus reproducing and reaffirming white superiority through images. Companies mass-produced derogatory images of non-White people, especially Black,

Asian, and Native American people, in several different forms. Caricatures of non-White people could be found on items like postcards, cleaning products, toys and games, ceramic figurines, ashtrays, golf tees, cast-iron banks, children's books, dinnerware, songbooks, tea towels, cookie jars, matchbooks, magazines, movies, gag gifts, salt-and-pepper shak-

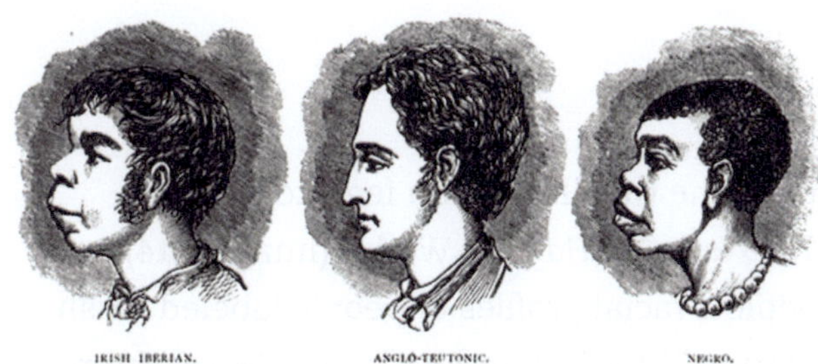

3.14 H. Strickland Constable, Illustration from *Ireland from One or Two Neglected Points of View*, **featured in** *Harper's Weekly,* **1899. Public domain.**

ers, planters, fishing lures, trade cards, ads, records, and tobacco tins.

Negative portrayals of those deemed not White, which would have included some European ethnic groups, contributed to their ongoing oppression. The Irish, for example, were characterized as uncivilized, unskilled, and impoverished. They were forced into labor that was considered "too diseased and too deadly" even for enslaved Black people.[29] Nineteenth century anti-Irish cartoons were featured in mainstream magazines like *Harper's Weekly* and *Puck*. Irish immigrants and their descendants were portrayed as drunken, ape-like barbarians who were lazy and lawless. The Irish were more closely associated with Black people than they were with Anglo-Americans.

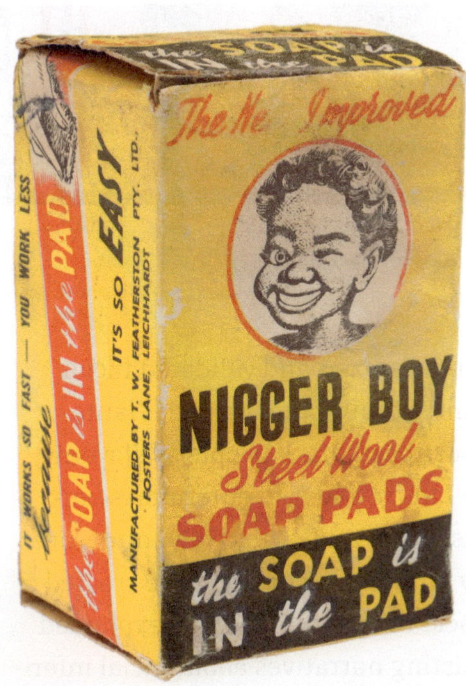

3.13 Nigger Boy Steel Wool Soap Pads. Museums Victoria. Copyright Museums Victoria / CC BY 4.0. https://collections. museumsvictoria.com.au/items/1371261.

Examine the illustration featured in the 1899 issue of *Harper's Weekly* (image 3.14). It depicts facial profiles of people labeled "Irish Iberian," "Anglo Teutonic," and "Negro," from left to right. It shows how the Irish were seen and more closely associated with Black people than with White people of English and Northern European ancestry. These visual representations drew from pseudo-scientific race theories that positioned non-White people as less than fully human.

Minstrelsy as Popular Culture

Exaggerated racial caricatures were presented to the public not only through mass media but also through **minstrelsy**, a form of live entertainment produced on local stages throughout the U.S. Minstrelsy was performed so widely that it became America's first national popular culture.[30] Minstrel shows, which included live comic skits, music, and dance, became popular in the 1840s as a way to depict Southern Black life to White people living in the Northern regions of the country. White men transformed themselves into "Black characters," painting their skin pitch-black with greasepaint or burnt cork and exaggerating their lips with red paint to resemble monkeys. This visual technique in minstrelsy is known as **blackface**.[31]

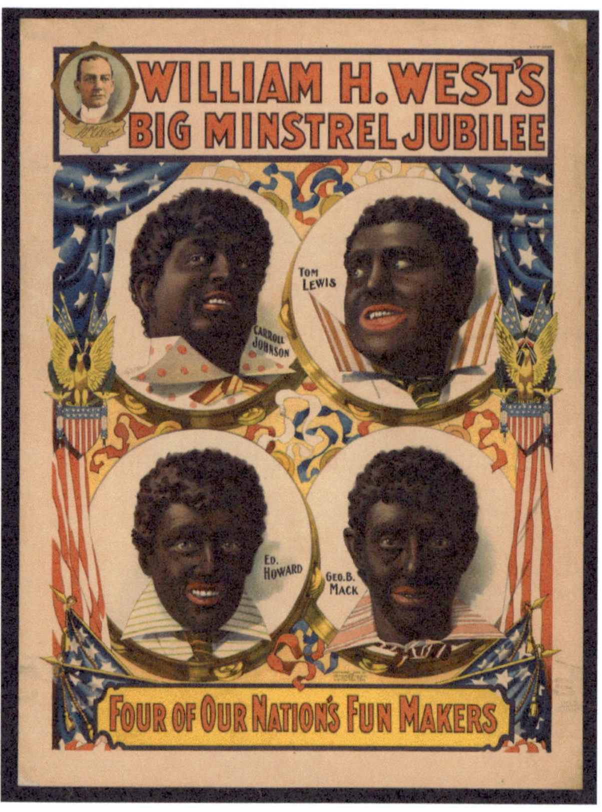

3.15 "Four of Our Nation's Fun Makers," Strobridge & Co. Lith.; Wm. H. West's Big Minstrel Jubilee, 1899. **Public domain.**

Blackface normalized and validated racial myths. Whites brought to life racial fantasies that portrayed Black people as slovenly, ignorantly happy, eager to entertain, sexually promiscuous, and cognitively immature. Minstrelsy and the use of blackface created a live spectacle that reinforced and expanded already existing narratives about racial inferiority encoded through earlier race paintings, race photography, and racial tropes like the hottentot.

White men even portrayed Black women in minstrel shows, as there were very rarely female performers in the early days of minstrelsy. As Black actors became more accepted on stage and in films, they also were forced to wear blackface. Ironically, White audiences often complained that the Black actors' faces were not black enough. The Black men needed to align more closely with the white fantasy.[32] As seen in the poster in image 3.15, the actors—all White men in blackface—are described as "Four of our nation's fun makers." Minstrel shows provided comic relief for the masses. With Black dehumanization at its center, minstrelsy cemented racist tropes of Black people as a pillar of U.S. popular culture.

TRY THIS!

White Reflections

Review all of the images in this chapter and consider the following questions:

- How do White people see themselves?

- How do White people depict themselves in relation to the racial Other?

- Where is whiteness present in the images of non-white peoples?

The Social Power of Face Paint, Yesterday and Today

Blackface minstrelsy was a visual exercise of racial power. It helped obscure the inhumanity of slavery by depicting it as amusing, and continued to shape how Black people were rendered as subjects in art and popular visual culture long after slavery had ended. Historian J. Stanley Lemons writes, "The minstrel show had the blackface character as its focus; vaudeville inherited him and passed him on to the musical theater, the movies, and radio."[33] Films in early history were dependent on blackface minstrelsy. A landmark example is D.W. Griffith's 1915 film, *The Birth of a Nation*, originally titled *The Clansman*. It is often cited as the first 12-reel film in the United States, and it was also the first film to be shown in the White House. President Woodrow Wilson's initial praise of the film lent credibility to White society's belief that Black people were inhuman and that the Ku Klux Klan's work needed to be continued. Still today, Griffith is acclaimed for his pioneering film production and cinematic innovations, like his use of close-ups, fade-outs, large battle scenes, color sequencing, and special use of subtitles that graphically verbalized imagery.

The Birth of a Nation influenced films produced long after. It is considered among the top 100 American films. Just as the film is praised for

Objects of Curiosity

Paul Rucker is a Black American interdisciplinary artist from Anderson, South Carolina. Rucker uses both visual art and music to layer his work, which creates multimodal opportunities and interactive experiences.

Conceptually, Rucker's work speaks explicitly to human rights issues, history (particularly slavery), and systemic racism. His 2015 exhibition, *REWIND*, explores the history of slavery and the objects that defined that era. He investigatively reappropriates objects, for example, recasting Ku Klux Klan robes using Kente cloth, camouflage, and silk fabric.

Rucker states,
These are the things that our parents don't tell us about. A lot of history is not taught in school, because there is shame on all sides. We're not taught to think as much as

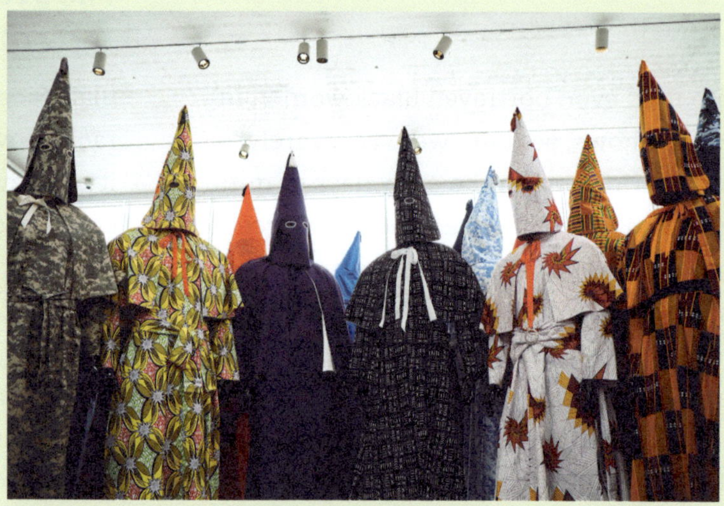

3.16 Paul Rucker, *Birth of a Nation Project*, 2015. Textiles and mixed media. Photo by Ryan Stevenson. Courtesy of the artist.

we're taught to be "good citizens." We're not taught to ask questions or challenge, because challenging preconceived ideas is hard, especially if it challenges why we have what we have…. If I cannot claim the words and symbols of those who killed and oppressed and make them my own, then I will turn them into an object of curiosity at least.[34]

establishing film as an art form, its content had an equally significant impact on race relations. The film claimed to represent American life after the Civil War, focusing on the impact of the abolition of slavery. Most members of the cast who portrayed the Black characters were White men in blackface. The visual rendering of Black men as violent rapists, unintelligent, and animalistic further solidified the already normalized belief that Black people were not humans but dangerous savages and their freedom would present a great danger to American society. The White actors in *The Birth of a Nation* vilified Black people so feraciously that the film ushered in the second wave of the Ku Klux Klan up to a decade after it was released. The racist film ignited a sense of urgency for White people to revitalize the work of the Ku Klux Klan in order to save White women from rape and the country from pillage.

White actors applied makeup to darken their skin to depict just about any race of people in film and on stage. Brownface was used to portray Native American, Latinx, and Middle Eastern people. Six years before D.W. Griffith presented *The Birth of a Nation*, he wrote and produced *Comata, the Sioux*, a 1909 film about a

Black American artist Michael Ray Charles asserts,

> A lot of Blacks don't want to see images like mine; perhaps they bring up too much pain…. A lot of whites are embarrassed and feel ashamed by them. But out of sight, out of mind doesn't mean that it doesn't exist. It happened, and I feel it has not been dealt with.[35]

> I think about so many people whose lives these images have affected. A lot of Black people have died and many are dying under the weight of these images. That's motivation enough for me to explore, and deal with, these things.[36]

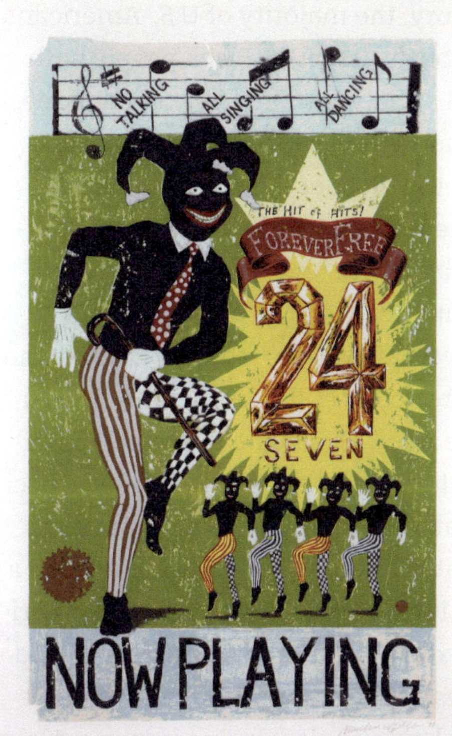

3.17 Michael Ray Charles, *(Forever Free) Twenty-Four-Seven*, 1995. Color screen print. Courtesy of the artist.

Native American woman who falls in love with a White cowboy.[37] All the actors were White, even those portraying the Native American characters.

While most of the racist media distributed in the 1800s and early 1900s have disappeared from wide circulation, the imagery has carried over and passively continues to enter our psyches. Research shows that even in the 21st century, the majority of U.S.-Americans unconsciously associate Black people with apes, and society is more likely to condone violence against Black criminal suspects based on the broader ideology that Black people are not fully human.[38] The iconography that blackface and brownface created still haunts this country, from culturally insensitive Halloween costumes to White and non-White actors still darkening their skin for movie roles. This is the historical underpinning that makes the black-and-red Gucci sweater at the beginning of this chapter so problematic. The sweater does not exist in a vacuum; it exists within a social and historical context. The failure to acknowledge and teach these historical underpinnings in art and visual culture classrooms is why a design team for a high-end clothing and accessories company like Gucci can forthrightly present a garment evoking violent imagery that dehumanizes an entire group of people.

Blackface Was Not an "Adults Only" Affair

Cartoon animation carried on traditions that originated in blackface minstrelsy. "With their white gloves, wide mouths and eyes, and trickerish behavior," Mickey Mouse and other popular characters carried "the tokens of blackface minstrelsy in their bodies and behaviors yet no longer immediately signif[ied] as such."[39] Animators would "blacken up" cartoon characters with exploding firecrackers and bombs that left soot on their faces. The Jim Crow Museum of Racist Memorabilia has an online collection of popular family cartoons that serves as an archive of racial iconography.

Blackvoice minstrelsy in cartoons and animation is the appropriation of racialized speech that is most closely associated with "blackness" or the culture of certain Black people.[40] Blackvoice in cartoons is most evident during interracial speech exchanges when certain dialects and speech patterns demarcate blackness, or otherness. Even animal characters in cartoons assume trope-like character traits that help audiences to "other" the characters. The hyenas in Disney's *The Lion King* are an example; they are sneaky, dangerous, and not to be trusted by the lion cub, Simba. The voices given to the hyenas imitate the qualities of speech—vocal intonation, accents, and cadence—commonly used in media representations of Black and Brown people living in inner-city neighborhoods. The Chihuahua Pedro in Disney's *Lady and the Tramp* displays brownvoice in its exaggerated vocal interpretation of Mexican and Mexican American accents.

In addition to voices, cartoon characters display slang, mannerisms, and fashion styles that read as "other," while the person behind the character is actually White. *The Simpsons* animated sitcom has received criticism for its brownvoice minstrelsy of the South Asian Indian character Apu Nahasapeemapetilon being voiced by Hank Azaria, a White actor from the U.S.[41] The show's writers and producers are White men, and despite years of criticism, the creators defended the practice as innocuous because it is intended as humor.[42]

Is It Ever Okay to "Try On" Another Culture?

Blackface and brownface was White America's attempt to dehumanize non-White people and popularize a particular racial narrative. However, darkening their own skin was also a way to "try on" different racial identities, ethnicities, and cultures. Cultural historian Eric Lott confirms,

> Minstrel performers often attempted to repress through ridicule the real interest in black cultural practices they nonetheless betrayed—minstrelsy's mixed erotic economy of celebration and exploitation.... The very form of blackface acts—an investiture in black bodies—seems a manifestation of the particular desire to try on the accents of "blackness" and demonstrates the permeability of the color line.[43]

A person's ability to take on and off certain racial and cultural ways of being represents social privilege but also reveals a desire to have certain experiences that are situated within a culture in which that person is not a member. The name for this is **cultural appropriation**. Cultural appropriation is the practice of using, borrowing, or "taking" another culture's intellectual property, expressive forms, artifacts, history, and ways of knowing.[44] Cultural appropriation becomes problematic when the group being "taken" from has been marginalized and even oppressed for having specific cultural habits and ways of being, but once these cultural habits and ways of

Mask On, Mask Off

In June 2015, Rachel Dolezal, a White American living in Spokane, Washington, became world-renown for her decades-long use of blackface to assume the identity of a Black woman. Using bronzer and a barrage of differently textured wigs and hair weaves, Dolezal passed as a light-skinned Black woman and taught Africana Studies at Eastern Washington University. She even headed Spokane's local chapter of the National Association for the Advancement of Colored People (NAACP) for a year.[45]

Since Dolezal's "outing," other White women have been exposed for engaging in similar offenses. In 2020, Jessica Krug, a Jewish White woman, co-opted blackness, specifically an Afro-Caribbean identity, and gained employ-ment as a college professor of African and Latin American Studies at George Washington University.[46]

In that same year, CV Vitolo-Haddad, an Italian-American non-binary graduate student at the University of Wisconsin in Madison took on both Black and Latin identities, utilizing one or the other depending on context.[47] Assuming Black and other non-White identities allowed Dolezal, Krug, and Vitolo-Haddad to insert themselves more comfortably into non-White organizing spaces, gaining social capital within the institutions they entered.

These stories of cultural appropriation illustrate the continued theft of Black identity, all the while profiting from it, unlike those who actually inhabit Black bodies. This is contempo-rary blackface minstrelsy.

being have been adopted by someone outside the group, then these traits are accepted and even desired.

For example, for centuries, Black women have worn their hair in braids known as cornrows for varying reasons, such as to protect their hair from environmental damage, to manage the volume of their curl, as well as to honor the Afrodiasporic connections passed on through ancestral traditions. However, there are workplaces, swimming pools, and even schools in the U.S. (e.g., Kentucky) that have banned cornrows, citing a range of reasons including the hairstyle is unprofessional, unsanitary, and a distraction to others. Non-White students have been suspended from school and barred from competing in athletic matches for wearing their hair in certain styles like twists, cornrows, and dreadlocks.[48] For example, Andrew Johnson, a 16-year-old Black boy, was forced to cut off his dreadlocks in order to wrestle in a championship match at his New Jersey high school.

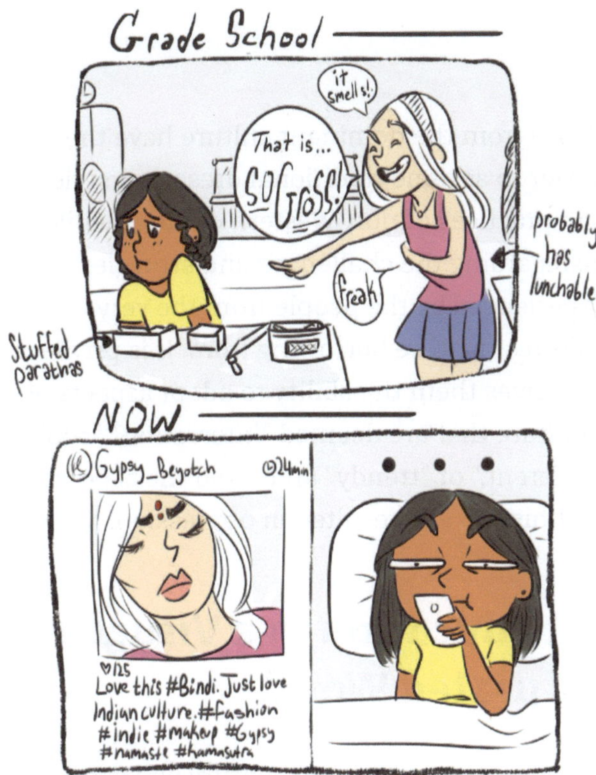

3.18 Sara Alfageeh, *Oh NOW You Like Me: Cultural Appropriation*, 2015. Digital comic, Photoshop. Courtesy of the artist.

Meanwhile, news outlets (e.g., *The Post*) featured cornrows as "the hot new trend" and even referred to them as "boxer braids," stripping the cultural history from the hairstyle. This rebranding occurred after reality star and social media personality Kim Kardashian and other high-profile White actresses and models appropriated the hairstyle. It has only been since the creation of the Crown Act of 2019 that Black Americans have been ensured protection from discrimination based on race-

based hairstyles.[49] This example represents the imbalance of power that often occurs with cultural appropriation.

But Artists Do It All the Time!

Visual and performing artists have been known to assume techniques, styles, and creative practices from other artists, mostly from the past, who have made a significant impact on the arts world across time. From a painter's brushstroke to a dancer's toe point, most artists have looked to others before them for not only inspiration but explicit direction in artmaking. So, how does artistic influence become an exploitative form of cultural appropriation? The answer is simple. Power.

One must consider relationships of power in the exchange of ideas. Cultural appropriation becomes exploitation when an artist who occupies a position of racial, social, and cultural privilege takes ideas and practices from a group of people who have suffered from cultural subjugation, creative oversight, and economic disadvantage for the very ideas and practices being taken. Let's consider the case of Amanda PL, a White, Canadian painter who was forced to cancel her art exhibition because of accusations of cultural appropriation of a form of Indigenous Anishinaabe painting known as the Woodland Style. The art gallery operators who canceled Amanda PL's show made a public statement that articulated the power imbalance at the core of cultural appropriation, stating,

> One question is whether it is appropriate to afford a non-Indigenous artist opportunities to show and sell work in the same style as Indigenous artists who don't have similar opportunities. We do not believe so.[50]

Further, Amanda PL openly shared that she has no Native American roots and that she did not try to pretend that her work held the cultural meanings that an Anishinaabe artist's work would. For this reason, Indigenous activists in Canada protested Amanda's work, claiming that it had the potential to erase the cultural heritage and ancestral memory that is embedded within the Anishinaabe style of painting. Tony Magee, one of the two proprietors of the art gallery, asserted,

> Our society has taken away the land, the freedom, the dignity, and even the children of indigenous people.… And it has done too little to make retribution. They don't have a lot left to claim as their own, not even their art, apparently.[51]

Those from the dominant culture have the power to assume traditional dress, hairstyles, and practices of non-Western cultures while disregarding the challenges and struggles experienced by the people from the very cultures they are borrowing from. It is privilege that gives them the ability to adopt aspects of a culture that are deemed "interesting," "cool," "different," or "trendy" and avoid the aspects that historically resulted in oppression.

Art Education in a Visually Saturated World

Art education in the 21st century will continue to face the challenge of racism via visual representation. But increasingly art teachers and their students also must contend with global media saturation where much of human-to-human interaction occurs through visuals and text on a screen. People of all ages watch television and stream videos, play video games, use the computer, swipe and tap their handheld mobile devices, and otherwise engage in mass-mediated digital content. For even the youngest children, digital media have become an integral part of childhood, particularly during the COVID-19 pandemic when many schools pivoted to online instruction.

Screen time was on the rise even prior to the pandemic. In 2018, the Pew Research Center found that 95 percent of teens ages 13 to 17 owned a smartphone. Forty-five percent of teens were connected to the Internet almost constantly. That figure is nearly double what it was only three years earlier. Social media usage is ubiquitous, but gaming is also significant, with 83 percent of girls and 97 percent of boys reporting that they played video games online, on a console, or on mobile device.[52]

Given what we know about the amount of time young people spend consuming and using media, visual racial literacy is vitally important. As we have seen throughout this chapter, racism is visually mediated and has evolved over time into racial tropes, iconography, and other cultural conventions that are actively used today. Without visual racial literacy to make sense of what they are presented with, young people (and adults, too) remain vulnerable to media's influence and manipulation, including cyberracism. Art teachers can develop their own literacy so they are better equipped to sensitize art students.

Visual racial literacy helps empower students in at least four ways:

1. Online Research for Artmaking

Many students use digital media to research artists, art movements, and potential subject matter for class projects. Social media and internet sites are abundant sources of inspiration for student artmaking both in and out of the classroom. It is important to be cognizant of the ways these powerful digital tools scaffold learning and development. Much like a teacher or more experienced peer, media technologies stand in as knowledgeable others.[53] They impart content and model habits of mind that may or may not be beneficial to young people's well-being. This is especially true for very young children or those who have not been given access to critical race histories and frameworks (like those presented throughout Chapters 2 and 3) and, as a consequence, have difficulty spotting racist content.

A good example is when students encounter a **cloaked website**. In a cloaked website, the domain name is used to undermine racial justice projects. "Martinlutherking.org" and "AmericanCivilRightsReview.com" are websites that actually espouse white supremacist ideas. Cloaked sites provide misinformation about history and distorted representations of the culture of particular racial and ethnic groups. When the duplicitous nature of cloaked websites is made known to the public, they lose much of their power. Once exposed, these sites may be decommissioned or transformed with a new name and URL. Cloaked sites are convincing because they trade on the visual and racial illiteracy of audiences. They may also use patriotism to disguise racist messages. Without visual racial literacy, young people remain vulnerable to manipulation.

2. Online Racial Discrimination

Youth often face racism directly in their online encounters. Young people may become a target or perpetrator of racial discrimination online, or they may witness a racist event. Psychologist Brendesha Tynes defines **online racial discrimination** as "denigrating or excluding individuals or groups on the basis of race through the use of symbols, voice, video, images, text, and graphic representations."[54] When she researched online racial discrimination among 6th through 12th grade Black American students, she found six types of cyberracism experiences:

- Racial epithets
- Statements that were untrue, stereotyping, and implicitly racist
- Racist jokes
- Symbols of hate, such as the Confederate flag
- Threats of physical harm or death
- Graphic representations and actual images of dead Black bodies

Nothing can capture the seriousness of cyberracism and harm to students as powerfully as the students' own words. Here are a few examples of what they said:

The worst thing that has happened to me on the internet is that someone threatened to kill me because of my race.

Almost every day on *Call of Duty: Black Ops* [a video game] I see Confederate flags, swastikas, and black people hanging from trees in emblems, and they say racist things about me and my teammates.

The worst internet experience that I received was online scrolling down my Facebook stream and seen a picture of an Obama doll hanging by a nuce [sic] at a gas station.... I showed it to my mom and my coworkers but really nothing we could do about it.

Me and my friends were playing Xbox and some kid joined the Xbox Live party we were in and made a lot of racist jokes I found offensive.[55]

Many schools have software called "hate filters" designed to filter out only the most overt forms of hate speech online. How effective do you think hate filters would be given what these students faced online?

3. Online Recruitment by Supremacist Groups

Social media applications have given White supremacists and eager racists a platform to disseminate hate speech and violent imagery. Neo-Nazis and the Ku Klux Klan use social media and video streaming applications like Facebook, Instagram, and YouTube to recruit and embolden previously closeted racists to be more vocal and active in their hate. The recruitment process is insidious. A reporter from *The Washington Post* investigated how extremist groups recruit children online. It goes something like this:

> With each tap of a finger, the memes grew darker: Sexist and racist jokes (for instance, a looping video clip of a white boy demonstrating how to "get away with saying the n-word," or memes referring to teen girls as "thots," an acronym for "that ho over there") led to more racist and dehumanizing propaganda, such as infographics falsely asserting that black people are inherently violent.[56]

In the current digital media landscape, it can be hard to discern what content is trustworthy. Visual racial illiteracy leaves children and teens more susceptible to being lured into extremist ideology and movements. Art teachers can help arm and protect children by making racial iconography, tropes, and their histories an integral part of visual literacy education in the digital era.

4. Digital Youth Engagement

Students use digital tools for various purposes. They connect with each other, create images and stories that reflect their perspectives, and participate in advocacy and activism. These online activities are not merely recreational. They enable young people to "restory" the world to include their perspectives.[57] Moreover, student and youth digital engagement has helped spur protest movements such as #BlackLivesMatter, #MarchForOurLives, and #FridaysForFuture, giving young people the opportunity to learn about and lead on issues that matter to

Where Brown Meets Green

Armed with visual racial literacy, young people engage with digital platforms and tools to change dominant advocacy narratives. Known as @browngirl_green on Instagram, youth activist and self identified "brown girl" Kristy Drutman uses podcasts, blogs, and a YouTube channel to "restory" traditional environmentalism and conservation.

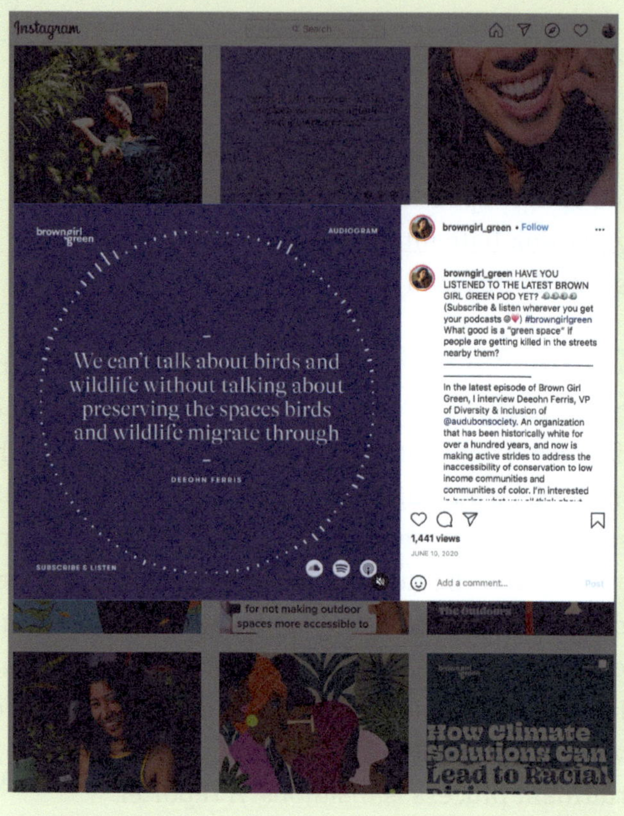

3.19 Brown Girl Green screen shot.

them and future generations. It is notable, too, that youth are injecting racial awareness into mainstream advocacy groups. Environmentalism is a good example of this.

Activism researcher Joe Curnow explains how traditional environmentalism and conservation had a cozy relationship with racism and colonization: "Indigenous communities and poor people have been removed, relocated, and displaced to protect privileged leisure access to 'nature,' or white settler economic interests."[58] Armed with visual racial literacy, more and more young people are pushing environmentalism toward environmental justice. (See Activists Speak, this page.) This change in language is significant. It reflects a recognition that seemingly unrelated social issues are intertwined and, as a consequence, there is a need for multifaceted, systemic changes rather than isolated reforms.

Young climate activists today tend to perceive climate change as the symptom of a broader systemic problem, connected to the same economic and political roots that produce other forms of violence, injustice, and inequality, including racism. They do not advocate making these systems sustainable. Their demand is climate justice and a new, more just global system.[59] Visual racial literacy is critical to being an informed digital citizen in the 21st century and participating in contemporary student- and youth-led movements for social change.

Conclusion

This chapter has focused on the idea that race and racism are visually mediated. We have provided examples of how race and racism are fundamentally practices of noticing and perceiving. We learn to see each other and the world in racialized ways through casual encounters with racially encoded pictures, objects, and moving images. To counter racist practices of looking, it is critical to (1) recognize racial iconography as an integral part of U.S.-American and global popular culture and (2) understand popular culture as a visually seductive medium through which racial hierarchy (white supremacy) is socially constructed, learned, and contested. It is important that people are able to recognize and respond to the dominant visualities of race because, if not, we can expect to see racist imagery resurface again and again with each new generation.

The technological means for producing and consuming popular visual culture increasingly is embedded in daily life. Cameras, camcorders, editing software, sharing sites, and screens for viewing content are less expensive and more readily available than ever before. Young people encounter images, text, and other modes of communication that provide racialized messages. They leave these encounters with ideas and mental images about themselves and others that are shaped by not only *what* they are looking at but also *how* they are doing the looking.

A curriculum that supports visual racial literacy includes opportunities for students to identify racial tropes as they are represented in art and visual culture of the past and as they are reiterated in newer forms, mediums, and contexts. Instead of avoiding racial stereotypes altogether, leaving students illiterate in the process, teachers can educate students to recognize and confront racist images, the visual techniques used to produce them, and their origins in supremacist ideology.

By having the tools to know "how it all works," students may develop a greater sense of agency, moving from mere objects of history to being cocreators of the world they wish to see. In the next chapter, we explore the relationship between young people's identity formation and their learning while growing up in racialized worlds, and the consequences for students when art teachers avoid talking about race.

Notes

1   Shawn Michelle Smith, *At the Edge of Sight: Photography and the Unseen* (Durham, NC: Duke University Press, 2013); and Marita Sturken and Lisa Cartwright, *Practices of Looking: An Introduction to Visual Culture* (New York: Oxford University Press, 2018).

2   Lani Guinier, "From Racial Liberalism to Racial Literacy: Brown v. Board of Education and the Interest-Divergence Dilemma," *Journal of American History* 91, no. 1 (2004): 92–118.

3   Lani Guinier, "Race and Reality in a Front-Porch Encounter," *The Chronicle of Higher Education*, July 30, 2009, para. 14, https://www.chronicle.com/article/RaceReality-in-a/47509/.

4   Ilona Katzew, *Casta paintings: Images of Race in Eighteenth-Century Mexico* (New Haven, CT: Yale University Press, 2004).

5   Laura Mulvey, *Visual and Other Pleasures* (New York, NY: Palgrave Macmillan, 1989).

6   Museo Central, "N°21 De Castas y Mala Raza: Claudia Coca," June 16, 2020, video, YouTube. https://www.youtube.com/watch?v=hGVGVH_SVN0.

7   María Elena Martínez, *Genealogical Fictions: Limpieza de Sangre, Religion, and Gender in Colonial Mexico* (CA: Stanford University Press, 2008).

8   Marcy J. Dinius, *The Camera and the Press: American Visual and Print Culture in the Age of the Daguerreotype* (Philadelphia: University of Pennsylvania Press, 2012).

9   bell hooks, *Black Looks: Race and Representation* (South End Press, 1992).

10 Molly Rogers, *Delia's Tears: Race, Science, and Photography in Nineteenth-Century America* (New Haven, CT: Yale University Press, 2010).

11 Sahil Chinoy, "The Racist History Behind Facial Recognition," *The New York Times*, July 10, 2019, https://www.nytimes.com/2019/07/10/opinion/facial-recognition-race.html.

12 Mark Lieberman, "I Know How You Felt This Semester," *Inside Higher Ed*, February 20, 2018, https://www.insidehighered.com/digital-learning/article/2018/02/20/sentiment-analysis-allows-instructors-shape-course-content

13 Lisa Gail Collins, *The Art of History: African American Women Artists Engage the Past* (New Brunswick, NJ: Rutgers University Press, 2002): 12.

14 Shawn Michelle Smith, *Photography on the Color Line: W. E. B. Du Bois, Race, and Visual Culture* (Durham, NC: Duke University Press, 2004).

15 Lisa Gail Collins, *The Art of History: African American Women Artists Engage the Past* (New Brunswick, NJ: Rutgers University Press, 2002).

16 Ibid.

17 Marita Sturken and Lisa Cartwright, *Practices of Looking: An Introduction to Visual Culture* (New York: Oxford University Press, 2018).

18 Christopher Emdin, *For White Folks Who Teach in the Hood and the Rest of Ya'll Too: Reality Pedagogy and Urban Education* (Beacon Press, 2017): 42.

19 PBS.org, "Who Owns the Media?" 2019, https://www.pbs.org/independentlens/democracyondeadline/mediaownership.html

20 Mary O'Brien, *The Politics of Reproduction* (London, UK and Boston, MA: Routledge & Kegan Paul, 1981).

21 Claude Denis, *We Are Not You: First Nations and Canadian Modernity* (Toronto, Ontario: Broadview Press, 1997).

22 Lorna Roth, "Home on the Range: Kids, Visual Culture, and Cognitive Equity," *Cultural Studies <—> Critical Methodologies* 9, no. 2 (2009): 141–148.

23 Darnell Hunt, Ana-Christina Ramon, Michael Tran, Amberia Sargent, Debanjan Roychoudhury, "Hollywood Diversity Report 2018: Five Years of Progress and Missed Opportunities," Institute for Research on Labor and Employment, UCLA, Division of Social Sciences, https://socialsciences.ucla.edu/wp-content/uploads/2018/02/UCLA-Hollywood-Diversity-Report-2018-2-27-18.pdf.

24 Phillip Atiba Goff, Jennifer L. Eberhardt, Melissa J. Williams, and Matthew Christian Jackson, "Not Yet Human: Implicit Knowledge, Historical Dehumanization, and Contemporary Consequences," *Journal of Personality and Social Psychology* 94, no. 2 (2008): 292–306.

25 John Gabriel, *Whitewash: Racialized Politics and the Media* (London: Routledge, 1998).

26 Eduardo Bonilla-Silva, *Racism Without Racists: Color-Blind Racism & Racial Inequality in Contemporary America* (Roman & Littlefield, 2010).

27 Sam Feder (director), *Disclosure*, 2020, film, Field of Vision; Bow & Arrow Entertainment; Level Forward.

28 J. Stanley Lemons, "Black Stereotypes as Reflected in Popular Culture, 1880-1920," *American Quarterly* 29, no. 1 (1977): 102–116.

29 Ibid.

30 Ibid.

31 Eric Lott, *Love and Theft: Blackface Minstrelsy and the American Working Class* (New York, NY: Oxford University Press, 2013).

32 Ibid.

33 J. Stanley Lemons, "Black Stereotypes as Reflected in Popular Culture, 1880–1920," *American Quarterly* 29, no. 1 (1977): 102–116.

34 Katherine Brooks, "Artist Paul Rucker Is Taking Back the Racists Symbols of America's Past," Huffpost: Culture & Arts, October 2, 2015, para. 9, https://www.huffpost.com/entry/paul-rucker-rewind_n_560d673ce4b0768127010cf5.

35 Steven Heller, "Michael Ray Charles: When Racist Art Was Commercial Art," *Print Magazine*, January 15, 2012,

para. 2, https://www.printmag.com/post/michael-ray-charles-when-racist-art-was-commercial-art.

36 Ibid, para. 13.

37 Brian D. Behnken and Gregory D. Smithers, *Racism in American Popular Media: From Aunt Jemima to the Frito Bandito* (Santa Barbara, CA: Praeger, 2015).

38 Phillip Atiba Goff, Jennifer L. Eberhardt, Melissa J. Williams, and Matthew Christian Jackson, "Not Yet Human: Implicit Knowledge, Historical Dehumanization, and Contemporary Consequences," *Journal of Personality and Social Psychology* 94, no. 2 (2008): 292–306.

39 Nicholas Sammond, *Birth of an Industry: Blackface Minstrelsy and the Rise of American Animation* (Durham, NC: Duke University Press, 2015): 3

40 Michael A. Chaney, "Coloring Whiteness and Blackvoice Minstrelsy: Representations of Race and Place in *Static Shock, King of the Hill, South Park*," *Journal of Popular Film & Television* 31, no. 4 (2004): 167–175.

41 Shilpa S. Davé, *Indian Accents: Brown Voice and Racial Performance in American Television and Film* (Urbana-Champaign: University of Illinois Press, 2013).

42 Hari Kondabolu (writer) and Michael Melamedoff (producer/director), *The Problem with Apu*, 2017, documentary film, US: Avalon Television, Marobru Inc.

43 Eric Lott, *Love and Theft: Blackface Minstrelsy and the American Working Class* (New York, NY: Oxford University Press, 2013): 6.

44 Bruce Ziff and Pratima V. Rao (eds.), *Borrowed Power: Essays on Cultural Appropriation* (New Brunswick, NJ: Rutgers University Press, 1997).

45 Leah Asmelash, "A White Professor Says She Has Been Pretending to Be Black for Her Entire Professional Career," CNN, September 4, 2020, https://www.cnn.com/2020/09/03/us/jessica-krug-gwu-black-trnd/index.html.

46 Hira Humayun and David Williams, "University of Wisconsin-Madison Grad Student Admits Pretending to Be a Person of Color," CNN, September 17, 2020, https://www.cnn.com/2020/09/17/us/wisconsin-grad-student-race-trnd/index.html.

47 Deborah Roberts, Ignacio Torres and Jasmine Brown, "As Natural Hair Goes Mainstream, One High School's Natural Hair Ban Causes Firestorm," ABCNews, September 15, 2016, https://abcnews.go.com/US/natural-hair-mainstream-high-schools-policy-sparks-firestorm/story?id=42100267.

48 The Crown Act, 2020, https://www.thecrownact.com/.

49 Kirk Johnson, Richard Pérez-Peña, and John Eligon, "Rachel Dolezal, in Center of Storm, Is Defiant: 'I Identify as Black,'" *The New York Times*, June 16, 2015, https://www.nytimes.com/2015/06/17/us/rachel-dolezal-nbc-today-show.html.

50 Alexander Nazaryan, "White Painter Loses Art Show Over Cultural Appropriation Debate," *Culture*, May 5, 2017, para. 3, https://www.newsweek.com/cultural-appropriation-outcry-succeeds-cancelling-gallery-show-white-painter-594924.

51 Ibid, para. 9.

52 Monica Anderson and Jingjing Jiang, "Teens, Social Media & Technology 2018," Pew Research Center, May 2018, http://publicservicesalliance.org/wp-content/uploads/2018/06/Teens-Social-Media-Technology-2018-PEW.pdf.

53 Ellen Wartella, Leanne Beaudoin-Ryan, Courtney K. Blackwell, Drew P. Cingel, Lisa B. Hurwitz, and Alexis R. Lauricella, "What Kind of Adults Will Our Children Become? The Impact of Growing Up in a Media-Saturated World," *Journal of Children and Media* 10, no. 1 (2016): 13–20.

54 Brendesha M. Tynes, "Online Racial Discrimination: A Growing Problem for Adolescents," *Psychological Science Agenda*, 2015, para. 4, http://www.apa.org/science/about/psa/2015/12/online-racial-discrimination.aspx.

55 Ibid, para. 11.

56 Caitlin Gibson, "'Do You Have White Teenage Sons? Listen Up.' How White Supremacists Are Recruiting Boys Online," *The Washington Post*, September 17, 2019, para. 15, https://www.washingtonpost.com/lifestyle/on-parenting/do-you-have-white-teenage-sons-listen-up-how-white-supremacists-are-recruiting-boys-online/2019/09/17/f081e806-d3d5-11e9-9343-40db57cf6abd_story.html.

57 Amy Stornaiuolo and Ebony Elizabeth Thomas, "Disrupting Educational Inequalities through Youth Digital Activism," *Review of Research in Education* 41 (2017): 337–357.

58 Joe Curnow, "#Fridaysforfuture: When Youth Push the Environmental Movement towards Climate Justice," *The Conversation*, September 15, 2019, para. 7, https://theconversation.com/fridaysforfuture-when-youth-push-the-environmental-movement-towards-climate-justice-115694.

59 Benjamin Bowman, "Fridays for Future: How the young climate movement has grown since Greta Thunberg's lone protest," *The Conversation*, August 28, 2020, para. 13, https://theconversation.com/fridays-for-future-how-the-young-climate-movement-has-grown-since-greta-thunbergs-lone-protest-144781.

Chapter 4

Growing Up in Racialized Worlds

Race and Racism in Students' Lives

> *"Racial considerations shade almost everything in America."*
>
> —Eduardo Bonilla-Silva

Racism is endemic in U.S. society. It shows up in the organization of neighborhoods, schools, and workplaces and is ever-present within media environments (see Chapters 2 and 3). Since young people grow up navigating these spaces, they cannot escape racism. Indeed, students walk into classrooms saddled with "racial baggage" from prior social and cultural experiences. The ways students absorb the weight of that racial baggage will differ depending on how they are situated in relation to social structures and hierarchies. Social structures, such as race, class, gender, and sexuality, play a key role in how students learn to perceive themselves and their place in the world. They can influence the way students take in and process new information as well as how they express their thoughts, feelings, and identities. Art educators are more prepared to support and guide students in meaningful, culturally relevant ways when they understand how racial structures can affect learning and development in and out of the classroom.

In this chapter, we focus on these key concepts:

- Identity formation
- Racial identity
- Colorblind racism
- Meritocracy
- Racial ecology

What Is Identity?

Racism is predicated on the ability to sort and categorize people as belonging to this racial group or that racial group. Visible markers are often used as indicators for sorting and categorizing people. For example, in the U.S., from the moment children are born, they are gendered, raced, and individuated with a name and unique identification number. The visible markers of the body are used to *identify* each person and thus begins the psycho-social process of **identity** formation.

From Categorization to Identity Formation

Because racial and gender categorization occurs early in life (prior to birth often), one learns early on to see the world through that schema, and racial and gender identity become salient parts of existence. Categorization is not a conscious process for many people. This is because in the midst of

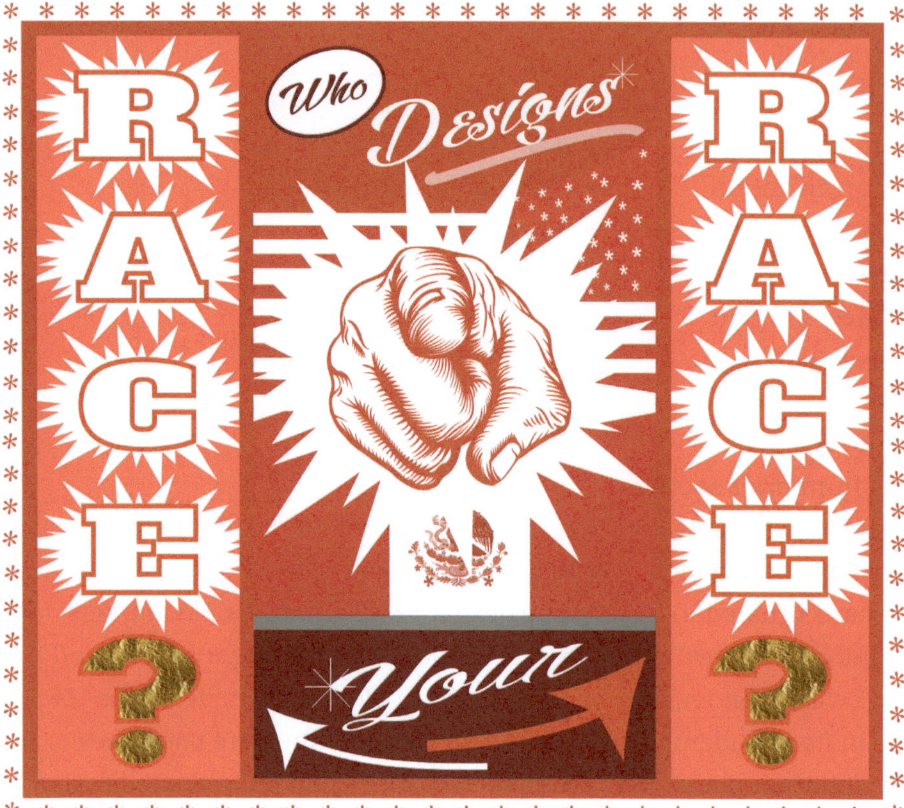

4.1 Collective Magpie, *Who Designs Your Race? Illustration no. 1*, 2018. Study for the public mural exhibited at the America Plaza Trolley Station as a part of the *In a Close(d) Relationship* solo exhibition, Museum of Contemporary Art San Diego. Courtesy of the artists.

any interaction, the human mind is capable of taking in information from the surrounding environment and using that information to make snap judgments. This innate capacity is useful for survival in the natural world, where quick responses to real threats are necessary, however, it poses a problem for social interactions in the modern world, particularly in diverse societies. This is because snap judgments can be and often are biased, wrong, or based on incomplete information.

Identity is a developmental process that involves categorization. It is what allows me to imagine myself as a particular kind of person and to enact that self-image as I navigate various social interactions and cultural settings. To put it another way, identity is a continual, lifelong process of self-identification that is rearticulated and performed over time. That repetition can produce a durable and deeply felt sense of self, particularly when others recognize me as the kind of person I long to be.

Taking on the concept of self-identification, Tae Hwang and MR Barnadas, who work under the name Collective Magpie, engage in social practice art. The larger-than-life poster-style artwork (see image 4.1) grew out of a race survey they created and circulated in San Diego, a city located in the racially, ethnically, and linguistically diverse borderlands between Mexico and the U.S.

Transnational students who live near the border cross back and forth daily to attend school. When in the U.S., they often are confronted with questions like "What race are you?" This question racializes them in ways they may not be familiar with. Taking the national census as its inspiration, Collective Magpie organized dialogues with many of the students and community members. They asked participants to fill out their own race survey (see images 4.2 and 4.3). It included more subjective questions like "Do you feel Korean? Not at all/Just a little/Somewhat/Moderately/Quite a lot/All the time. Where and when? How often?"

In an interview, Collective Magpie's Tae Hwang describes the intention of their survey to serve as a pedagogical tool:

What we hope to do as artists is provoke a question.... We certainly don't have the solutions of how to solve a race war. Our intention isn't to create a survey that would cure any kind of race issues, but just to have

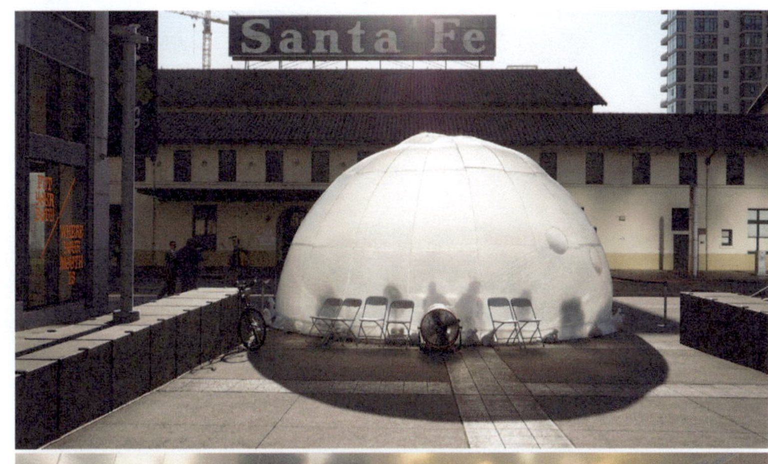

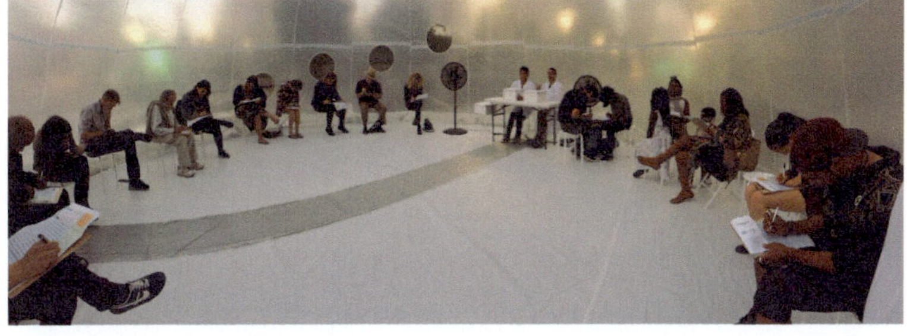

4.2 Collective Magpie, *Poetic Exploration of Race Survey*, 2017. Participatory event and performance, Museum of Contemporary Art San Diego at the America Plaza Trolley Station. Courtesy of the artists.

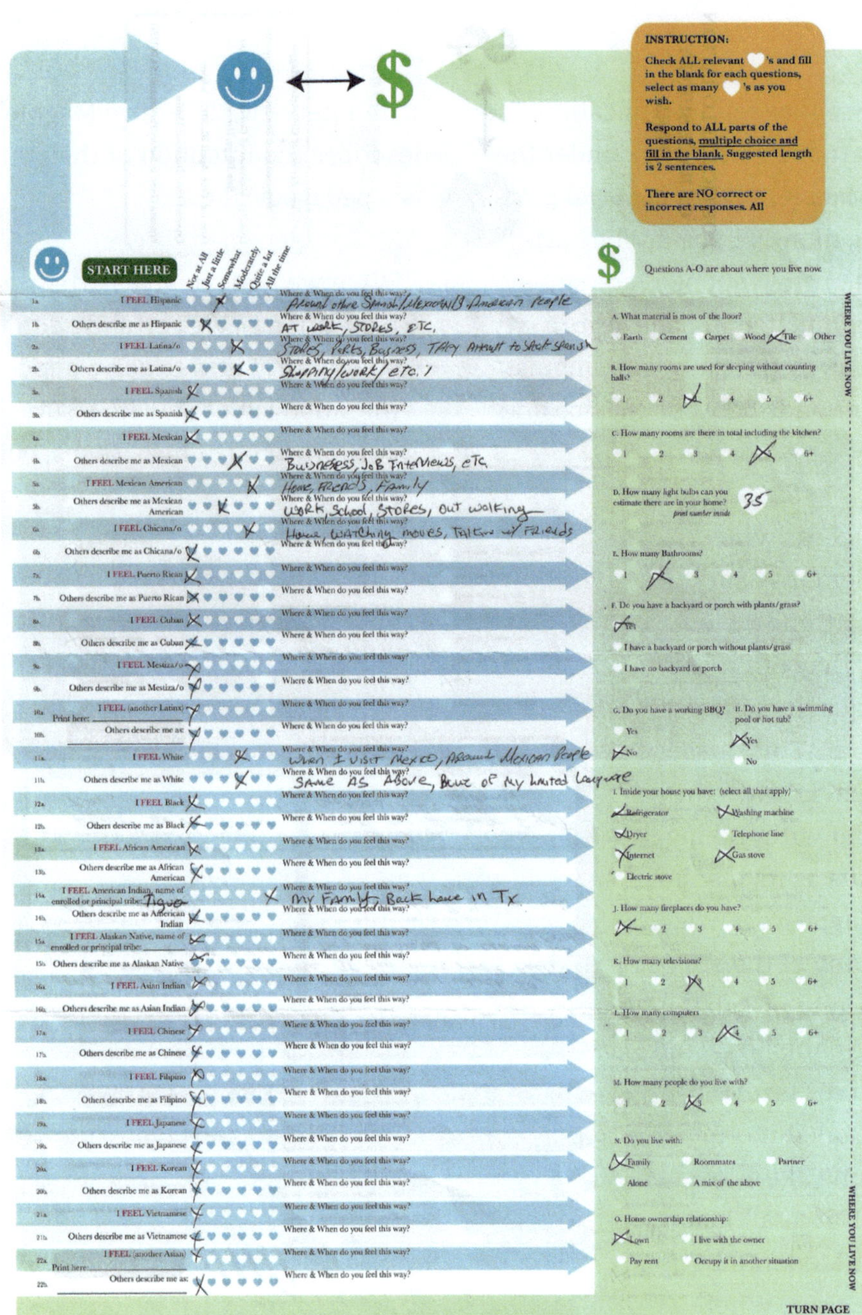

4.3 Collective Magpie, *Poetic Exploration of Race Survey form*, 2017. The front side of a participant-completed form; one of 100 forms collected on April 20, 2017. Courtesy of the artists.

people think about these issues. If you live in Mexico people might call you a blonde, basically something that would be considered "White," but when they come into the U.S. they're clearly not blonde anymore—they're "Mexican."[1]

Collective Magpie's art practice reveals how arbitrary and messy racial categories are. It makes visible the complex ways race intersects with socioeconomic realities to shape one's class identity. Artworks such as this provide an entry point for dialogue about the experience of racialization and what it feels like depending on one's background and the kind of physical body they inhabit.

Identity and the Black-White Binary

The power of identity formation is that it provides an orientation to the world that guides decision making and behavior. Identification often determines one's status within a community, and identities mediate associations, later internalized as feelings, about where and with whom a person belongs.[2]

Chapter 2 discussed the history of how White identity came into existence and the manner in which white supremacy was institutionalized to shore up that identity and the privi-leges attached to it. History sets the stage for what comes next, and the history of whiteness is anchored to anti-blackness. It is important to go back to this history because in many ways it is an undertow that directs racial categorization and racial identity today.

No matter how varied the hues and ancestries that make up the population today, racial identification is still often guided and limited by what is known as the **black-white binary**, a way of thinking and talking about race that assumes Black and White are the only racial categories that matter.[3] We see this binary in the way disparities in educational achievement are often described by school leaders and the media. White achievement often functions as a standard against which Black achievement is compared, even though other groups with even higher achievement levels than White students might provide a better benchmark for the improvement of educational outcomes.

Not only does the black-white binary center White identity and the realities of so-called White people, it does not attend to the experiences, voices, or actual presence of "other people of color," that catch-all category for anyone not easily identified as either White or

During student teaching, Cherise designed and taught a lesson based on the work of Romare Bearden. Cherise, a Black American, modeled for the students how to create their own collage self-portraits with papers hued to match different skin tones:

> When I was doing my demonstration, I picked a skin color that was similar to [Anthony's] skin color. At first they were like, "Well, why are you picking that? That's not your skin color." And I was like, "Well, I like this color. It's your project. It's how you see yourself." And they were like, "Oh, okay"… This one girl—a White student—was like, "Well, what if we're not African American?" They always want to emulate what it is that I'm doing, and I'm like, "Well, that's why we have all these different skin tones available for you." She's like, "Oh, okay"… Other students made some comments because I had some darker brown skin tones that were available, and one of the students started laughing and they were like, "Oh, that's Anthony's color." Anthony's darker skinned. I went up to the student, and I just asked, "So why are you laughing? How is that funny?" and just kind of questioned him and things like that. [He answered with] "Oh, I don't know."

Black.[4] This includes people who self-identify as Indigenous, Latinx, of Asian descent, or mixed race. Binary thinking can prevent recognition of the ways these groups also are subject to different forms of racism.

Negotiating the Binary

Although racial oppression experienced by non-Black people of color may be distinct, it would be ahistorical to view their plight as divorced from anti-Black racism. Like race itself, the black-white binary is a social construction that has real consequences for people perceived as Black or White. Ignoring it will not make racism go away. Indeed, ignoring has a way of making problems fester. So how might we think constructively about the black-white binary in the context of a demographically complex, global society?

We take the position that to abolish racism against any non-White people requires, among other things, an understanding of how whiteness and white supremacy are fundamentally linked to anti-blackness. Recall that the idea of whiteness was invented by Europeans who imagined that whiteness represented one side of a binary, a symbolic system involving only two parts. The color white is associated with light, that which is

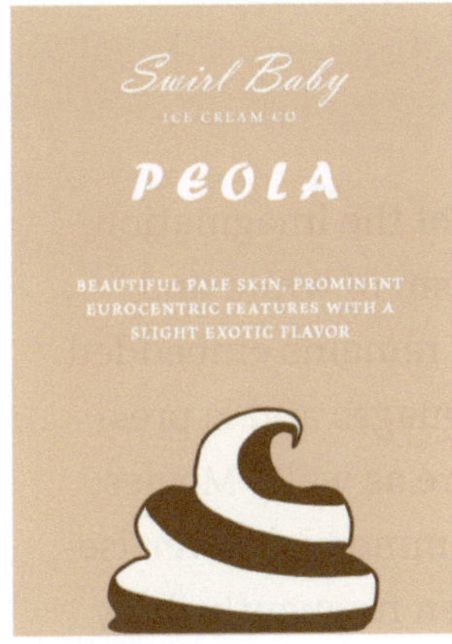

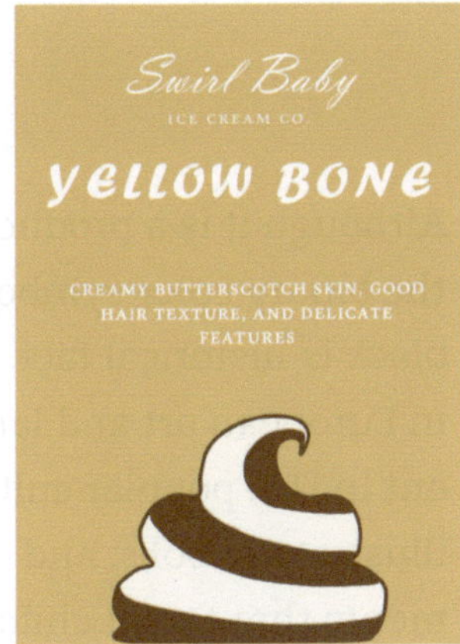

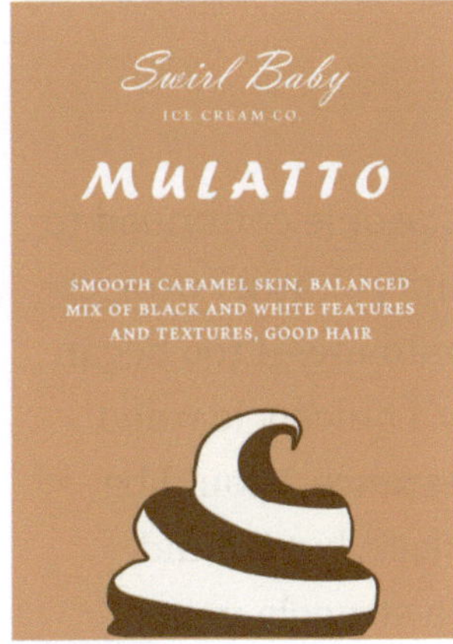

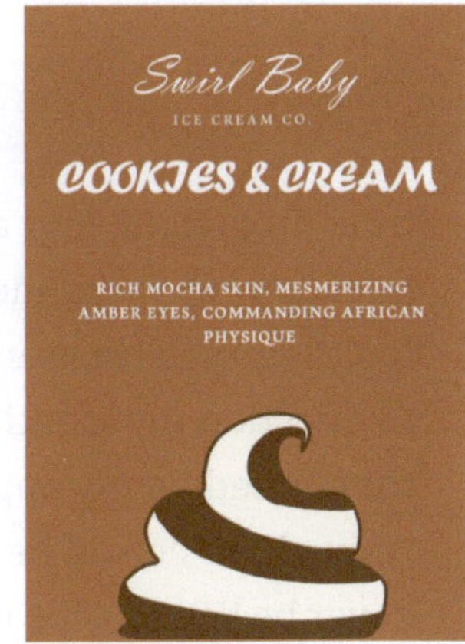

Aesthetic Facts

1 Serving Per Container
Serving size — 1 Baby

Amount per serving
Beauty — 88

	% to Standard*
Skin	95%
Body Type	85%
Hair Texture	85%
Eye Color	85%

* The % to Standard tells you the average beauty percentage on a 100 point scale of the four categories of beauty established by the current standards of beauty.

Ingredients

White dad (Scandinavia, Great Britain, Ireland/Scotland/Wales, Iberian Peninsula, Germany), Black mom (Ireland/Scotland/Wales, Ivory Coast, Nigeria, Ethiopia, Great Britain)

Aesthetic Facts

1 Serving Per Container
Serving size — 1 Baby

Amount per serving
Beauty — 86

	% to Standard*
Skin	93%
Body Type	86%
Hair Texture	84%
Eye Color	80%

* The % to Standard tells you the average beauty percentage on a 100 point scale of the four categories of beauty established by the current standards of beauty.

Ingredients

White mom (Great Britain, Ireland/Scotland/Wales, Germany, France), Black dad (Great Britain, Gahna, Ivory Coast, Nigeria, Ethiopia)

Aesthetic Facts

1 Serving Per Container
Serving size — 1 Baby

Amount per serving
Beauty — 83

	% to Standard*
Skin	90%
Body Type	75%
Hair Texture	75%
Eye Color	95%

* The % to Standard tells you the average beauty percentage on a 100 point scale of the four categories of beauty established by the current standards of beauty.

Ingredients

White mom (Great Britain, Ireland/Scotland/Wales, Iberian Peninsula, Scandinavia, Germany), Black dad (Ivory Coast, Ghana, Nigeria, Great Britain)

Aesthetic Facts

1 Serving Per Container
Serving size — 1 Baby

Amount per serving
Beauty — 70

	% to Standard*
Skin	67%
Body Type	80%
Hair Texture	66%
Eye Color	60%

* The % to Standard tells you the average beauty percentage on a 100 point scale of the four categories of beauty established by the current standards of beauty.

Ingredients

Black mom (Ivory Coast, Nigerian, Ethiopia, Ghana, Ireland/Scotland/Wales, Benin-Togo), White dad (Great Britain, Ashkenazi Jewish Ireland/Scotland/Wales, Iberian Peninsula, France)

4.4 Marynn Robinson, *Swirl Baby: Aesthetic Facts*, 2018. Digital print, 14" x 9 1/2" (35 x 24.13 cm), cut to 3 1/2" x 9 1/2" (8.89 x 24.13 cm). Courtesy of the artist.

morally good, and civilization itself, whereas Black is said to be the opposite of white and, thus, associated with dark, danger, and evil. This color symbolism sets up a tension between white and black such that they are antagonistic and irreconcilable.

Marynn Robinson, a former art student and current art teacher, created a series of artworks that visualized how she negotiates the black-white binary (see images 4.4 and 4.5). In a conversation with her instructor, Gloria Wilson, she reflected on how her racial identity was formed in childhood:

As a child, I remember being very proud of having a White mom and a Black dad. To me, it was something that made me unique, just the same as being left-handed. I reveled in how people were different. However, as time progressed and as people continued to question my racial identity—rather projecting their racial biases onto me—I too began to question my identity. I quickly learned that, based on my appearance, I could be "mixed," or I could be Black, but I could never be White. This is a struggle many people of a mixed-race have in common, the never-ceasing identity crisis.[5]

Although it is a product of the imagination, the binary color symbolism of white and black is historical fact. It remains embedded in European art and languages and is present in U.S. popular culture as well.[6] Movies, illustrated books, and commercial advertisements that target children frequently draw on the opposition of black-white dualities in their depictions.[7] For instance, when visiting a

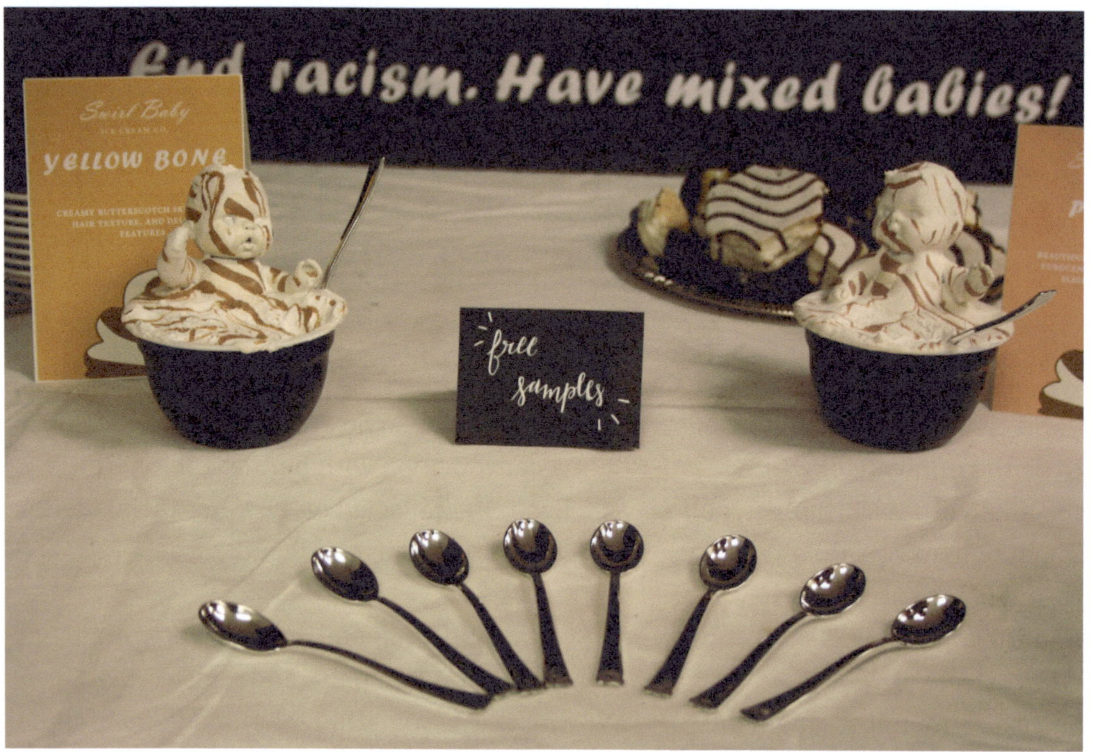

4.5 Marynn Robinson, *Swirl Baby Ice Cream Co. Table Setting*, 2018. Baby dolls, plaster, tin bowls, acrylic, Oreos, Zebra Cakes, plastic spoons, paper cups, laserjet prints, 84" x 48" x 30" (213.4 x 122 x 76.2 cm). Courtesy of the artist.

popular family restaurant for breakfast, Amy's children were handed menus illustrated with cheerful kids' faces. Take a moment to look at the menu (image 4.6). What is the hidden curriculum of such seemingly innocuous drawings? What might children internalize when they see light and dark skin colors presented as a duality within a hierarchy of value?

In a curriculum she taught with eighth graders, art educator Olivia Gude and her students analyzed and interpreted the use of color in *The Lion King* movie. Here's how they developed visual racial literacy to combat the pernicious influence of binary color symbolism:

> Over and over, we discovered that lightness is associated with good and darkness with evil. Simba and his father, "the true king of the lions," have light manes; the evil brother who wants to usurp the throne has a black mane and nails. We contrasted the good light animals with the threatening dark ones; the high chroma kingdom with the dusky and fearsome land of the marauding hyenas. We considered what this means in a story which opens with the lines, "...every living thing has its place in the great circle of life."[8]

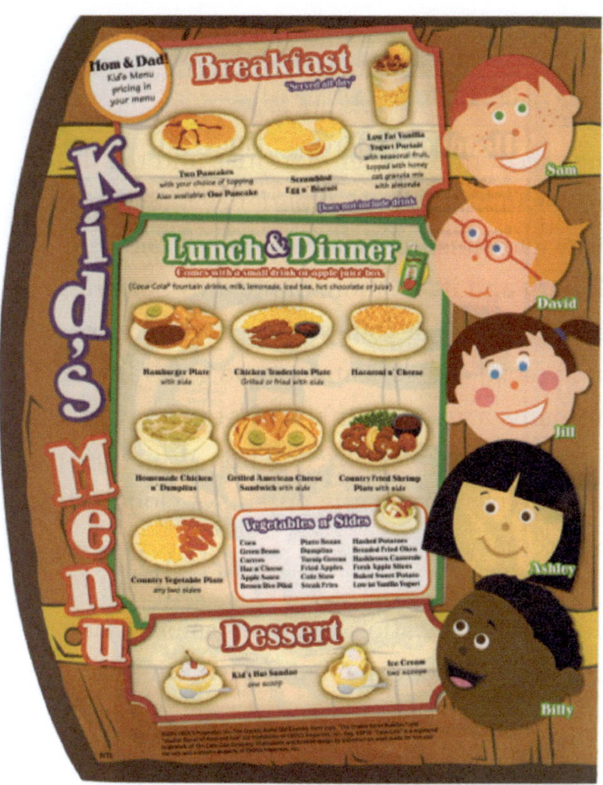

4.6 Children's menu from popular food chain in the U.S., 2013.

Of course, symbolic systems are not simply cultural conventions. They are sense-making systems that people use to give order and meaning to the real world. The system of thinking in black and white is acted upon, nowhere more obvious than in its mapping onto the bodies of actual people through racial identification.[9]

Some thinkers call for moving beyond the conversation about black and white. The argument is that the black-white binary does not account for other identities and the differences in how people experience racialization. However, it is important to understand the binary and its relationship to anti-blackness because it is the foundation of whiteness and racial categorization more generally. It remains a way of thinking that influences self-identification of White and non-White people and helps animate the pursuit of global white supremacy.

Racial identification and oppression of non-Black people of color is different but not divorced from the history of Black oppression and resistance.[10] The U.S. Civil Rights Movement offers an instructive example. Though the movement focused on addressing inequality between Black and White people, its implications went far beyond the black-white binary. Leaders of the movement understood this as well. The legislative wins not only made racial discrimination against Black people illegal, but they also benefited other non-White people and set the groundwork for women's rights, disability rights, and LGBTQ rights struggles. Addressing anti-Black racism opened the door for many non-White immigrants through passage of the U.S. Immigration and Naturalization Act of 1965. This law overturned legalized racial discrimi-nation that sought to "preserve the ideal of American homogeneity" by limiting immigration to only people coming from Northern and Western Europe.[11]

Art and Identity

Having discussed identity formation in general and racial identity in particular, now let us look at how race influences art learning and the making of art identities.

Art and art education are especially invested in the idea of identity. We conducted a quick Internet search using the words *art*, *project*, and *identity* to gauge the strength of the association between terms. The search generated about 378,000,000 results. In one of the top results, a blogger wrote the following introduction to an art project about identity: "Art is a wonderful outlet for self-expression and a great way for kids to show the world who they truly are." How often do you or the people around you talk about art as a mode of self-expression or a way to explore identity? This question is deceptively simple but important to ponder in the interest of learning something about how identities work and, by extension, how racial identities work in art education.

Art Work as Identity Work

Art is commonly taught through projects that are aimed at giving students a way to explore their identities. Students are given artistic materials and shown technical processes so they may explore who they are through media. To explore is to search for something or travel through an unfamiliar area. The focus on searching or figuring out *who they are* often assumes that identities exist already formed, that identity is basically a stable thing waiting to be discovered.

A similar assumption is at work in the ways people commonly talk about and appreciate art as a creative expression of the artist. The word *expression* comes from the Latin for "a pressing out." Many of us take for granted that a work of art is an outward representation or "pressing out" of the inner feelings and ideas of the artist. Maybe this is why it is difficult for some people to accept an interpretation of an artwork's meaning other than what the artist intended, as though artworks are primarily extensions of the artist's inner self (rather than a representation of ideas existing in the larger society).

Identity is not so much a thing inside a person waiting to be expressed, rather, it is what we do. Identities happen, they take place, and they sometimes afford opportunities for improvisation of a new self. Identity is, therefore, not *who we are* but rather a process of *becoming* that we participate in each day through social interactions and cultural associations with others.[12] Who we are is always a work in progress. The self is never finished. There is an openness to who we might yet become and how we perform new iterations of ourselves with cultural signs, such as dress, speech, hair style, bodily posture, facial expressions, icons, and group associations. How others perceive us is never settled but is open to new interpretations. In short, who a person can and will become is continually negotiated.

Resisting Racial Constructions through Art

Racially marginalized people push back and resist meanings assigned to them. In *Self-portrait* by artist Jimmie Durham, the artist draws viewers' attention to the contested nature of identities and the role racial categorization plays in self-identification (see image 4.7). The artist's self-portrait is a sculptural object constructed from a tracing of his body on canvas. The figure was cut, painted, and inscribed with hand-written messages. On the mounted figure, viewers find two kinds of

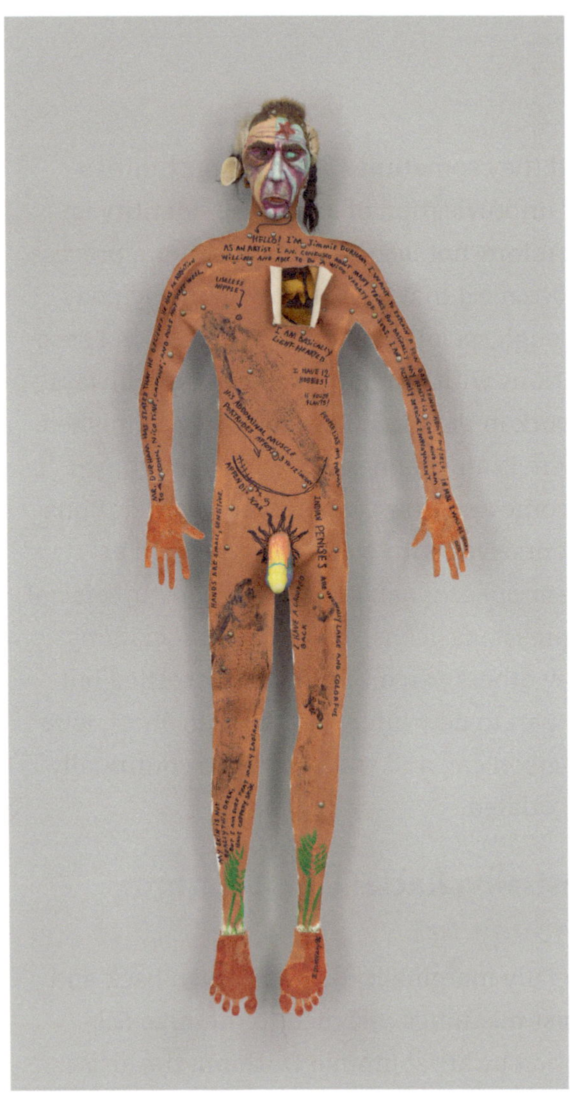

4.7 Jimmie Durham, *Self-portrait*, 1986. Canvas, wood, paint, metal, synthetic hair, for, feathers, shell, and thread, 78" x 30" x 9" (198.1 x 76.2 x 22.9 cm). Digital image © Whitney Museum of American Art/Licensed by Scala/Art Resource, NY. Courtesy of the artist and Sprovieri Gallery, London.

statements. Some affirm his humanity—"I am basically a lighthearted person" and "Some people like my poems"—while others racialize his body, in effect rendering it "Indian" through disparaging words and phrases written onto the figure's surface—"Mr. Durham has stated that he believes he has an addiction to alcohol, nicotine, and caffeine, and does not sleep well" and "My skin is not really this dark, but I am sure that many Indians have coppery skin." The ironic tone of the statements underscores how the construction of racial identity is a social process that is contested. It is never settled. Durham exemplifies this, showing how art can be a way to resist and transform conceptions of self and others.

Racial Identity in the Art Classroom

It is common to think of schools as places where students develop competence in school subject matter, like art, music, mathematics, and science. When visiting art classrooms, a person will likely see student learning goals and objectives posted on the board or noted in the teacher's written lesson plans. These goals and objectives usually concern subject knowledge and technical skills in art that students are to learn. Of course, teachers know there is more to what students learn in the course of classroom interaction than subject matter alone. Now, a growing body of research in the learning sciences echoes what teachers have long observed. Schools are important places where social identities are created, reinforced, and resisted as young people interact with each other, the curriculum, and other institutional structures.[13] Art classrooms provide opportunities for students to learn about art, but they also are spaces in which students' art identities commingle with their social identities. At the same time students are developing an understanding of what it means to be an artist, they are also negotiating their sense of self as racialized, classed, gendered, sexed beings.

"Everyone Is an Artist!" ... If Only It Were That Simple

Although it would be nice to accept the mantra that "everyone is an artist" or can learn to think like one, there are certain barriers in U.S. art education, many of them invisible at first glance, that make becoming an artist or constructing an artist self potentially fraught for some non-White students and an easier fit for others, particularly those who identify with whiteness.

To learn more about invisible barriers, we can listen to the stories of adult artists who "grew up" in art education. These stories reveal much about the centrality of whiteness and racism in art curriculum and pedagogy. Kehinde Wiley, a Black American contemporary artist whose larger-than-life portraits often feature Black men as subjects, shares this recollection about his art education:

Who Can Be an Artist?

Type the word "artist" in any search engine (e.g., Google Chrome, Safari, Internet Explorer). Click search and go to the photos that are populated in the results. Take stock of who is there.

What is the racial designation of the majority of the "artists" in the search? Is there a fixed message that can be inferred from the image results? In what ways might this message impact White students? How might this message impact non-White students? How are the messages distinctively different? Can the images in the results be labeled as stereotypical? How might the stereotype yield varying consequences as far as different students' identification as an artist in the future?

It's arguable that I knew how to paint White women better than I do Black men because so much of my educational history came from the tradition of having nude female models in live art classes. And to that degree I think it's really fascinating to know there is very little in the way of a rule book on how to get the blues and the crimsons and the greens that go into shadows and highlights of Black skin.[14]

This snippet of Wiley's art education biography resonates with our experiences as well in which White women's bodies are centered in the art curriculum. His observations are revealing in the way they illustrate how in art education students learn not only the stated art objectives, but also encounter hidden messages about what is most beneficial for an artist to know. In art class, students learn what *bodies of knowledge matter* and are accorded value while simultaneously learning what *actual bodies matter* and how they are assigned value in the dominant system of art.

The notion that artists are good drawers is a powerful identity narrative that equates being an artist with having realistic representational drawing skills. How many times have you heard someone say, "I'm not an artist because I'm not a good drawer"? It is especially common to hear among U.S. children entering adolescence, when many of them begin to practice **disidentification**, a process of distancing themselves from the idea of an artist as it has been culturally defined, practiced, and valued by others in their social group.[15] We raise this familiar example of the *artist as good drawer* to highlight how repetition of identity scripts like this may be difficult for an individual child or teenager to overcome unless they are exposed to different messages that provide persuasive counter narratives and images with which to construct an art identity.

Amy Sherald, a Black American artist who painted the portrait of First Lady Michelle Obama for the National Portrait Gallery, described how her own racial identity and art identity co-developed during her early years:

> I was always very interested in drawing. I don't even think I knew in the 2nd, 3rd, and 4th grades that there were artists, that people did that kind of stuff. What was so shocking when I first went to a museum, was to find out that art wasn't something in a book, in an encyclopedia, that people did [art] a long time ago…. And then, when I saw an image of a person of color, it all

came together in that moment—that this was something real, that somebody created this who was alive at the same time that I was alive…. My art teacher brought me into my own work, and…helped me understand my own relevance. As much as I was enchanted by art history, I was disconnected from it. It wasn't about me.[16]

This window into Sherald's art education biography highlights the role of racial counter narratives and images in developing an art identity starting at a very young age. Racial counter narratives and images can dislodge old scripts and stereotypes that are hidden within the art curriculum and tacitly reinforce the association between art and whiteness.

Racial Stereotypes and Stigma

Stereotypes are fixed, overgeneralized beliefs about a group of people or an idea that often are transmitted through stories and images. Although stereotypes can be connected to some aspects of truth, they are most often erroneous and become blanket expectations for whole groups of people, leaving little room for them to be anything outside of that stereotype.

For example, young people who identify as Black or Latinx are commonly stereotyped as menacing, "troubled" youth. Negative racial stereotypes like this shape how young people experience school. Black and Latinx children are disproportionately more likely to be reprimanded by teachers and more harshly disciplined by school authorities for the same behaviors exhibited by students who are racialized differently.[17]

Social stigma stemming from tacitly held stereotypes can prevent a young person from being recognized by others as creative and as one who belongs in artistic spaces.[18] This is the case whether the stereotype is perceived as positive or negative. For example, Asian Americans are frequently cast as the "model minority."[19] This stereotype is held up as the ideal against which all non-White persons are compared. The model minority identity constructs Asian Americans as intelligent, hard-working high-achievers. However, this seemingly positive construction of identity also leads Asian Americans to be perceived as lacking in creativity and the social skills needed for leadership.[20]

Whether positive or negative, stereotypes are problematic. They flatten and reduce the complexity and diversity of human beings. They also have real-world consequences.

Stereotypical stories and images are widespread, traveling from one social environment to another. They can be found in curriculum representations, entertainment media, and news sites. No boundaries or walls can keep them out of schools and play yards. Eventually, they are taken up and repeated in the words and actions of unwitting children and well-meaning adults.

Stereotypes can also threaten student learning and engagement when they are internalized. This phenomenon is known as **negative stereotype threat**. Research shows that when a person identifies with a group that is the target of a negative stereotype, the stereotype can actually undermine that person's performance in measurable ways.[21] When a negative stereotype is connected to the racial group a person identifies with, their desire to ward off that stereotype may impact their ability to self-define, engage with people, and perform tasks in ways that are authentic to them. Unfortunately, negative stereotype threat can result in people trying to distance themselves from central aspects of their identity or racial group.

The stigmas associated with some stereotypes are not easy to ignore. Stigma operates in ways that are largely unconscious and, among those

What Are You?

Ken Tanaka's short film, *What Kind of Asian Are You?*, went viral on YouTube in 2013. Tanaka, a White American adopted by a Japanese family, uses parody to explore the stereotype of Asian Americans as perpetual foreigners. The website that has archived Tanaka's video, titled Re-Imagining Migration, offers teacher-friendly discussion questions that could follow a class discussion on stereotypes and racial identity development. Some questions include:

- Why do you think the White man kept trying to find out where the jogger's ancestors were from?

- What do you think was his motivation?

  Go to reimaginingmigration.org/what-kind-of-asian-are-you/ for more reflection questions and prompts for teacher and student writing.

targeted by negative stereotypes, stigma can lead to lowered performance. One research study suggests that in art, stigma associated with artist stereotypes can combine with racial stereotypes in ways that lead some students of color to feel disconnected from art.[22] Consider: What racially coded stereotypes might threaten the performance and engagement of students in art?

Time to Retool

In 2009, Bree Picower, a White American education researcher, published a study in which she examined the experiences of eight White preservice teachers as they learned about race and other differences during a course on multiculturalism.[23] Picower found common patterns in the ways the teachers responded to content that challenged their preconceived and often stereotypical racial narratives. She calls these "tools of whiteness" that the individuals used not only to resist learning but also to protect their own racial narratives and white supremacy as the status quo. There are three types of tools—emotional, ideological, and performative—shown below. Teachers can learn to recognize them and reflect critically on their usage in everyday life.

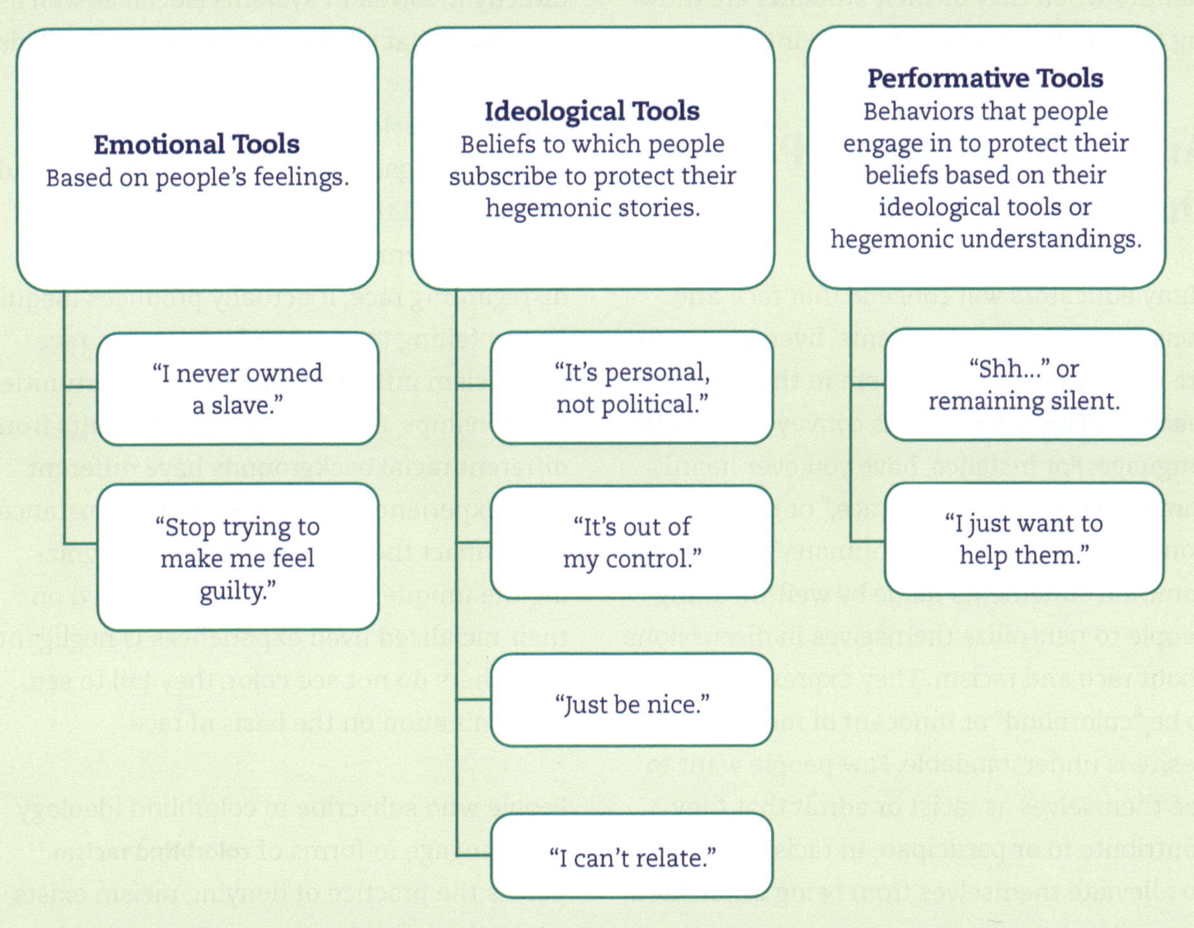

Racial stereotypes have staying power. Once learned, they remain operative as part of a person's mental schema. Stereotypes have a way of creeping into teachers' lesson plans, students' artworks, critiques, and other assessments. Art teachers need to be knowledgeable about racial stereotypes to be able to identify when they or their students are drawing from them and take steps to intervene.

Aren't We All Just a Part of the Human Race?

Many educators will concede that race and racism are factors in students' lives, yet some are reluctant to address them in their roles as teachers. This reluctance is conveyed through language. For instance, have you ever heard someone say, "I don't see race," or better yet, "I don't see color; I only see humans"? These are common statements made by well-meaning people to neutralize themselves in discussions about race and racism. They express a desire to be "colorblind" or innocent of racism. This desire is understandable. Few people want to see themselves as racist or admit that they contribute to or participate in racist systems. To alleviate themselves from being implicated as such, a person might say they do not see racial differences.

When we as art educators claim to notice only "the human" but not the racial identities and experiences of our students, we are positioning ourselves as not responsible for or directly involved in systems (social as well as cognitive) that produce racial inequality. This evasive stance is called colorblind ideology. **Colorblind ideology** argues that all people are the same, regardless of race, and thus should all be treated the same. Although colorblind ideology attempts to support equality by disregarding race, it actually produces inequities by failing to account for the ways race and racism influence a person's opportunities, relationships, and perceptions. Students from different racial backgrounds have different lived experiences and different circumstances that impact their education. Not recognizing the unique needs of students based on their racialized lived experiences is negligent. If teachers do not see color, they fail to see discrimination on the basis of race.

People who subscribe to colorblind ideology often engage in forms of **colorblind racism**.[24] This is the practice of denying racism exists while also behaving in ways that uphold racist systems. One example is using euphemistic "non-racial" words like "culture" and "ethnicity" instead of race. Language is a powerful and often subtle tool used to deny racism exists and deracialize discussions about how to create equitable and inclusive classrooms. Bree Picower, a researcher who studies teachers' understandings of race, found additional tools used by preservice teachers to resist examining racism and racial privilege. These "tools of whiteness," as she calls them, are noted to the left in Scholar Speaks. They are protective strategies that preserve the status quo. Small though they may be, these tools are components of colorblind racism. They are most often deployed by those in privileged racial positions (e.g., people who identify as White). Groups of people who are negatively impacted by racism generally do not have the luxury to "not see color," as race mediates every aspect of their lives, all day, every day.[25]

Race in the Mind of a Child

Children spend more time at school during their adolescent lives than they do in their own homes. Therefore, school classrooms are ideal spaces for children to learn how to engage with conversations about race. Many teachers will say that young children do not see color and are unaware of differences between themselves and classmates. However, research shows that children note racial differences as early as preschool. In her book *"Why Are All the Black Kids Sitting Together at the Cafeteria Table?" and Other Conversation About Race*, Beverly Daniel Tatum writes, "Learning to spot 'That stuff'—whether it is racist, or sexist, or classist—is an important skill for children to develop."[26]

All children make correlations between how they are treated in comparison with other children who are different from them. However, non-White children are more likely to realize these differences at an earlier age than their White counterparts because there are significant differences between the ways in which White children and non-White children are introduced to and experience race. Families raising non-White children commonly engage in a **race talk** to prepare their children to be racially literate in a world that is structured by colorblind racism. A race talk is an open discussion about police brutality and killing of unarmed Black and Brown people, adults as well as children. It instructs the young on how to respond if they are stopped by the police. The talk is intended to safeguard the community's children in the face of physical and symbolic racial violence. Non-White children

In Formation

Black American psychologist Beverly Daniel Tatum studies racial identity formation in non-White and White communities. She offers stages that people experience as they learn about racial construction.

6 Stages for White People

Contact — Lacks awareness of cultural and institutional racism and their own racial/cultural white privilege. Limited knowledge/awareness of racial issues and interactions with non-White people.

Disintegration — Increased interactions with non-White people may lead to a new understanding of racial/cultural issues.

Reintegration — Desire to be accepted by the individual's own race/culture may lead to accepting covert/overt racism and racial/cultural superiority. A negative encounter or a need to survive in one's circumstance can heighten the need for reintegration.

Pseudo-Independent — Information-seeking about non-White people and abandoning cultural (white) superiority beliefs. May still unintentionally perpetuate institutional systems of racism.

Immersion/Emersion — Feelings of discomfort with whiteness but understands that whiteness is a part of personal identity/culture. Searches for Whites with similar experiences and seeks to resist racism in their environment.

Autonomy — Acquires positive feelings about self as White. May form alliance with other races/cultures more easily. Positive feeling and encounters may lead the individual to confront racism and oppression in daily life.

5 Stages for People of Color

Pre-encounter — Seeks to assimilate into the dominant culture.

Encounter — Individual is forced to acknowledge their differences through an event or series of events.

Immersion/Emersion — Strong desire to surround themselves with visible symbols of racial/cultural identity.

Internalization — Secure in racial/cultural identity and seeks to establish meaningful relationship with racial/cultural identity.

Internalization-Commitment — Discovers ways to communicate commitment to the concerns/needs of their own racial/cultural group.

of all economic levels do not have the privilege to move through the world without recognizing that they are raced because acknowledgement of how others may misperceive them can be the difference between life and death. It is less common for White children to engage in similar discussions that build critical racial awareness.[27] If White parents and guardians do not engage in explicit conversations about race with their White children, then those children may struggle to perceive racist acts and the ways white supremacist thinking manifests in their lives and the lives of others.

Children's ways of looking at the world and interacting with people, curriculum, education, and art differ based on their lived racial experiences. This is in part a function of children internalizing the racial ideologies that play out day-to-day in their environment. The prevalence of colorblind ideology in White-dominant communities affects how children raised in those communities observe and interpret the world around them. For example, oftentimes non-White students quickly realize when there are no non-White teachers on staff in their entire school, whereas White students may not come to this realization until it is pointed out to them. The invisibility of racial dynamics among White children is normal-

Have You Had "the Talk"?

Watch *The Talk: Race in America* on pbs.org.

Reflect on what you just watched, then doodle a narrative sketch that illustrates what "the talk" looked like in your household as a child, teen, or even adult. Things to consider: Can you remember an actual race talk? Who gave you the talk? Was the conversation dialogic or was it instructive? How did you feel during and after?

ized, as is the general disregard for how racism affects non-White children. For instance, having to work twice as hard as their White counterparts to get half as far is one of those effects that non-White children, in particular Black children, have the burden of carrying.[28]

"If You Just Work Hard Enough..." Then What?

"If you just work hard, you can be whatever you want to be and do whatever you want to do." While growing up, we frequently heard statements like this from teachers and other adults. It was their way of encouraging us to believe in our own abilities, to dream big and aspire to do great things. Their words taught us to think that everybody is in charge of their own destiny and success is a measure of an individual's effort.

Looking back now, we can see how problematic these encouragements were, even if they were well intended. They assume that everyone's economic and social advancement rests entirely in their hands. If this is true, then it also must be the case that failure rests solely in the hands of individuals. This way of thinking is based on a belief in **meritocracy**, a social system in which political and economic power is earned by individuals who work hardest, develop their innate talents, and excel based

"Whenever I reflect on my understanding and knowledge of colorblind racism, racial order, or hegemonic practices, there is one specific experience that stands out as the most transformative and as the one that made me even aware of such topics. It happened in my sophomore year at [college], when writing an assignment in my Ethnic Arts writing course. Our professor asked us to write a paper about our culture, describing it from our own understanding and in relation to the rest of society. Having never been asked to talk about my culture, I started off by saying that I didn't really know what my culture was. After struggling to think of ways to describe it, I started explaining that I am pretty much just a typical American, pretty generic in comparison to other cultures…. It wasn't until my professor graded my paper and gave it back to me that I was brought to awareness of my own ignorance. She added little notes of recognition and advice here and there, but at the end of her comments was the question "Have you ever thought that your description of your 'lack of culture' might come off as offensive towards others in the way that it assumes you are the norm and it's everyone else who is different?" Boom. It hit me like a brick wall. How in the world was I able to write this entire paper about how "I don't really have culture" without even once thinking about how ignorant this sounded? I had always prided myself on my equal treatment of people no matter their culture or color of their skin. I spent some time feeling lost and, to be honest, disappointed and slightly disgusted with myself. This led to my decision to delve into my past a bit, not necessarily in search of my culture, but in search of my own biases and perspective of myself and the world and the experiences that shaped them."

—Anonymous, White American art teacher

on personal achievements alone.[29] The vision
of a meritocracy is an admirable ideal. For
many Americans and people around the world,
this ideal is an integral part of the American
Dream, but it is not currently a reality. It is
unlikely any parent or educator would argue
that hard work is not important, but to suggest that with enough hard work a child will
be able to determine the future for themselves
is to ignore the unearned advantages of racial
privilege. The resulting message is that members of certain (privileged) groups can righ-
teously justify their accumulation of resources
because "if you work hard enough" you can get
your own, "just like my family did."

The dream of living in a meritocracy is
reflected in the centuries-old idiom "pull
yourself up by your bootstraps," a saying that
promotes independence and self-determina-
tion as personal qualities that lead a person
to choose success. When a person is unable to
pull themselves up by their bootstraps, then
this also is viewed as a choice. Ultimately,
failure to advance artistically, educationally,
or economically is seen as the fault of the
individuals for having made bad choices or
not working hard enough. Bootstrapping is a
seductive form of victim-blaming. It offers an
easy explanation for disparities in artistic and

"I connected personally to the Picower
2009 reading when Dawn [a research
participant] described her father's story
about immigrating to America. I have had
similar thoughts about my father, who
also immigrated to America from Italy and
became very successful through his hard
work…growing up overcoming a language
barrier, going to college, and starting his
own business. However, this article has
made me [wonder] that although he put in
hard work and determination, if he was a
different race, like African American, would
he have become just as successful."

—Anonymous, White American art
teacher responding to Bree Picower's
article "The Unexamined Whiteness of
Teaching: How White Teachers Maintain
and Enact Dominant Racial Ideologies"[30]

academic achievement. Such explanations are
erroneous and deceptive because they take for
granted that everyone has the same opportunities and access to resources, like good
teachers, food security, health care, economic
means, and so on. To the contrary, as we show
in Chapters 2 and 3, the world children are
born into is not a level playing field. It is rife
with social and racial inequalities owing to
past and present discriminatory attitudes,
practices, laws, and policies. It is an ahistori-

cal fallacy to act as though intrinsic resources, such as talent, effort, and motivation, are the only or primary determinants of one's success or failure. Likewise, interlocking systems of race, class, and gender inequality cannot be dismantled solely by individuals. To create a more level and just playing field will require policies, laws, and education that offer solutions beyond bootstraps.

Drawing Lines

"Why don't they just go to a better school?" This common sense question bespeaks another fallacy about individual choices. Access to a better education is simply a matter of parents making better choices for their children, so the thinking goes. Strongly related to bootstrapping, this way of thinking is persuasive, particularly among people who benefit from socioeconomic and racial privileges that empower them to make a wide array of choices that are in their child's and families' best interest.

Setting aside the false assumptions implied by the question, if we take the question at face value, we need to consider some important facts in order to understand school choices and how they are related to institutionalized racism.

One of these facts is **gerrymandering**. Gerrymandering is the practice of redrawing the boundaries of electoral districts to favor the voting power of one political party over another (see chart 4.8). Gerrymandering is akin to the practice of redlining, which we introduced in Chapter 2. It involves officials literally drawing lines around and throughout certain neighborhoods to reconstitute communities and manipulate their voting power.[31] Gerrymandering is technically illegal because it suppresses the electoral power of certain non-White communities. Nonetheless, politicians and lawmakers have found boundless excuses to redraw district lines while escaping crimination. Unfortunately, public schools are frequently ensnared by political parties and their leaders jockeying for greater and greater electoral advantage. Gerrymandering sets off a domino effect of systemic educational inequity, with non-White students negatively impacted most.

Choice or Confinement

It is generally the case that students are assigned to neighborhood schools. In some cities across the country, neighborhoods can include families from a range of socioeconomic levels that live in single-family houses, apartments, condos, and mobile home communities. However, when lines are drawn around specific parts of an existing neighborhood to impact political power, as is what happens during gerrymandering, usually people with similar socioeconomic status are grouped together. Out of this process, "new" neighborhoods are created, which means "new" school zones are established. It has been shown that as a result of redrawing district lines, public schools become more and more segregated, keeping students from low socioeconomic backgrounds (a population that is disproportionately non-White) out of schools with students from higher socioeconomic backgrounds.[32]

In the U.S., schools are largely funded through revenue generated from local taxes on homes and commercial property. When neighborhoods shift, property taxes shift and, consequently, school resources shift. Certain schools and, thus, certain students are left with

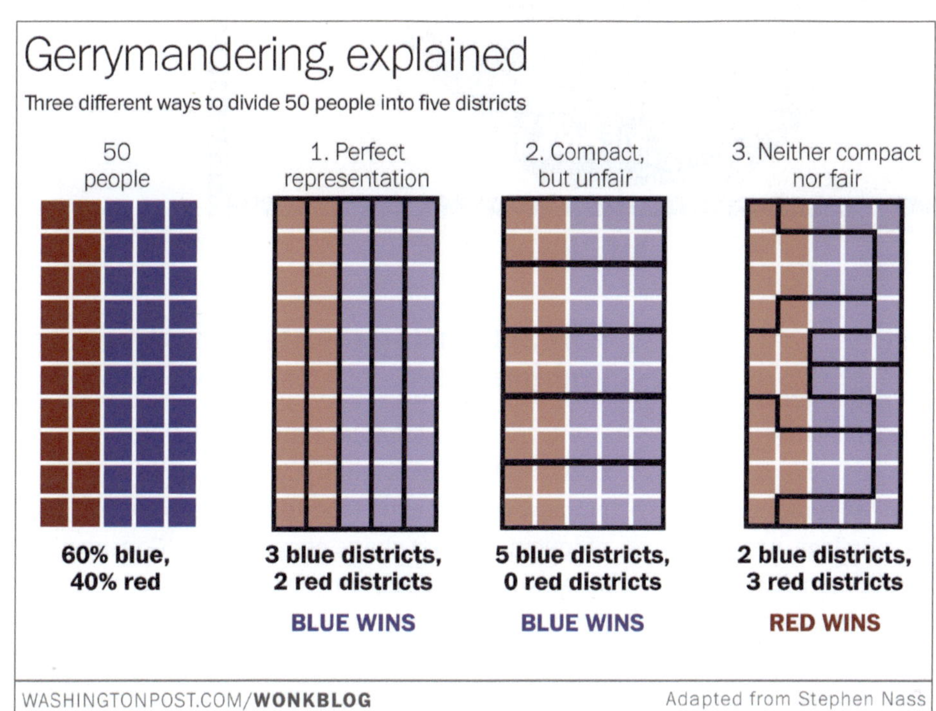

4.8 Visualization to illustrate gerrymandering. From The Washington Post. © 2015 The Washington Post. All rights reserved. Used under license.

Poverty Narratives

An art teacher displayed this poster on the classroom wall for high school students, saying, "I just want to help these students stabilize their lives and in some cases change their family tree for positive, healthy growth."

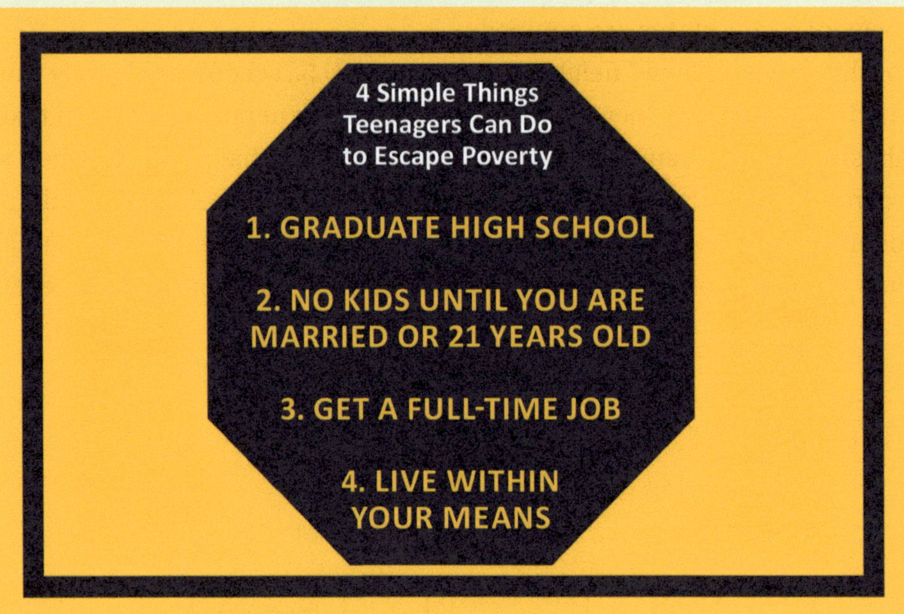

Part 1: Critical analysis

How are the myths of meritocracy encoded in the poster's message? Describe what you imagine the intended audience demographics are for this poster. What principles of meritocracy do you see (bootstraps, privilege, American Dream, independent, determination, individualism, choice)? How do the words and images together convey the message of meritocracy?

Part 2: Creating counter narratives and images

Design a poster to replace this one that supports students' racial literacy—their ability to perceive, name, and respond to larger systems of inequality that shape people's lives. Consider what words, images, and compositional strategies would be most persuasive and effective for teens.

minimal access to important resources (e.g., highly qualified teachers, updated textbooks, robust curricular offerings, advanced technology) and comfortable learning conditions (e.g., working drinking fountains, air conditioning). At the same time, other schools and students become the beneficiaries of highly concentrated wealth. In the art classroom, this economic disparity can be the difference between having a $35 annual material budget versus a $3,500 annual material budget, or only having printer paper and markers in the classroom versus having a designated digital photography lab with access to programs like Adobe Photoshop and Illustrator.

Understanding gerrymandering helps art teachers move beyond bootstrapping and other victim-blaming explanations for systemic racial and socioeconomic inequities. Consider the case of Kelly Williams-Bolar, a Black woman from Akron, Ohio, who used her father's address on school papers when she enrolled her daughters in a "better" school district with greater resources. Williams-Bolar was charged with and convicted of falsifying residency records, jailed for months, and ordered three additional years of probation. School officials said she was "cheating [the system] because her daughters received a quality

CRITICAL QUESTIONS
FOR CRITICAL CONSCIOUSNESS

Access Denied

Kelly Williams-Bolar's situation brings forth much larger questions to ponder regarding the origin of race-based educational disparities. How have certain groups of people been forced into such desperate situations that they must make life-altering decisions like Williams-Bolar? Outside of education, what other laws and institutional policies can you identify that may have peripheral but real, material effects on children's educational opportunities?

education without paying taxes to fund it."[33] On the one hand, the school district's claim is accurate. Her taxes did not pay for a quality education. On the other hand, most school districts assign children to schools based on the neighborhood they live in, despite gross disparities caused by gerrymandering.

No matter how "hard" Williams-Bolar worked, she could not have provided a decent, valuable educational opportunity for her daughters since her failing neighborhood school was the only legal option she had. Aside from moving her family to another neighborhood, which brings up other systemic barriers based on race and socioeconomic status, she is at the mercy of the law. This mother's story illustrates a lack of access to quality education, but when we zoom out a bit more, we can see a larger ecosystem of inequality.

Racial Ecologies of Art Education

Although the art classroom may be enclosed by walls made of brick and mortar, the practice of art education is inseparable from its context. Like all aspects of schooling, art education is intertwined with the wider social, cultural, economic, and political dynamics. Although it may be tempting to focus solely on what happens inside the four walls of the art classroom, racial equity and justice in art education necessitate a critical awareness and responsiveness to the context of students' lives.

In an online post to a popular art education forum, an art teacher asked for ideas on how to respond to the Black Lives Matter demonstrations and racial justice movement. Another art teacher remarked, "I am usually too busy teaching students how to draw, paint, and sculpt for this, but I am an advocate for social change." This sentiment expresses a common misunderstanding that can be broken down in two ways.

First, art and art learning often are treated in a detached manner, as though they exist in an immaculate bubble devoid of issues that concern the broader world. Is the world really so neatly ordered into compartments that children and teachers can check their experiences at the door? Like a piece of luggage, do they set aside their identities and histories

"Growing up I always had the desire to make things, but going to art school was too expensive. My background implied that if I went to college, I should major in something that would provide me with a secure salary. I didn't even contemplate going to art school because I felt there was, and is, a certain class perspective built into being an artist, which I couldn't do because I needed a real job. For many years I did work a job because that was my social and economic reality. I hate it when people tell young kids 'you can do anything you want' without qualifying it. Economic, social, and ethnic realities play a big role in young people's choices. These realities need to be discussed almost in conjunction with their artistic aspiration."[34]

—Black American artist Mark Bradford

Literacy as a Constitutional Right

In 2016, seven Detroit students sued the state of Michigan for the deplorable conditions in their public schools. The lawsuit cited that mice, cockroaches, and other vermin overwhelmed the school, so much so that teachers came into the classroom early every day to clean the feces before the students arrived. Other unfathomable learning conditions were cited in the lawsuit, such as classroom temperatures above 90 degrees or sometimes below freezing because of failed heating and cooling systems, the employment of long-term subs for years at time, and noting that in one case, "an eighth-grade student was put in charge of teaching seventh- and eighth-grade math classes for a month because no math teacher was available."[35]

The foundation of the students' complaint was that without access to basic literacy, they cannot access other constitutionally guaranteed rights like voting, military service, and civic responsibilities like jury duty. A federal judge in Detroit rejected their lawsuit in 2016. However, in May 2020, a 6th Circuit U.S. Court of Appeals panel reversed that decision and deemed, by law, that literacy is a constitutional right. The Governor of Michigan, Gretchen Whitmer, agreed to pay $2.7 million to Detroit Public Schools Community District, create two task forces to make long-term recommendations for improving education in Detroit, ask legislators for an additional $94 million to fund evidence-based literacy programs, propose legislation to allow the school district to borrow money (it had been previously barred from doing so), and finally, develop a trust for the seven plaintiffs for $280,000 to be used for their future education.[36]

the moment they pass across the classroom threshold? Can it really be true that "in here" we do art and "out there" is where problems live? This seems like magical thinking that may result in missed opportunities to build upon students' diverse experiences and prior knowledge. When teachers miss opportunities to scaffold student knowledge, art education can leave students feeling alienated from themselves, their communities, and school.

The remark posted to the online forum displays an uncritical attitude about one's own teaching, as if to say, "Social change may be needed elsewhere, but *my* art classroom is just fine as it is." The fact of the matter is there is growing evidence that this is not the case. Race-based inequities in students' art education experiences have been documented and studied, though many art teachers may not be aware of the findings and the implications of those findings for themselves and

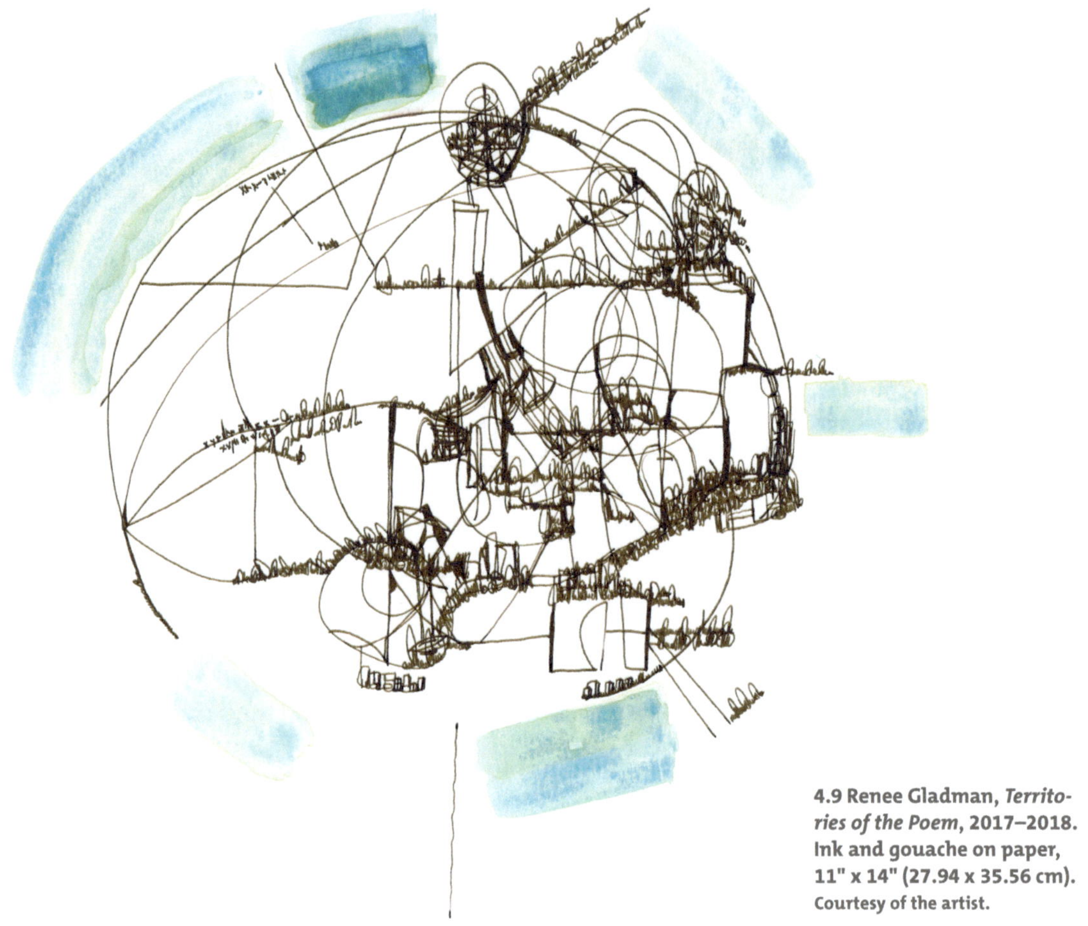

4.9 Renee Gladman, *Territories of the Poem*, 2017–2018. Ink and gouache on paper, 11" x 14" (27.94 x 35.56 cm). Courtesy of the artist.

their students.[37] Many art education teacher preparation programs do not teach about how racial injustice is structured within art education (e.g., art curriculum, pedagogies, assessments, classroom climate, etc.).[38] Moreover, teacher education standards and state boards overseeing educator certification do not hold teacher preparation programs accountable for knowledge about how race influences student learning, how racism intersects with other forms of oppression to produce disparate arts and educational opportunities and outcomes, and how to teach for racial equity through professional best practices.[39]

Understanding race and racism in the lives of students demands that we take an **ecological approach**, which is to say we need to view art learning not in isolation but instead as a reciprocal interaction between what happens with learners in art classrooms and the dynamics taking place in the broader biological, ideological, and economic environment.[40] This enables art teachers to understand how they and the students they teach are part of a larger network or web of relationships that produces racial inequalities.

What we begin to see when we adopt an ecological perspective is that art education is not simply shaped by a context of racial inequality "out there" somewhere. No, the story of art education is much knottier than that. It is organized and embodied in classrooms by individuals interacting with ideas, symbols, materials, and each other. This interplay of people and environment is similar to the graphic renderings of artist Renee Gladman in which single words, entire phrases, and the gaps in between them evolve into an architectural form that threatens to cohere into an opaque structure (see image 4.9). If we were to picture the racial ecologies of art education, they might look something like Gladman's image. Art classrooms (art teachers, art curriculum, art pedagogies, art resources, etc.) tie into a larger PreK–20 educational system, which is itself constitutive of an even larger social environment.

In other words, what happens in art classrooms is not racially innocent. To be innocent is to be without responsibility or involvement in racism. All the elements of art classrooms described in this chapter—the identities that are formed, cultural stereotypes and scripts that are invoked, and the materials and supports that differentially constrain and enable participation in art—are shaped by and, in turn, help shape the social, cultural, economic, and political processes that sustain racial inequality. Grasping this reciprocal relationship is crucial to an anti-racist practice of art education where art classrooms become transformative spaces that spark students' critical racial awareness, creating the potential for social change.

Our goal in this chapter was to explore race and racism in students' lives. In the next chapter, art teachers take center stage. We build on the idea of racial ecologies of art education to see how racial identities and awareness filter art teachers' perceptions, decision-making, and enactments within and beyond art classrooms.

Notes

1   Nicole Rupersburg, "Collective Magpie Explores the Concepts of Race and Identity in Cultural Borderlands," *Creative Exchange*, November 19, 2018, para. 27, https://springboardexchange.org/collective-magpie-explores-the-concepts-of-race-and-identity-in-cultural-borderlands/

2   Dorothy Holland, William S. Lachicotte, Debra Skinner, and Carole Cain, *Identity and Agency in Cultural Worlds* (Cambridge, MA: Harvard University Press, 1998).

3   Juan F. Perea, "The Black/White Binary Paradigm of Race: The Normal Science of American Racial Thought," *California Law Review* 85 (1997): 1213–1258.

4   Ibid.

5   Gloria J. Wilson, "The Table Setting as Medium: Lived Curriculum and Mixed Race Identity," *Art Education* 73, no. 4 (2020): 14–21.

6   Richard Dyer, *White: Essays on Race and Culture* (London, UK: Routledge, 1997).

7   Miguel Picker (director), *Mickey Mouse Monopoly: Disney, Childhood & Corporate Power*, 2002, film, Media Education Foundation.

8   Olivia Gude, "Drawing Color Lines," *Art Education* 53, no. 1 (2000): 44–54.

9   Frantz Fanon, *Black Skin, White Masks* (New York, NY: Grove Press, 1967). C. L. Markmann, trans. Original work published 1952.

10 Roy L. Brookes and Kristen Widner, "In Defense of the Black/White Binary: Reclaiming a Tradition of Civil Rights Scholarship," *Berkeley Journal of African-American Law & Policy* 12, no. 1 (2010): 107–144.

11 Office of the Historian, The Immigration Act of 1924 (The Johnson-Reed Act), Department of State, United States of America, para. 8, https://history.state.gov/milestones/1921-1936/immigration-act.

12 Stuart Hall, "Introduction: Who Needs 'Identity,'" in Stuart Hall & Paul Du Gay (eds.), *Questions of Cultural Identity* (London, UK: Sage, 1996): 1–17.

13 Stanton Wortham, *Learning Identity: The Joint Emergence of Social Identification and Academic Learning* (New York, NY: Cambridge University Press, 2006).

14 Kehinde Wiley, "Kehinde Wiley Reimagines Classic Art," televised interview, *ABC News*, December 28, 2015, https://www.youtube.com/watch?v=oiGxR4e8lEQ

15 Neil Cohn, "Framing 'I Can't Draw': The Influence of Cultural Frames on the Development of Drawing," *Culture & Psychology* 20, no. 1 (2014): 102–117.

16 Janice Hughes, "A Conversation with Amy Sherald," *Art Education* 72, no. 2 (2019): 51–54.

17 Ann Arnett Ferguson, *Bad Boys: Public Schools in the Making of Black Masculinity* (Ann Arbor, MI: University of Michigan Press, 2000).

18 James Haywood Rolling, Jr. and Sharif Bey, "Stargates: Managing Stigma, Challenging Representations, and Mediating Identity Through Narrative," *Studies in Art Education* 57, no. 4 (2016): 307–317.

19 Stacey J. Lee, *Unraveling the Model Minority Stereotype: Listening to Asian American Youth* (New York, NY: Teachers College Press, 2009).

20 Min Zhou and Jennifer Lee, "Hyper-Selectivity and the Remaking of Culture: Understanding the Asian American Achievement Paradox," *Asian American Journal of Psychology* 8, no. 1 (2017): 7–15.

21 Claude M. Steele and Joshua M. Aronson, "Stereotype Threat and the Intellectual Test Performance of African-Americans," *Journal of Personality and Social Psychology* 69 (1995): 797–811.

22 William Charland, "African American Youth and Artist's Identity: Cultural Models and Aspirational Foreclosure," *Studies in Art Education* 51, no. 2 (2010): 115–133.

23 Bree Picower, "The Unexamined Whiteness of Teaching: How White Teachers Maintain and Enact

Dominant Racial Ideologies," *Race Ethnicity and Education* 12, no. 2 (2009): 197–215.

24 Eduardo Bonilla-Silva, *Racism Without Racists: Color-Blind Racism and the Persistence of Racial Inequality in America*, 5th ed. (Lanham, MD: Rowman & Littlefield, 2018).

25 Ibid.

26 Beverly Daniel Tatum, *Why Are All the Black Kids Sitting Together in the Cafeteria? And Other Conversations About Race* (New York, NY: Basic Books, 1997).

27 Lani Guinier, "From Racial Liberalism to Racial Literacy: Brown v. Board of Education and the Interest-Divergence Dilemma," *The Journal of American History* 91, no. 1 (2004): 92–118.

28 Christopher D. Desante, "Working Twice as Hard to Get Half as Far: Race, Work Ethic, and America's Deserving Poor," *American Journal of Political Science* 57, no. 2 (2013): 342–356.

29 Stephen J. McNamee and Robert K. Miller, *The Meritocracy Myth*, 2nd ed. (Lanham, MD: Rowman & Littlefield, 2009).

30 Bree Picower, "The Unexamined Whiteness of Teaching: How White Teachers Maintain and Enact Dominant Racial Ideologies," *Race Ethnicity and Education* 12, no. 2 (2009): 197–215.

31 Brent Tarter, *Gerrymanders: How Redistricting Has Protected Slavery, White Supremacy and Partisan Minorities in Virginia* (Charlottesville, VA: University of Virginia Press, 2019).

32 Genevieve Siegel-Hawley, "Educational Gerrymandering? Race and Attendance Boundaries in a Demographically Changing Suburb," *Harvard Educational Review* 83, no. 4 (2013): 580–612.

33 Andrea Canning and Leezel Tanglao, "Ohio Mom Kelley Williams-Bolar Jailed for Sending Kids to Better School District," *ABC News*, 2011, https://abcnews.go.com/US/ohio-mom-jailed-sending-kids-school-district/story?id=12763654.

34 Marc Mayer, "Art21 at NAEA: An Interview with Mark Bradford," *Art21 Magazine*, April 7, 2009, https://magazine.art21.org/2009/04/07/mark-bradford-at-naea-an-interview-with-art21/#.X-zm5HqSk2w.

35 John Wisely, "Despite Settlement, Detroit Literacy Lawsuit Heads Back to Court," *Detroit Free Press*, May 19, 2020, https://www.freep.com/story/news/education/2020/05/19/federal-appeals-court-overturns-detroit-literacy-lawsuit-ruling/5225188002/.

36 Nancy Kaffer, "Whitmer Settled the Detroit Literacy Lawsuit. What It Means (and What It Doesn't)," *Detroit Free Press*, May 15, 2020, https://www.freep.com/story/opinion/columnists/nancy-kaffer/2020/05/15/detroit-schools-right-read-literacy-lawsuit/5191807002/.

37 Amelia M. Kraehe, Joni B. Acuff, and Sarah Travis, "Equity, the Arts, and Urban Education: A Review," *Urban Review* 48, no. 2, (2016): 220–244.

38 Amelia M. Kraehe, "Sounds of Silence: Race and Emergent Counter-Narratives of Art Teacher Identity," *Studies in Art Education* 56, no. 3 (2015): 199-213; Hannah Kim Sions and Amber C. Coleman, "The Team Is All White: Reflections of Art Educators of Color on Whiteness," *Journal of Cultural Research in Art Education* 36, no. 1 (2019): 29-55; Sunny Spillane, "The Failure of Whiteness in Art Education: A Personal Narrative Informed by Critical Race Theory," *Journal of Social Theory in Art Education* 35 (2015), https://scholarscompass.vcu.edu/jstae/vol35/iss1/6/.

39 Amelia M. Kraehe, "Multicultural Art Education in an Era of Standardized Testing: Changes in Knowledge and Skill for Art Teacher Certification in Texas," *Studies in Art Education* 51, no. 2 (2010): 162–175.

40 Urie Bronfenbrenner and Pamela A. Morris, "The Bioecological Model of Human Development," in William Damon and Richard M. Lerner (eds.), *Handbook of Child Psychology: Theoretical Models of Human Development* (New York, NY: Wiley, 2006): 793–828.

Chapter 5

Awakening an Abolitionist Mindset in the Art Classroom

"What we do echoes through the generations."

—U.S. President Barack Obama

Amy   *Joni, when did you first learn about race? What was your "aha" moment? When was that? Where were you? What was that like?*

Joni   *I didn't learn about race or to recognize racism in one sitting. You know, it wasn't like my parents sat me down and talked about race. I learned about race through experiences and observing the people in my environment.*

Amy   *Yes, same for me.*

Joni   *So, I learned about race mostly through my daddy's and mama's actions. Their interactions with White people always seemed peculiar and very…timid. Also, I learned through the conversations that I wasn't supposed to hear but would listen in on.*

Amy   *Give me an example of that, Joni.*

Joni   *The ways my parents, grandparents, aunts, and uncles talked about White people, about whiteness, taught me that there were differences between Black people and White people. For example, observing my parents engage with White people outside of my home made it very clear that there was a different way of being when in their company. Language changed, speech patterns changed, even body positions changed. My mother would always give me these corrections, like she'd say, "Stand up straight. Don't slouch." So my recognition and comprehension of race was gained through an accumulation of reflections and experiences in the presence and absence of White people.*

Also, at times, it was really confusing because White people in the South are really nice.

Amy   *I'm from the South, too, so I get that.*

Joni   *Yeah, so they would smile, greet you at every corner, but when I would get home, my daddy would unpack those actions. He would pick apart the acts of kindness and explain, pretty explicitly, that what we witnessed was basically racism packaged with a bow. For example, it may be something like a White person's interest in our new car, a comment like, "Wow, Maurice, nice car. How much did that run you?" might translate into, "How did you afford that by hauling manure?" My father worked for UPS but also hauled manure on the weekends to make extra cash for our family. The families that he worked for on the weekends were all White. They couldn't* *see how a Black man who hauled manure for them could afford a Cadillac. Thinking back now, while I may have questioned his translations at the time, at my young age, his interpretations were spot on…based on what I know now about microaggressions, implicit bias, and so forth.*

Amy *Critical race scholars like Charles Lawrence, Chester Pierce, and many others have helped explain how effective microaggressions are and how real they are.*

Joni *Yeah, and at a very young age I learned to read racial slights and recognize the biased undertones of conversations, even though I didn't know exactly what I was learning at the time. What about you?*

Amy *Well, I learned about race very much like you, Joni, in the smallest day-to-day gestures. It wasn't a single spectacular event like a grand talk or lesson. It was just part of the world that I lived in. I am the product of a biracial marriage. My parents were married for decades, and my brothers and I were raised by them in a biracial household. So I had a biracial upbringing. But I lived in the suburbs of Atlanta, Georgia, in the 1970s through the 1990s. Growing up, everybody read me as Black. You know, the rules around race in the United States are such that if you have just one drop of so-called "Black blood," you're Black.*

Joni *Right.*

Amy *And in that context, I think everyone understood that I was Black because there's a range of complexions that are Black, right? So, that's how things were in that social context, but at home, we were just us, and there were no categories, really. Well, I remember one day—I must have been around elementary school age, maybe fourth grade, maybe fifth grade—I said to my parents, "I'm mixed. I'm both. I'm Black and White together." And they just sort of stared.*

Joni *Ha ha!*

Amy *They didn't communicate anything much beyond that. They just stared. So, I kept talking, going on and on as young children do, and I started talking about my skin color. And I described myself. I said, "I'm right in between Dad and Mom, pinkish beige and milk chocolate brown. I'm right in between. I'm tan." I was trying to come up with some vocabulary to name my color. "I'm peach. I'm light brown." I didn't have more sophisticated names than that.*

And then my mom said, "Yeah, but always remember that when you're out there in the streets, all they're going to see is a nigga." Her clear, matter-of-fact articulation of the state of race relations as they actually are— what Derrick Bell might call racial realism—may sound harsh to folks who grew up "colorblind" and "colormute," learning to avoid acknowledging the way racial categories operate. My dad was probably raised that way, never talking openly about racism. This is the misleading idea that if we never acknowledge race and treat everyone as if they were the same, racism will just go away. Of course, this underestimates the power of unconscious bias and racially discriminatory policies and practices set in place hundreds of years ago.

The past is always present. Nowhere is this more true than in teaching. As art teachers, we carry the imprint of our life histories into the classroom every day. It is impossible not to. The people and places that have been a part of our upbringing "show up" in our sense of humor, the stories we tell, our language and cultural references, our affinities and aversions toward certain subject matter, and even our attitudes about particular students.

Research has shown that teachers view students through their own biographical lenses and rely on their own personal beliefs and experiences as a teaching guide.[1] The images teachers consumed from literature, television, and movies while growing up contribute to their perceptions of what is normal, expected, and desirable.[2] So much of what art teachers believe about the purposes of art in education and what makes someone a good art teacher is shaped by their past experiences. Those experiences motivate many artists and students to become professional educators. Some dream of being the kind of art teacher that they remember, someone who supported them and made a transformative difference in their lives. Others are driven by less positive experiences to be the art teacher they wish they had had growing up. In both cases, life histories and future aspirations powerfully influence teachers' identities and their curricular and pedagogical decision-making in ways that are not always obvious.

Given the importance of teachers' biographies, this chapter illuminates how art teachers' prior experiences are situated within specific racial contexts. These contexts, which we introduced as racial ecologies in the previous chapter, influence art teachers' understandings of race, their emotional responses to racism, and their mental models of what it means to be a "good teacher" in relation to anti-racism. We move through these three topics and provide supporting concepts and sidebar activities for readers to use for critical race reflection. Subjecting our own biographies to critical race reflection is an important part of developing an anti-racist teaching practice because it opens up a space to reimagine other ways of living, teaching, and being. At the same time, history holds valuable lessons for today and tomorrow. Hence, we look to past and present abolitionists and allies working to dismantle racist structures as inspiration for an anti-racist art education led by teachers who hold a commitment to developing the capacities for racial equity and justice.

In this chapter, we focus on these key concepts:
- Critical race reflection
- Anti-racism
- Critical race consciousness
- Good teacher as abolitionist

Critical Race Reflection

The journey of developing anti-racist teaching practices requires that art teachers reflect critically on racism in their biographies and the contexts that have shaped their thinking.[3] In sharing parts of our own stories in this chapter's opening, we show that personal and social histories are products of broader racial ecologies that can be difficult to discern in the midst of managing all the activity that goes on in the course of an art class. This is especially so for people who were socialized as White and those who benefit from racial inequality.

To illustrate, we invite readers to explore the Racial Dot Map online. (See Try This, page 118.) The map is a visualization of the 2010 U.S. Census. It plots the racial makeup of the United States one person at a time. The map makes visible an otherwise invisible history of racial inequality and its sedimentation in the landscape in the form of racially segregated neighborhoods. With the map's zoom function, viewers can "step back" to get a fuller picture of the entire country and "get up close" to see the smaller details of how cities, neighborhoods, and even individual blocks have been built up over time.

One can literally see the geography of racism. It defines who individuals are likely to be in community with and their proximity to people who are racially different. In addition, the map makes apparent environmental inequities, for example, where public resources and enrichments are located. What racial patterns exist in the placement of services and amenities? Is there a relationship between some groups of people living near art museums, shady parks, playgrounds, and grocery stores with fresh, affordable produce while others are relegated to live near highways and polluting industries? In what ways are these environmental disparities related to the geography of racism? What does a racially segregated landscape imply about other quality-of-life indicators, like health and well-being? What does the dot map visualization tell you about your own racial ecology?

The dot map illustrates the spatial dimensions of racial ecologies. If we add to this the other dimensions explored already—socioeconomic structures in Chapter 2 and visual cultures in Chapter 3—then we begin to realize how each person is neither autonomous nor entirely individual. Rather, each of us participates in and contributes to a larger system of interconnected contexts. Even if we are largely unaware of their full impact on our thoughts, feelings, and actions, racial ecologies tacitly shape our biography.

Of course, racial ecologies are inherited from previous generations, but this does not absolve people living today from responsibility for racial justice. Indeed, if we collectively were to do nothing, racial inequality would continue and likely worsen. Doing nothing is tantamount to acceptance, as if to say, "Well, that's just how it is." Therefore, it is important to realize that being non-racist is not the same as being anti-racist. **Non-racism** is a complacent stance that is satisfied with and uncritical of the way things are. It gives a wink and a pass to racial injustice. **Anti-racism** is a stance that refuses to accept and actively disrupts the societal norms that privilege the ways of whiteness. The shift from non-racist mindset to anti-racist mindset is both a process and an outcome of critical race reflection. But it takes practice to make critical race reflection a habit. In the next section, we support art teachers

Connecting the Dots

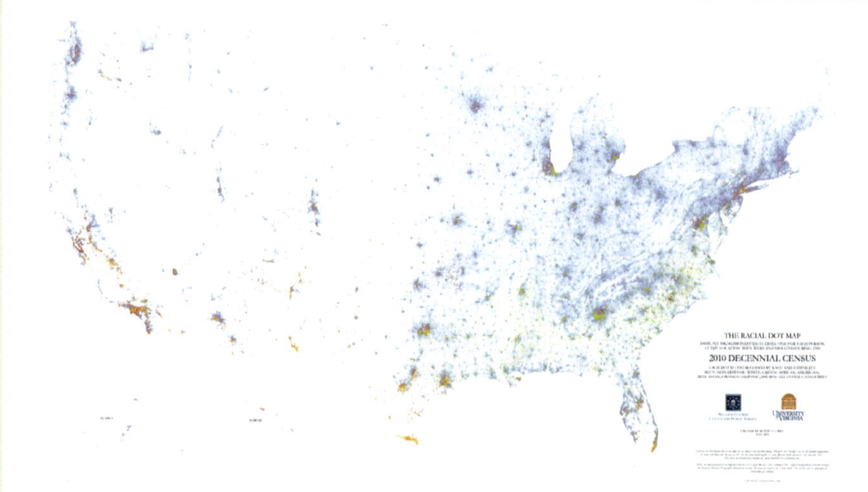

5.1 Racial Dot Map. Image © 2013, Weldon Cooper Center for Public Service, Rector and Visitors of the University of Virginia (Dustin A. Cable, creator).

The U.S. Census is a constitutionally mandated count of the full population of the country. It is conducted once every 10 years. Every resident is counted one by one. The purpose of the census is twofold: to distribute federal tax dollars to local communities and to allocate political power fairly to the people through the number of seats assigned to each state in the U.S. House of Representatives. The census is also a racial document in that it asks residents to indicate a racial identity. The Weldon Cooper Center for Public Service at the University of Virginia converted the 2010 Census into a visual map by plotting the racial makeup of the United States one person at a time.

In the screenshot of the Racial Dot Map pictured here, we can see the geography of race.

The map is interactive, enabling viewers to see how racism defines the way people interact and their proximity to resources. The map's zoom function allows the country to be viewed from a macro perspective down to a micro view of cities, neighborhoods, and even blocks.

Open up the interactive Racial Dot Map published for free use on the website of the Weldon Cooper Center (demographics.coopercenter.org/racial-dot-map). Take time to examine the map by zooming in to a place that has significance for you. It may be where you grew up and went to school or where you teach now. Perhaps it is a place that has gained attention from the news media. Use the color-coded dot key to analyze how race is structured into the landscape.

Consider these questions:

- What can the dot map tell you about your own racial ecology?

- What is the relationship between dot patterns and clusters shown on the map and racial disparities in schools? What further connections can be made to inequities in arts education?

- Many cities, large and small, have invested public resources in the creation of arts districts. These are hubs of creative activity. Locate an arts district on the map. How does the placement of the arts district contribute to the racial ecology of the area?

- What surprises you most when looking at the Racial Dot Map?

- How can the Racial Dot Map be used with students to inspire research, reflection, artmaking, and community dialogue about race and racism?

Go further: To explore the impact of geographic racism on health and wellbeing, visit the interactive visual article "How Decades of Racist Housing Policy Left Neighborhoods Sweltering," published by The New York Times. www.nytimes.com/interactive/2020/08/24/climate/racism-redlining-cities-global-warming.html

"Every city has its own story. In Denver, formerly redlined neighborhoods tend to have more Hispanic than Black residents today, but they remain hotter: parks were intentionally placed in whiter, wealthier neighborhoods that then blocked construction of affordable housing nearby even after racial segregation was banned. In Baltimore, polluting industries were more likely to be located near communities of color. In Portland, zoning rules allowed multifamily apartment buildings to cover the entire lot and be built without any green space, a practice the city only recently changed. The problem worsens as global warming increases the number of hot days nationwide."

—Brad Plumer and Nadja Popovich in "How Decades of Racist Housing Policy Left Neighborhoods Sweltering," an interactive visual article published by The New York Times[4]

in developing that habit by illuminating racial ecologies that characterize many schools and art classrooms, including those that serve racially homogeneous populations. We provide concepts and examples that art teachers can use to understand racism, non-racism, and anti-racism within their own practice.

Seeing Color in a Colorless Art Room

While reading the daily postings to a well-known online art education forum, we came across a comment that led us to pause and reflect. The contributor wrote, "Skills-based art education excludes no one because it's not about gender, race, or culture. It's just about mastering the visual." If you, dear reader, have ever heard this or anything similar to it, then you know what non-racism sounds like in an art classroom.

Art classrooms have their own racial ecologies. From the psychology of color symbolism to the materials and technologies that we teach students to use and make art with, colorblind ideology animates many seemingly neutral, non-racist ideas commonly promoted through the teaching of art.

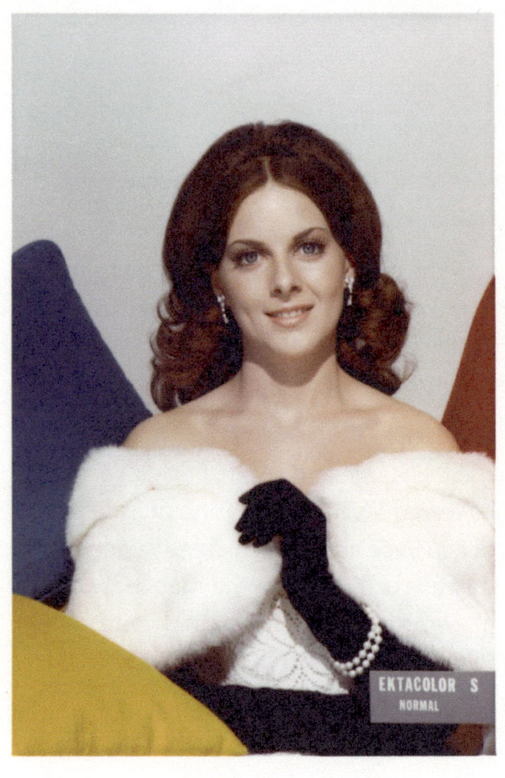

5.2 Kodak Shirley Card, 1974. Kodak. Photo: Hermann Zschiegner. From the Collection of Hermann Zschiegner.

Seemingly non-racial artmaking materials carry their own racial histories that are passed along to each generation through colorblind teaching. For example, did you know that in the mid-1950s, Kodak, the largest, most successful photo company in the U.S., developed "Shirley cards" to calibrate light and shadows during their printing process?[5] Shirley cards were cards that featured a White woman named Shirley. Her skin tone was used as a baseline to correct the color of all other skin tones during photo processing. The result is that darker skin can, when photographed, appear irregular and unattractive. The technology itself creates the illusion of light-skin beauty, an objective disguise for anti-black racial bias encoded in the tools. Other photo companies around the world also began using Shirley cards to calibrate skin tones. A succession of other White women eventually stood in for the original model, but the cards retained her name. "Shirley" was the standard. Even today, newer technologies and materials that appear neutral and non-racial can and do have biases built into their basic functions.[6]

Anti-racism requires that art teachers first acknowledge that race and the arts are inextricably intertwined. Shirley cards are one of many tangible examples of this and why anti-racism is needed in art classrooms. The art discipline, with its seemingly innocuous tools, processes, and techniques, can and often does promote a black-white binary and white supremacist thinking. For this reason, all art teachers, ourselves included, have a responsibility to develop the knowledge and skills for anti-racism in the discipline, lest we become part of perpetuating racism through the content we so love to teach.

"I Didn't Know…"

With the advancement of 21st century technology and widespread access to Wi-Fi, anyone with a computer, smartphone, or tablet can complete a Google search and get information in mere milliseconds. Information on any topic is now at our fingertips, that is, if we want it to be. The question to ask oneself is, "Do I want it to be?" The decision to either learn about something or avoid learning about it is what defines ignorance.

Philosopher Linda Alcoff explains that when people avoid learning about the construction of race and racism's detrimental impact on non-White communities, they are engaging in an act of willful ignorance by choosing to be uninformed.[7] **Willful ignorance** is a non-racist strategy. It is used to absolve oneself of responsibility for dealing with racism. Courtnie N. Wolfgang, a White American art education scholar, writes, "Lesson one that I have been taught is that we (White and White-presenting people) have to do the work… to acknowledge how legacies of racism and violence continue to deeply impact curriculum and pedagogy in the arts; to make space where we have failed in the past; and to reconsider pedagogy as a step toward reparation or mitigating the effects of white supremacy in Art Education on our students, our colleagues, and our communities."[8]

Some tactics of willful ignorance are avoiding certain news sources, college courses, and even people with different beliefs so that a facade of ignorance remains plausible.[9] In a large-scale study of how White people talk about race, sociologist Eduardo Bonilla-Silva found consistent patterns in White people's statements of denial (e.g., "I don't believe that, but…") and claims of ignorance (e.g., "I don't know") when asked about their racial views.[10] Age-old excuses like "I didn't know" and "I had no idea" are no longer acceptable or believable responses to dismiss the realities of racism. Ignorance is anything but innocent. Instead, not knowing protects white privilege and leaves racism as the problem of those who experience it. Willful ignorance is a non-racist strategy taught and learned through generations.

In the classroom, willful ignorance allows teachers to ignore privilege and the ways that it advances certain students while extending

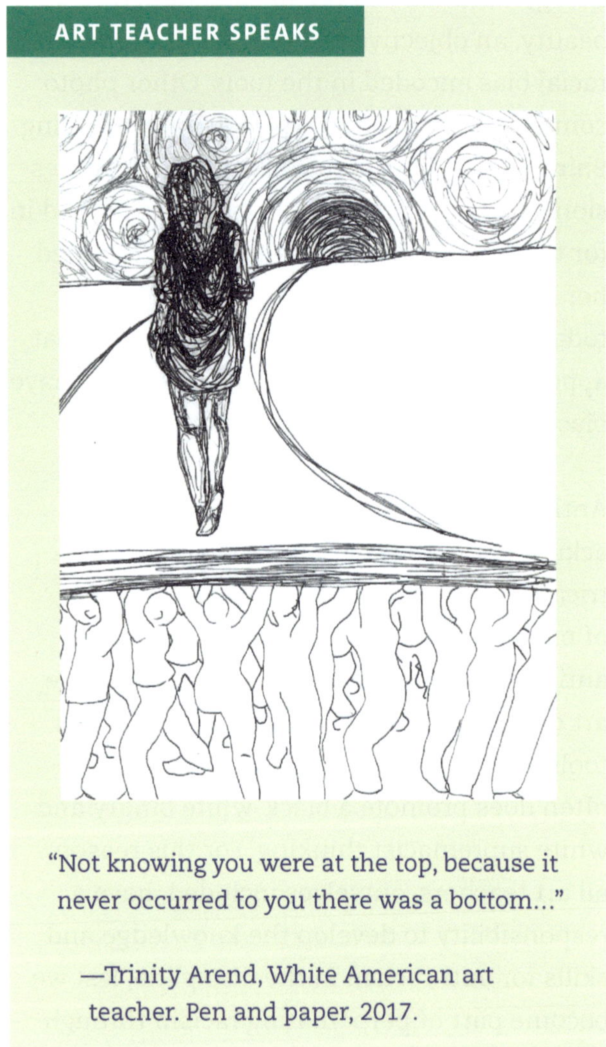

"Not knowing you were at the top, because it never occurred to you there was a bottom…"

—Trinity Arend, White American art teacher. Pen and paper, 2017.

the finish line for others. Willful ignorance allows teachers to disregard the effect that an unarmed Black man being killed by police officers or an Asian person being assaulted on the street can have on students' motivation and interest in completing schoolwork the very next day. Willful ignorance allows teachers to claim that the classroom is not the place for conversations about social inequalities and human rights. Willful ignorance is teachers believing that when they close their classroom doors, the problems of the world are shut out, too.

Critical Race Consciousness

Moving from willful ignorance to critical race **consciousness** is a lifelong process. Consciousness is awareness. A critical consciousness is an awareness of structural causes of social problems that is awakened every time we pose questions that get at root causes of everyday living conditions.[11] An uncritical awareness of social problems leads to the acceptance of dominant ideas as truth. Recognizing, naming, and interrogating white supremacy are ways of practicing more critical race consciousness.

We find joy in being part of the struggle for justice and a better way of life through art and education, but we also admit to feeling fatigued by racism. When talking to pre-

dominantly White art teachers about race and racism in art education, we notice that they experience a variety of emotions, too—from curiosity and eagerness to fear and exhaustion. One day after I, Joni, facilitated a group discussion on race, a White female art teacher said to me, "I look forward to having these discussions about race, but then I don't look forward to having these discussions about race because when I'm done, I feel so heavy. I can't stop thinking about our conversations all day." In response, I let her know that the heaviness she feels twice per week is the same heaviness many non-White people feel every day, moment to moment as they navigate white-dominant institutions.

Another art teacher shared that learning how to identify racism in her everyday life has caused her to reflect on her relationships with her parents, grandparents, and other family members. She began to ask hard questions about how the words and actions of the people she cares about reflect a belief in the innate superiority of White people, and a sense of entitlement to the advantages they enjoy. "I was so sure about who I was when I started taking this anti-racism workshop," she said. "Now I just don't know. That's scary but also a bit exciting." Uncertainty is a part of self-transformation. When a person begins to ask questions about what has always been "normal" for them, they start to reflect on the ideals that they learned from their family members. They come to understand that if they are not attentive to the ways racism touches their day-to-day lives and the lives of their students, they will inflict trauma on their students through their use of alienating curricula and teaching practices built on white supremacist frameworks.

There is range in the consciousness-raising experience when it comes to non-White art teachers. The path toward critical race consciousness depends on whether they have internalized white supremacy. For example, while I, Joni, was having a discussion with a Black woman art teacher about race-centric pedagogies, she insisted, "Everything isn't always about race." As a self-reflective activity, I asked her to write down some stories that she associated with blackness and also to identify the ways systemic racism had impacted her and her family on a personal level. After taking some time with these tasks, examining some contemporary events plagued with clear racial undercurrents, and reading key critical race texts, the teacher came to the realization that she was assuming a colorblind ideology. She

Sick from Racism

Racial battle fatigue is not only mental and emotional stress, it also results in actual physiological responses like suppressed immunity, tension headaches, trembling and jumpiness, chronic pain in healed injuries, and elevated blood pressure. When anticipating racial conflict, non-White people have also described bouts of diarrhea, frequent urination, uncontrollable sweating, anxiety, insomnia, conflict-specific dreams, rapid mood swings, and even social withdrawal.

acknowledged that she had been **deracializing** events and experiences, ignoring race when race was indisputably implicated in situations.

This particular Black art teacher's erasure of race was a means to cope with and avoid being fatigued by the injustices she saw happening to other Black people daily. Ultimately, she was attempting to avoid racial battle fatigue. **Racial battle fatigue** is the cumulative stress caused by racism. Usually experienced by non-White people, racial battle fatigue can cause a person to lose confidence in themselves and question their life's work and even, tragically, their life's worth.[12] It is not uncommon for non-White people to experience race-based trauma so often that it induces racial battle fatigue.

I interacted with another Black woman art teacher who described having an awakening after taking the Harvard Implicit Bias Test, an assessment tool that detects the strength of a person's subconscious associations between racial groups and stereotypes about those racial groups. Her results revealed that she had a slight preference for White individuals over Black individuals. She shared with the class that she was embarrassed but not surprised. She admitted that she had always struggled with self-hatred because of internalized white supremacy. She reflected on the racial ecologies of her upper middle-class upbringing and came to recognize that she had accepted as true many dominant racial tropes about blackness (see Chapter 3 on tropes). In her

suburban elementary and high school days, she received her White peers' statements, "You're different!" and "You're not *Black* Black," as if they were giving her compliments for not performing blackness in the stereotypical way they understood it from watching television and consuming other forms of popular visual culture. She remembered feeling proud for being accepted by her White peers but simultaneously confused about what their comments meant. Her school experiences and peer-to-peer interactions explain why, as an adult, her implicit bias test showed she preferred other racial groups over her own.

These examples illustrate that non-White art teachers are as capable of promoting white supremacy as White art teachers who are willfully ignorant and unaware of their racial privilege within a society structured by racial inequality.[13] Whiteness, as mentioned in Chapter 2, is a set of assumptions and beliefs that place people who are perceived as or believe themselves to be White at the center of what is considered normal. Regardless of their racial identity, anyone can internalize and, thus, perpetuate whiteness as a standard. It takes practice and a developed critical race consciousness to push against this dominance.

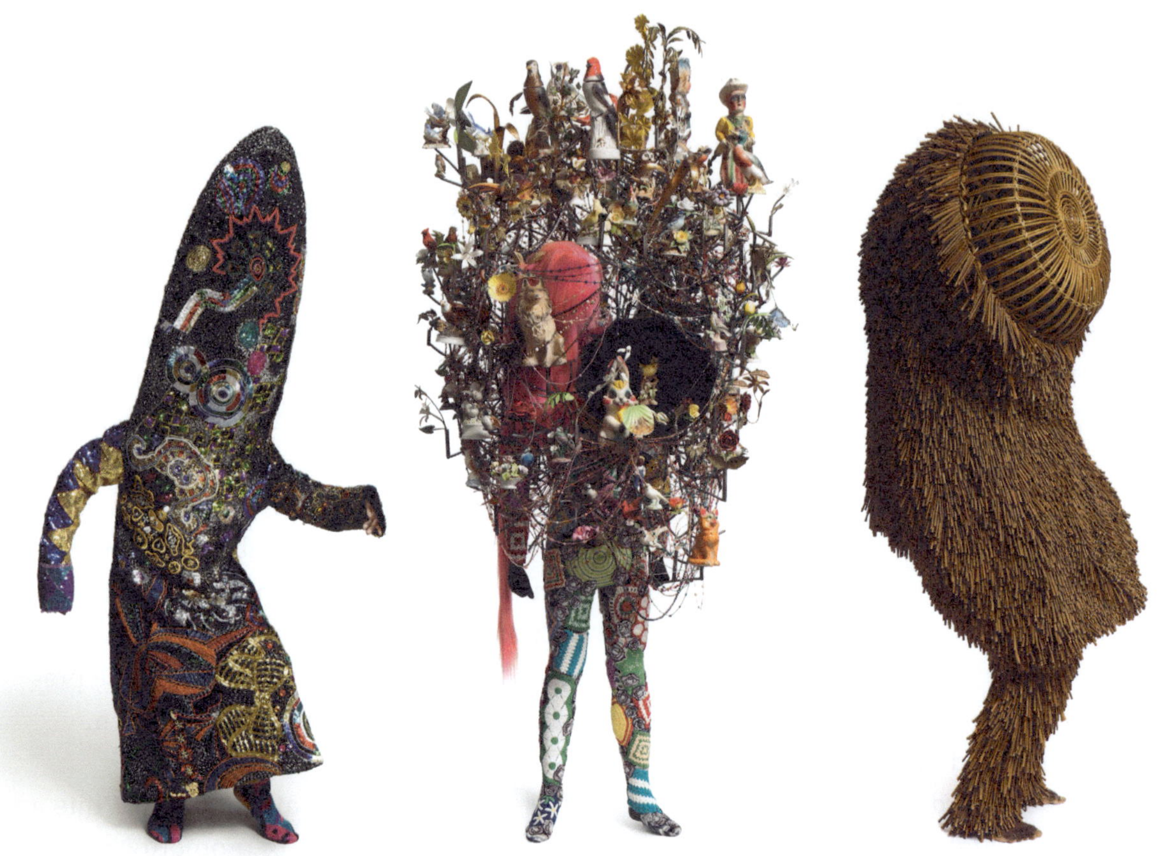

5.3 Nick Cave, Soundsuits, (from left) 2008, 2011, 2012. Mixed media including beaded and sequined garments, metal, mannequin, embroidery, fabric, metal flowers, dogwood twigs, wire, and upholstery. © Nick Cave. Courtesy of the artist and Jack Shainman Gallery, NY.

What If I'm Already There?

Some art teachers have well-developed racial literacy. They already understand the significance of social and historical circumstances, so they might feel frustrated with peers who exhibit racial illiteracy. This can occur particularly in peer-to-peer discussions about racial privilege. In situations like this, White colleagues and those who are invested in white-ness can become defensive, angry, withdrawn, or consumed with guilt.[14] This emotional response is called **white fragility**, and it is triggered by discomfort and stress. White fragility is often accompanied by tears that can indicate a need for more practice and stamina in conversations about race.[15]

Art teachers with more developed critical race knowledge may be overlooked in settings that cater to white fragility. This is another way whiteness is re-centered even in conversations that are about decentering whiteness. Art education researcher Sunny Spillane writes about her struggle to create an anti-racist pedagogy as a White woman. She says, "many Whites—including myself—are neither accustomed to nor comfortable with thinking about ourselves in racial terms."[16] To support art teachers who are still developing critical consciousness about racism, it is detrimental to center, yet again, ways of whiteness. Instead, critical race artistic practices can provide content and experiences that foster visual racial literacy. Because the arts "speak" to human senses and sensibilities in ways words alone cannot, they can also be used to inspire critical race reflection and anti-racist art pedagogies.

For example, Black American contemporary artist Nick Cave is known for his life-sized soundsuits, wearable sculptures that can obscure the racial identity of the wearer. According to Cave, his art objects enable him, and those who suit up in them, to unleash personal experiences, especially racial profiling and witnessing police brutality. His work has been described as "vehicles of empowerment."[17] Cave uses his knowledge from lived experience to build an anti-racist practice of artmaking.

How Do I Perceive My Students?

Teachers' beliefs about and expectations for students impact students' performance. It is common for teachers to have a mental image of the ideal student. As they organize the curriculum and arrange the classroom so it is set up for instruction, teachers imagine how students will behave and what they will learn. Unfortunately, we do not often recognize the intellectual, behavioral, moral, and cultural standards embedded in those ideals. It is critical to consider how and why the standards we have adopted as our own were conceived. Where do our mental images of the ideal student come from? How have they been shaped by the racial ecologies in which we were raised? How might standards and expectations for students mask whiteness, traditional notions of gender, heterosexual norms, and middle-class values and lifestyles?

Deficit Ideology and Implicit Bias

Today's art teachers are often encouraged to identify and support students' individual needs through differentiated or customized instruction. To do this, they work to get to know students as individuals. They use a battery of instruments to measure and evaluate individual factors like student motivation, aptitude, and readiness to learn. They are encouraged to "diagnose" students' motivations for art with interest inventories, their prior art knowledge with portfolios and performance tests, and their abilities with benchmark examinations. This information is used to find out each student's needs and strengths. Some students are understood as having more needs than others. Once identified, these needs are targeted with instructional remedies intended to ameliorate shortcomings so every student makes progress toward a norm or standard that has been set for learning.[18]

This storyline is so familiar that it feels like common sense. It is hard to imagine anyone disagreeing. Yet the assumptions underlying assessments of students' motivations, talents, and abilities can be problematic. First, they are too often devoid of context, which makes it easier to miss the role social and cultural differences play in learning. When left to make judgments about students with-

Filling In the Gap

Look at the graphic below. How many triangles do you see?

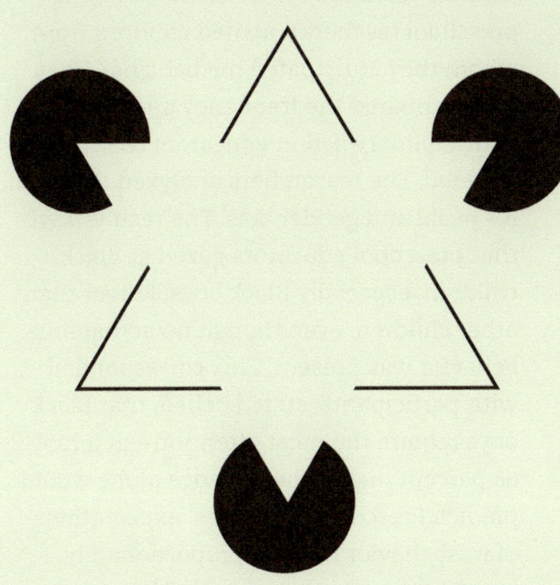

Now turn the book over to learn more …

There are no triangles. Our brain fills in the spaces where it wants to see triangles. This simple exercise demonstrates how the brain plays tricks on us all the time, filling in gaps in our information with assumptions that are often biased. The brain does this in fractions of seconds, almost instantaneously. It is a process that precedes conscious thought. This process is useful for survival in wilderness but can be harmful in social environments and human relationships. The racial assumptions we rely upon are acquired over time, not through direct lessons so much as by being around other people, seeing how they respond differently to groups who might have different skin color, hair texture, facial features, and personal style.

In other words, we make snap judgments that are positively or negatively biased based on our place within social hierarchies and cultural upbringing. What implications might this have for the routine snap judgments teachers must make in a classroom environment? How might snap judgments be involved in teachers' perceptions of students and their communities or families? What can a teacher do to guard against filling in knowledge gaps with biased and faulty assumptions?

out adequate context, teachers can miss key pieces of the puzzle that make up the conditions of a person's life and development. As a consequence, teachers can end up acting on their prejudices.

Another problem with this way of thinking is that it expresses a **deficit ideology**, a disposition toward students that focuses on what is perceived as lacking, missing, or deviant. Deficit ideology is the belief that achievement gaps and other inequalities result from individuals' intellectual, cultural, familial, or moral deficiencies, not from social inequalities such as institutional racism or economic and environmental injustices.[19] Deficit ideology is often led or influenced by a teacher's **implicit biases** toward certain groups of people. Implicit biases are deep-seated, pervasive beliefs, mental images, and assumptions that combine to form stereotypes that impact thinking and guide behavior on an unconscious level. Implicit biases cause humans to pay more attention to things that confirm preconceptions and justify their existing beliefs, regardless of whether they are situated in fact or reality. Implicit biases are mental shortcuts that enable a person to save time and make quick decisions. Unfortunately, at times, these shortcuts are based on racism.

Teacher Bias and Students' Futures

The **school-to-prison pipeline** is an example of the ways in which deficit ideology and implicit bias lead educators to take disparate disciplinary actions for different groups of students, resulting in the over incarceration of Black and Brown people, especially young men.[20] The school-to-prison pipeline refers to a system in which Black, Indigenous, and other non-White students are disciplined more harshly

Watchful Gazes

In a recent study, researchers at the Yale Childhood Study Center used an eye-tracking technique to measure how long preschool teachers watched children from whom they anticipated misbehavior. They also compared the frequency and severity of disciplinary action educators recommended. The researchers analyzed the data for racial and gender bias. The results were that preschool educators gazed at Black children, especially Black boys, longer than other children, even though no actual misbehavior was present. This corresponded with participants' stated beliefs that Black boys require the most attention—at a rate 68 percent higher than chance alone would predict. Preschool educators' expectations of misbehavior were disproportionately high for boys in general, with 76 percent of participants endorsing the idea that boys required the most attention, a rate of 52 percent more than predictable by chance alone.[21]

than White students, creating a funnel for them from the classroom into the juvenile and criminal justice systems.[22] In this case, a prison sentence does not begin when a person commits a crime as an adult; it begins when a child is profiled in the preschool classroom by their teacher, principal, or school counselor.

The pipeline contains a disproportionate number of Black, Indigenous, Latinx, and Asian American subgroup (e.g., Hmong) students singled out and labeled as "disruptive" or "trouble-makers."[23] These students are suspended at higher rates for committing the same or similar offenses as their White counterparts and are about four times more likely than White students to be placed in special education, a more restrictive learning environment with lower academic standards than they would find in the regular classroom.

Through videos that go viral online, the world has seen White police officers handcuff, fingerprint, and transport non-White students as

Proliferation

In 2009, Black American artist Paul Rucker engaged in a thematic art exploration titled *Proliferation*, in which he delved into the topic of prisons. In his work, which can be viewed in its entirety on YouTube, he animated a digital visualization of the prison system and composed an original score to accompany a visual illustration of the rapid growth of prisons in the U.S. The prisons are represented by dots on a U.S. map. The map starts with only one dot, but as each second passes, new dots appear. New dots appearing correlate with the rhythms of Rucker's composition. Rucker utilizes the pioneering work by Prison Policy Initiative to provide accurate data on prison growth and location. The audience witnesses 232 years of growth in 10 minutes and 45 seconds. Watch his work at youtu.be/ySH-FgMljYo.

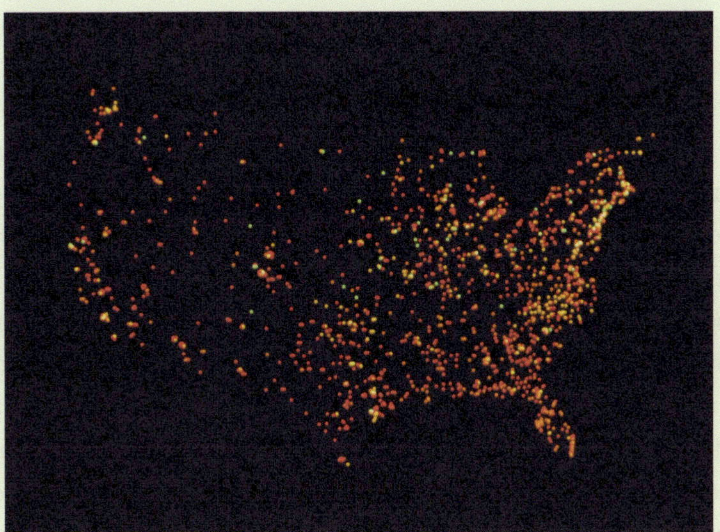

5.4 Paul Rucker, *Proliferation*, 2009. Courtesy of the artist.

young as six years old to juvenile detention for having age-appropriate "temper tantrums."[24] The world has seen a White school resource officer flip a teenaged Black girl out of her desk and slam her to the ground for not putting away her cell phone.[25] These are not random actions. Such drastic disciplinary tactics are not used on *all* students. These are patterned behaviors that some people approve of because their implicit bias and deficit thinking leads them to view young non-White children as prone to criminality.

The school-to-prison pipeline is but one example of the many long-term consequences of deficit ideology and implicit biases. However, teachers can adopt an assets orientation when thinking about and engaging with students, especially non-White students. An **assets-based approach** to education means having an intentional focus on the strengths of not only the child but the child's cultural community. An assets-oriented art teacher might ask, "What is present in this child that can be built upon?" instead of "What is missing in this child that needs to be fixed or attended to?" This approach perceives diversity in thought and culture as positives, not challenges or gaps to overcome. Assets are the starting points for curriculum and instruction.[26] The intentional

shift in a teacher's focus to strengths instead of deficiencies and possibility instead of despair affirms students' humanity and supports their potential in the classroom.

Do My Actions Align with My Beliefs?

Mispronouncing a minority, immigrant, or international student's name during roll call every morning. Asking Asian students with names you find hard to remember if they have a nickname. Complimenting a Black student on how "articulate" they are. Completing a painting demonstration on making "flesh tones" where all of the colors are variations of peach. Or moreover, beginning the flesh tone demonstration with a pale color and going darker. What do all of these seemingly minor acts have in common? They are all **racial microaggressions**. Racial microaggressions are the subtle slights, putdowns, and questions of one's competence that reflect implicit racial biases about individuals from non-dominant groups.[27] Non-White people are the targets of racial messages and misinformation that tacitly reinforce a social hierarchy based on the assumed inferiority of racially minoritized persons.[28] The examples above illustrate com-

Racial Messages

Chinese American psychologist Derald Wing Sue and his colleagues studied the various ways microaggressions manifest. They found that racial microaggressions are not limited to human interactions but can be communicated through non-human environmental elements as well.[29] Explore the categories of microaggression to better understand the different forms of microaggression.

Microaggressions

Microassault
"A verbal or nonverbal attack meant to hurt the intended victim through name-calling, avoidant behavior, or purposeful discriminatory actions."

Microinvalidations
"Communications that exclude, negate, or nullify the psychological thoughts, feelings, or experiential reality of a person of color."

Microinsults
"Communications that convey rudeness and insensitivity and demean a person's racial heritage or identity."

mon ways that teachers contribute to microaggressive learning environments, causing great harm to the psyches of non-White students. You may wonder, how does mispronouncing a name have a racial undertone? To understand the harm of mispronouncing a name, one first needs to understand the history of racism in schools.

As early as the 18th century, the education system in the U.S. has codified and affirmed a hierarchy of knowledge that prioritizes and privileges White middle-class culture. Teachers have been trained in curriculum and pedagogy designed to assimilate Native Americans, Mexicans, Catholic Irish, and other groups to a White, Protestant ideal by stripping them of their language, cultural knowledge, and lifeways. New language, clothes, culture, and even names were imposed upon these students. This historical backdrop is what makes the repeated mispronunciation of a student's name a racial microaggression.

Microaggressions do not occur in a vacuum. They are not simply actions that happen to a person in a singular moment. Instead, they are part of the larger historical context of racism and racial injustices enacted against non-White people. It is this historical baggage that makes microaggressions violent. Additionally,

Resource Audit

Think about environmental microaggressions, specifically microinsults, that could be happening in your classroom. Did you know that some of our most beloved children's films and books have been heavily criticized for being overtly racist? For example, the film *Peter Pan* depicts Native Americans in stereotypically inaccurate ways in which they skin other humans (specifically pirates in *Peter Pan*), grunt, speak incomprehensible English, play instruments, and howl and chant around fires with feathered headdresses all day and night. In the film, they call Native Americans "Injuns" and "Red skins," which are derogatory names that helped Europeans establish Natives' identity as primitive, violent, savage beasts that are not human. In a book adaptation of *Peter Pan*, also written by its film creator J.M. Barrie, the character Tiger Lily has a tribe of "picaninny warriors" that speak in "pidgin." Examples of pidgin talk from the "tribe" include "Ugh, ugh, wah!" and "Ugga-wugga-wigwam." Tiger Lily is characterized as a bit more intelligible. She says, "Peter Pan save me, me his velly nice friend. Me no let pirates hurt him." Tiger Lily and her "tribe" call Peter "the great white father."

Other heavily critiqued films and books include *Mary Poppins*, *Charlie and the Chocolate Factory*, and *Dr. Doolittle*. These are all characterized as microinsults, as they demean racial heritage and identity of non-White people. The characterizations of non-White characters in these childhood cultural artifacts convey hidden messages about the humanity, intellectual capacity, and likability of certain groups of people. What kind of microinsults may be present in your classroom resources and the images on your walls?

White and non-White students who are not the target of racist messages nonetheless are affected by them, and they, too, may learn to perpetrate microaggressions.[30]

What Is Anti-Racist Pedagogy?

In the remaining pages of this chapter, we present some ideas for art teachers who wish to develop an anti-racist pedagogy. By **pedagogy** we are referring to a set of commitments that guide and orient teaching and teachers' reflection on their practices. This goes beyond the usual definition of pedagogy as the science of teaching. We take a more encompassing view than this because pedagogy is as much about the teacher's beliefs and ethical sense of responsibility as it is about the mechanics of instructional methods. We can see pedagogy in how art teachers design lessons, the artworks and other artifacts displayed on classroom walls, the way a teacher talks to students, the allocation of time for particular activities, and the explicit and implied rules of classroom life.

Anti-racist pedagogy is a commitment to understanding and grappling with racism in classrooms and in one's own life as a teacher. One challenge in adopting an anti-racist pedagogy is that many people and institutions already speak the language of "equity" and "social justice," but too often these and other change-oriented vocabularies are hollowed out by a lack of shared definitions. This makes it easier for them to be appropriated in the service of aims that have little to do with justice, and over time, they lose their original power to inspire understanding and action.

To illustrate, we offer a cautionary tale. It is based on an experience I, Amy, had in the aftermath of George Floyd's murder in summer 2020 that inspired a global racial justice uprising. Readers may recall that a White police officer in Minneapolis pressed his knee on Mr. Floyd's neck, killing him, while fellow police officers looked on. Cell phone video footage went viral showing Mr. Floyd, a Black man, pinned to the ground and pleading for his life for more than nine minutes, repeatedly saying, "I can't breathe." The world responded in outrage. Many people who had never before engaged in activism took to the streets to demonstrate. Other people supported the demonstrations. For example, store owners provided food and water to protesters, and many people donated money to bail bonds funds for activists who were arrested and jailed. Schools, universities, and cultural institutions expressed their support, too, by issuing statements denouncing racial discrimination and hatred. Parents and teachers formed reading lists and book clubs to learn more about racism, white supremacy, and what it means to be an anti-racist.

It was during that time that I received a letter from my child's preschool. In it, the administrative leadership wrote that the school community stands with Black Lives Matter (BLM). Its first action would be to hire consultants to help the school's teaching staff, the majority of whom were White, become more knowledgeable and responsive to this moment of racial reckoning. "We are listening," the letter stated. "Now, more than ever, we commit ourselves to a deeper practice of anti-bias curriculum."

I reread the letter several times. With each reading, my concerns grew. Were they saying that *racism* is the same as *bias* and *bias* the same as *racism?* The BLM protestors were demanding an end to systemic, institutionalized racism, not individual biases. As we know from Chapter 2, racism is a system, a way of thinking and behaving upheld by structures such as laws, institutional policies, economic disparity, language and cultural norms, as well as the threat of state-sanctioned violence. Racism is compounded by other systems of inequality, and its effects on people's well-being and life chances are profound.

Although anti-bias curriculum may address prejudices in general, it is not an adequate response to systemic racism. In fact, one could teach an anti-bias curriculum without ever mentioning race or social structures that reproduce racial inequalities. Avoidance of racial topics is common among White teachers and parents who themselves were taught to think of race as a taboo or rude topic.[32] Some teachers think that the mere mention of race is itself racist and teaches children to be racist. In the end, race avoidance undermines good intentions and generates little to no change in policies and practices that maintain racial inequities. To guard against this, anti-racist pedagogy goes beyond awareness of biases. It is a clear-eyed stance against racism with two primary goals:

1 tear down educational systems that maintain racial inequality, and

2 replace them with new ways of teaching and learning that support an egalitarian society, thriving communities, and education as a practice in freedom.

"We Been Knew That"

Some readers are learning about anti-racism for the first time; however, it is not a new concept. As we would say, *We been knew that!* The past is full of inspiring examples of anti-racism that we draw from when building an anti-racist pedagogy. We find our inspiration in the way enslaved people invented creative strategies to resist white supremacy and, often at great risk, shared that knowledge in house-

"I talk to other artists about this because I find it important to hear other perspectives in case I have a blind spot, but at the end of the day, a lot of people agree with me. When we talk about the art world, we're talking about the art industry, the monetizing of artwork. Art can exist outside the industry of art. Our industry is predominantly run by heterosexual white men. So my question and statement is this: where does my queer and person-of-color work fit into that industry when there is very little representation of people who look like me and people whose lifestyles reflect my lifestyle? This is the problem that women have had in the art world since the beginning. For the most part, the people in power who validate artists don't understand artwork that comes from another experience than their own. Even in the film industry, the stories told are the stories that reflect the people in power. That's why there's a lack of diversity. They need to tell stories of women, stories of people of color. What we need is more people that are minorities, women, other marginalized communities, to be in positions of power so that they can also champion artists who are not just heterosexual white men."

—Guatemalan-born artist Gio Black Peter in an interview for *ArtSpace*[33]

holds, churches, and other informal places of education.[35] In the antebellum abolitionist movement, Black people and White allies worked together for liberation and an end to slavery. Their anti-racism sought to change the hearts and minds of a complacent nation. The same commitment to racial justice ignited the 20th-century Civil Rights Movement, where people of diverse hues dared to imagine and articulate a world different from that in which they existed, a world of possibility. Not only are these inspiring examples of anti-racism, but they show us what liberatory education can look like. Knowledge is created. People's critical race consciousness is altered. And in the process, new relationships and ways of being take shape.

A lesson to be learned by looking to the past is that anti-racism requires work, even struggle, at the level of everyday thoughts and actions by ordinary people. We are heartened to see young people, particularly high school and university students, using activism to channel their discontent with an educational system that has not served them well. Many of them are calling for specific actions that align with the goals of Black Lives Matter and the Movement for Black Life to dismantle rather than assimilate to institutions that maintain white supremacy.[36] They are demanding an educational system in which they can thrive, not just survive. Students cannot wait for Superman or anyone else to create the change they know is needed for education to be equitable and life-affirming. How can we as art teachers use our agency to co-conspire to transform schools into racially just institutions? We believe the answer lies, at least in part, with a critical assessment of what it means to be a good teacher.

It's Time to Reimagine "The Good Teacher"

Just about everyone has a good teacher metaphor, a mental image of what a good teacher is. Teacher metaphors do two things at once. They reflect deep-seated beliefs and values about what makes for an effective educator, and they drive teacher decision making and behavior in and out of the classroom.[37]

What makes a good art teacher is, for many people, based on their own biographies as art students, what they observed, and how they felt about their previous art teachers. Art education researcher Beth Thomas found that among preservice art teachers, "Being a good art teacher meant re-creating an influential art teacher's interactional style so that future students will feel about them the way they felt about the cherished teacher."[38] These meanings are also informed by fictional representations and storylines about art teachers found in television and popular movies.[39]

In a society that is racialized, good teacher metaphors are also shot through with racial meaning. Education researcher Nora Hyland conducted a study with teachers who identified as White, including one who was Latina but held a strong affinity to whiteness. She looked at the metaphors each one used to define their roles as good teachers of non-White children. The metaphors included the teacher as

- *a helper* who meets students' needs;
- *an assimilator* who helps students conform to the desires, values, and behaviors associated with an idealized White norm that is also middle class, heterosexual, able-bodied, and Christian;
- *an intercultural communicator* who respects cultural differences and adopts students' cultural and linguistic patterns in the classroom; and
- *a radical* who engages in self-reflection and justice-centered critique of schooling.[40]

Before reading further, take a moment to ask yourself: *Do I agree with any of these metaphors? Why or why not? What other metaphors embody the role of a good teacher in contexts marked by racial differences?*

Though Hyland did her research with teachers who identified as White, these metaphors are common among White and non-White teachers (and teacher educators) alike. At first glance, the four good teacher metaphors seem harmless. Yet when set within the art classroom, they can play out in unexpected and potentially harmful ways.

What Is a Good Teacher?

The good teacher as helper metaphor is a common plot device in Hollywood. In the movies *Blackboard Jungle, Dangerous Minds,* and *Freedom Writers*, just to name a few, the White teacher helps save non-White students. These movies place non-White characters in roles subordinate or subservient to the White teacher protagonist who, in godlike fashion, helps the helpless non-White student overcome obstacles. The *Mad* TV skit "Nice White Lady" (Season 12, Episode 15), offers a satirical critique of the good teacher as helper. Looking at classrooms through the lens of the good teacher as a helper places primary importance on the behaviors and attitudes of individuals, while root causes of why students might not be thriving in schools are overlooked. As a basis for one's pedagogy, the helper metaphor can lead teachers to desire band-aid solutions to deeply entrenched problems caused by institutional racism.

For example, the **"good teacher as helper"** metaphor reinforces the idea that non-White students are lacking and their families are unable to support their education. Conversely, it positions the teacher as more capable and a savior. In the art classroom, a teacher might help students with materials they are unable to afford from the supply list. Art teachers may feel it is their role to help students find something they are passionate about or help them develop creativity or technical competence. Perhaps by learning art, they can craft and sell their own work to lift themselves out of poverty.[41]

This metaphor expresses a deficit ideology. But more than that, the helper image guides teachers toward assuming the position of someone who always knows more and better than the student. It is a patronizing relationship to students that dismisses the root causes of the problems many students face. That is, non-White students and their families are not simply less privileged; every day they navigate a society and educational system that are unequal and designed to benefit White people. The flip side of the helper metaphor is that correlations between arts attainment and social advantages—for example, food security, stable residence, time for cultural enrichment, proximity to wealth, and access to consistent, high-quality educational experiences—are frequently overlooked. As a consequence, the art teacher as helper attributes talent, giftedness, and creativity in students to individual traits without recognizing how artistic ability is also a byproduct of unequal opportunities and hoarding of resources that are less matters of merit than they are systemic inequalities.[43]

The **"good teacher as assimilator"** metaphor encourages teachers to view students from racially marginalized backgrounds as "other" or different from an imagined White norm. Often this difference is expressed through stereotypes that cast students' communities as dangerous, primitive, lazy, or uninterested in education—reflecting representations of non-White people in popular media (see Chapter 3).[44]

For instance, at a district-level professional development meeting, "assimilator" art teachers might organize a system-wide curriculum redesign to incorporate more lessons on perspective drawing and "the Great Masters" in elementary and middle school curricula so that students have a grasp of the "fundamentals" of graphic representation when they enter high school. The assimilation of students occurs not only through art curriculum but also in the course of managing classroom etiquette. For example, an elementary art teacher

facilitating an art criticism exercise reprimands a Black child for shouting out answers when other students are speaking, rather than raising her hand. This child is one of just three non-White students in an otherwise all-White school. The teacher feels the child is not used to being in a school environment, but over time and with redirection, she will learn from the other children how to behave "properly."

The assimilator image reinforces racial prejudices. It promotes the idea that White and non-White people are distinct and that White ways of being are preferred. It fosters a sense of distance between the teacher and non-White students, with teachers of any race feeling closer to whiteness than they do to their non-White students. Moreover, assimilationist teaching is subtractive when it devalues the social resources and cultural repertoires non-White students bring into the art classroom.[45] It leads to contempt for anything that does not approximate White cultural achievements and creates low expectations for non-White students. In the end, this metaphor can limit students' potential rather than expanding the scope of opportunities for success.

The **"good teacher as intercultural communicator"** embraces students' cultures in order to improve instruction and garner students' trust. The desire to embrace other cultures often results in teachers learning the speech patterns, behavioral norms, and aesthetic preferences of non-White students and then mimicking them as a teaching style. For example, an art teacher working in an inner city middle school might teach students the traditional elements of art and principles of design using a rap. The purpose of switching cultural codes is to make non-White students more amenable to the traditional art curriculum that reflects White artistic achievements and cultural references.

The "intercultural communicator" may seem to be a helpful metaphor, but only to a point. We agree that understanding and incorporating students' cultures into the classroom is important, especially when it enables teachers to interpret students' prior knowledge and behavior through an assets orientation, as discussed earlier in this chapter. However, the adoption of stylistic features of another group's cultural practices is superficial and likely to be experienced by non-White students as fake or, even worse, as a racial microaggression. It erases the experiences, worldviews, and contexts that gave rise to those practices and continue to enliven them in the present. It also ignores how whiteness dominates the art curriculum. For racially marginalized people, sustaining culture is often about reclaiming power, joy, and beauty under oppressive and hostile conditions. Cultural preservation and reinvention are acts of resistance to white supremacy and erasure.

The **"good teacher as a radical"** is a familiar metaphor in social justice art education. It offers art teachers a mental image tied to democratic ideals such as open dialogue to share diverse points of view and participation among equals. The "radical" approach helps art teachers go against the grain, for example, by questioning widely accepted practices, like student tracking, that target certain students for advancement into upper level art classes and specialized art schools while others fall into regular classes or out of art education altogether. These structures form an artist education pipeline. From advanced secondary art classrooms through post-secondary art graduates, White and affluent students are overrepresented, and non-White students are underrepresented. The racial inequities in art participation and opportunities continue as one moves through the K-20 pipeline.[46] The consequences can be seen in the racial disparities in who stays in the arts and who leaves to pursue other careers.[47] The "radical teacher" metaphor orients educators toward critiquing tracking and other in-school mechanisms that exploit and exacerbate existing social inequalities in the education of artists.

Radicals also reflect on their teaching practices to detect the subtle ways their implicit racial biases impact their decision making and the culture of the art classroom. But the "radical" art teacher can also be socially and culturally disconnected from students. This disconnection can manifest as feeling uncomfortable and reluctant to engage with students and their families beyond the narrow instructional role of classroom teaching. In contrast, anti-racist pedagogy demands art teachers see their own future bound up with and deeply invested in the well-being and struggles of non-White people beyond the classroom. It is more than viewing students and their families positively.[48] It involves a feeling of kinship and love that comes not from biology but from proximity, spending time in communities, learning from families, and valuing the knowledge and lifeways they impart to their young.[49]

Abolitionist Teaching

As we reimagine teaching from an anti-racist lens, we find ourselves drawn to the metaphor of the **"good teacher as abolitionist."** The image of an abolitionist reflects a sense of shared responsibility for racial justice in and through one's teaching as well as beyond the classroom. Curriculum theorist Bettina Love reminds us, "Abolitionist teaching is dependent on spaces…to create art for resistance, art for (re)membering, art for joy, art for love, art for healing, and art for humanity."[50] We understand anti-racist art teachers as abolitionists because we believe institutionalized racism must be dismantled, and educators have a role and responsibility to play in that. Abolitionist teaching is not about reform. How does one reform racism anyway? Is there any aspect of racism worth keeping? These are rhetorical questions aimed at highlighting the need to transform the system of education and teaching—this includes art education and art teaching. We know from abolitionists who sought the end of slavery that transformation requires both privileged and oppressed people within and outside of institutions to tear down structures—mental structures as well as policies and processes that structure behavior. We also know that it requires time, persistence, courage, creativity, and healing. Abolitionist teachers see their work in classrooms *not apart* *from but as part of* a larger historical movement to construct a racially just society.

Abolitionist art teachers model and teach students how to critically interpret and resist racism in the arts. These are acts of protective care that enable artists of color to thrive in an art world marred by racism and its intersections with other supremacisms. When asked by an interviewer from *Great Women Artists* how being a woman had affected her career, Egyptian-born artist Ghada Amer did not miss a beat. She responded by reframing the interviewer's question to address the racism

"That painting was my way of addressing the problem that we have in America with law enforcement targeting people of color. There's been so many crimes against people of color, especially black men who have been shot and killed by police. The central figure in that painting is a man of color. Next to him is a trans woman. The reason they connect—something they share besides being marginalized—is that police have a history of not protecting them. There are a lot of crimes against trans people with no follow-up. So the painting is about that. When you make a painting, you can make it about anything. For me, it's important that my work talks about things that I think are important to discuss, and it opens that dialogue."

—Guatemalan-born artist Gio Black Peter in an interview for ArtSpace[51]

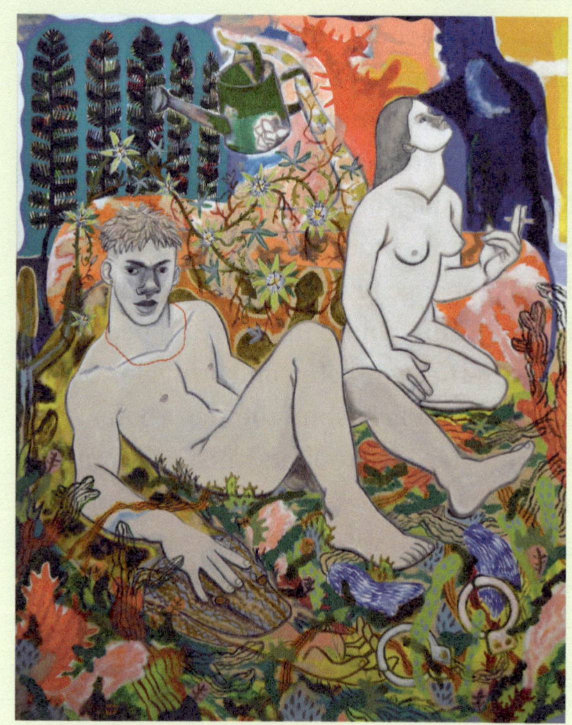

5.5 Gio Black Peter, *Bad Cops Make Good Snacks*, 2016. Oil on canvas, 60" x 48" (152.4 x 121.9 cm). © Gio Black Peter. Courtesy of the artist.

and related economic exploitation she had experienced as a woman, stating, "It makes me sell for much less money than if I were a male (and White) and it closes all doors for solo museum shows."[52] Abolitionist art teachers help young artists who identify as Black, Indigenous, and non-White to navigate and sustain themselves, like Ghada Amer, in the face of oppressions that await them.

Abolitionist teaching benefits White-identified students as well. They learn to be allies with marginalized people in the work of creating a

more egalitarian environment for artists of all backgrounds.[53] **Allyship** is when a person who is not the target of racism willingly stands with those who are and proactively takes on the problems borne of racial injustice as their own. It is more than caring about a cause. Genuine allies are accomplices who co-conspire to end racism and repair the damage it has caused.

So how does one begin to enact the image of the **"good art teacher as abolitionist"**? How do we model allyship in our pedagogies so that our journey toward anti-racist art education embodies racially just relationships with others? The following are some tips for getting started. They are a list of "do's and don'ts" that we modified from #WhatIsAnAlly (guidetoallyship.com). We advocate posting them in the classroom as a reminder and point of reflection for art teachers and students alike.

What to do

- **Do** be open to listening and learning inside and outside the classroom.
- **Do** accept criticism with grace, even if it's uncomfortable.
- **Do** be aware of your implicit biases.
- **Do** the inner work to figure out a way to acknowledge how you participate in racism.

Ally Guide

The Guide to Allyship is open source. This means you or anyone else may contribute to it. In the collective spirit of abolitionist movements, ask yourself, *What do I have to contribute to allyship? What do artists and art teachers know that could be useful in tearing down systems that maintain racial inequality and replacing them with new ways of teaching and learning that support an egalitarian society, thriving communities, and struggle for universal freedom?* Based on your answers, add one "do" or "don't" to the Guide to Allyship at guidetoallyship.com.

- **Do** the outer work to figure out how to change racist institutions and structures.
- **Do** use your privilege to amplify historically suppressed voices.
- **Do** your research to learn more about the history of anti-racism struggles.
- **Do** the work *every* day to learn how to be a better ally.

What not to do
- **Do not** expect to be taught or shown. Take it upon yourself to use the tools around you to learn and answer your questions.
- **Do not** compete for the gold medal in the "Oppression Olympics." (You do not need to compare how your struggle is "just as bad as" a marginalized person's.)
- **Do not** assume and act as though you know best. (This is likely an implicit bias.)
- **Do not** take credit for the labor of those who are marginalized and did the work before you stepped into the picture.
- **Do not** assume that every member of an underinvested community feels oppressed.

This chapter focused on the importance of teachers reflecting on their biographies. So much of what a person knows and how they think about race is learned implicitly while growing up in families, communities, schools, and media cultures. Together these various contexts comprise the racial ecology in which a person is socialized to have a particular mindset about real and imagined differences. In the U.S. and other settler colonial nations, white supremacy has been and continues to be a defining feature of the racial ecology. It shows up in social institutions, the economy, visual cultures, and the landscape itself. No living thing can develop apart from its ecology. This is true for teachers as well who, like all living things, carry within them and express through their behaviors traces of their environment.

For many art teachers, developing an anti-racist pedagogy will require a shift in mindset in order to adopt an assets orientation toward non-White students, families, and communities. This begins with a careful and honest examination of one's personal and professional biography, shaped as it is by racial ecologies. It also entails reimagining what it means to be a good teacher and recognizing the limitations of the dominant cultural models and metaphors of the good teacher learned from a combination of influences. Historical examples of abolitionists provide a replacement teacher metaphor to guide practitioners of anti-racism. In the next chapter, we suggest strategies for anti-racist art pedagogy, along with methods for activating visual racial literacy with students.

Notes

1 Brad Olsen, *Teaching What They Learn, Learning What They Live: How Teachers' Personal Histories Shape Their Professional Development* (Boulder, CO: Paradigm, 2008).

2 James D. Trier, "The Cinematic Representation of the Personal and Professional Lives of Teachers," *Teacher Education Quarterly* 28 (2001): 127–142.

3 Joyce E. King, "Dysconscious Racism: Ideology, Identity, and the Miseducation of Teachers," *The Journal of Negro Education* 60, no. 2 (1991): 133–146

4 Brad Plumer and Nadja Popovich, "How Decades of Racist Housing Policy Left Neighborhoods Sweltering," *The New York Times*, August 24, 2020, interactive visual article, https://www.nytimes.com/interactive/2020/08/24/climate/racism-redlining-cities-global-warming.html?smid=url-share.

5 Lorna Roth, "Looking at Shirley, the Ultimate Norm: Colour Balance, Image Technologies, and Cognitive Equity," *Canadian Journal of Communication* 34 (2009): 111–136.

6 Ruha Benjamin, *Race After Technology: Abolitionist Tools for the New Jim Code* (Cambridge, UK: Polity Press, 2019).

7 Linda Martín Alcoff, "Epistemologies of Ignorance: Three Types," in Shannon Sullivan and Nancy Tuana (eds.) *Race and Epistemologies of Ignorance* (New York: State University of New York Press, 2007): 39–57.

8 Courtnie N. Wolfgang, "The White Supremacy of Art Education in the United States: My Complicity and Path Toward Reparation Pedagogy," *Journal of Cultural Research in Art Education* 36, no. 1 (2019): 14–28.

9 Linda Martín Alcoff, "Why Trump Is Still Here," *The Philosophical Salon*, February 8, 2016, http://thephilosophicalsalon.com/why-trump-is-still-here/.

10 Eduardo Bonilla-Silva, *Racism Without Racists: Color-Blind Racism & Racial Inequality in Contemporary America* (Roman & Littlefield, 2010).

11 Paulo Freire, *Pedagogy of the Oppressed* (New York: Continuum Publishing, 1970).

12 William A. Smith, Tara J. Yosso, and Daniel Solórzano, "Challenging Racial Battle Fatigue on Historically White Campuses: A Critical Race Examination of Race-Related Stress," in Christine A. Stanley's (ed.), *Faculty of Color Teaching in Predominantly White Colleges and Universities* (Bolton, MA: Jossey-Bass, 2006): 299–327.

13 Monique Cherry-McDaniel, "Skinfolk Ain't Always Kinfolk: The Dangers of Assuming and Assigning Inherent Cultural Responsiveness to Teachers of Color," *Educational Studies* 55, no. 2 (2019): 241–251.

14 Cheryl E. Matias, *Feeling White: Whiteness, Emotionality, and Education* (Rotterdam, Netherlands: Sense Publishers, 2016).

15 Robin DiAngelo, *White Fragility: Why It's So Hard for White People to Talk About Racism* (Boston, MA: Beacon Press, 2018).

16 Sunny Spillane, "The Failure of Whiteness in Art Education: A Personal Narrative Informed by Critical Race Theory," *Journal of Social Theory in Art Education* 35, (2015): 57–68.

17 Katherine Brooks, "Stunning 'Soundsuits' Address the Realities of Racial Profiling in America," *HuffPost: Arts and Culture*, October 7, 2016, https://www.huffpost.com/entry/nick-cave-soundsuits_n_57f79dcae4b0e655eab37e67?fbclid=IwAR1wtDzmwfyD-QFaY6Qz0gl6-kLeYGoqLbkWUtN5ovfpb4Ed0hX1Dns5tQk.

18 Richard R. Valencia, *Dismantling Contemporary Deficit Thinking: Educational Thought and Practice* (New York, NY: Routledge, 2010).

19 Paul C. Gorski, "Unlearning Deficit Ideology and the Scornful Gaze: Thoughts on Authenticating the Class Discourse in Education," in Roberta Ahlquist, Paul Gorski, and Theresa Montaño's (eds.) *Assault on Kids: How Hyper-Accountability, Corporatization, Deficit Ideologies, and Ruby Payne are Destroying Our Schools* (New York: Lang, 2011): 152–176.

20 Advancement Project, "Test, Punish, and Push Out: How 'Zero Tolerance' and High-Stakes Testing Funnel Youth into the School-to-Prison Pipeline," March 2010, https://b.3cdn.net/advancement/d05cb2181a4545db07_r2im6caqe.pdf.

21 Walter S. Gilliam, Angela N. Maupin, Chin R. Reyes, Maria Accavitti, and Frederick Shic, "Do Early Educators' Implicit Biases Regarding Sex and Race Relate to Behavior Expectations and Recommendations of Preschool Expulsions and Suspensions?" Research study brief (New Haven, CT: Yale University Child Study Center, 2016).

22 U.S. Department of Education Office for Civil Rights, Civil Rights Data Collection, Data Snapshot: School Discipline, Washington, DC, 2014, http://ocrdata.ed.gov/Downloads/CRDC-School-Discipline-Snapshot.pdf.

23 Bach Mai Dolly Nguyen, Pedro Noguera, Nathan Adkins, and Robert T. Teranishi, "Ethnic Discipline Gap: Unseen Dimensions of Racial Disproportionality in School Discipline," *American Educational Research Journal* 56, no. 5 (2019): 1973–2003.

24 Ebony Bowden, "Florida 6-Year-Old Arrested, Handcuffed for Elementary School Tantrum," *New York Post*, September 22, 2019, https://nypost.com/2019/09/22/florida-6-year-old-arrested-handcuffed-for-elementary-school-tantrum/.

25 Richard Fausset and Ashley Southall, "Video Shows Officer Flipping Student in South Carolina, Prompting Inquiry," *The New York Times*, October 26, 2015, https://www.nytimes.com/2015/10/27/us/officers-classroom-fight-with-student-is-caught-on-video.html?_r=0.

26 Norma González, Luis C. Moll, and Cathy Amanti (eds.), *Funds of Knowledge: Theorizing Practices in Households, Communities, and Classrooms* (Mahwah, NJ: Lawrence Erlbaum Associates, 2005); Tara J. Yosso, "Whose Culture Has Capital? A Critical Race Theory Discussion of Community Cultural Wealth," *Race Ethnicity and Education* 8, no. 1 (2005): 69–91.

27 Derald Wing Sue, *Microaggressions in Everyday Life: Race, Gender, and Sexual Orientation* (Hoboken, NJ: Wiley, 2010).

28 Rita Kohli and Daniel Solórzano, "Teachers, Please Learn Our Names! Racial Microaggressions and the K-12 Classroom," *Race, Ethnicity and Education* 15, no. 4 (2012) 441–462.

29 Derald Wing Sue et al., "Racial Microaggressions in Everyday Life: Implications for Clinical Practice," *American Psychologist* 62, no. 4 (2007): 271–286.

30 Amelia M. Kraehe, "Sounds of Silence: Race and Emergent Counter-Narratives of Art Teacher Identity," *Studies in Art Education* 56, no. 3 (2015): 199–213.

31 Dani McClain, "The Freedom and Fulfillment of Home-Schooling," *The New York Times*, August 22, 2020, para. 2, https://www.nytimes.com/2020/08/18/parenting/homeschool-families.html?searchResultPosition=1.

32 Brigitte Vittrup, "Color Blind or Color Conscious? White American Mothers' Approaches to Racial Socialization," *Journal of Family Issues* 39, no. 3 (2018): 668–692.

33 Loney Abrams, "'We're All Brothers and Sisters': Artist Gio Black Peter on Uncensoring Queer Lifestyles," *ArtSpace*, May 10, 2019, para. 14, https://www.artspace.com/magazine/interviews_features/qa/were-all-brothers-and-sisters-artist-gio-black-peter-on-uncensoring-queer-lifestyles-56064.

34 Anna Deavere Smith, *Letters to a Young Artist: Straight-up Advice on Making a Life in the Arts—For Actors, Performers, Writers, and Artists of Every Kind* (New York, NY: Anchor Books, 2006): 157–158.

35 Stephanie M. H. Camp, *Closer to Freedom: Enslaved Women and Everyday Resistance in the Plantation South* (Chapel Hill: The University of North Carolina Press, 2004).

36 Roby Chatterji, "Fighting Systemic Racism in K-12 Education: Helping Allies Move From the Keyboard to the School Board," Center for American Progress, July 8, 2020, https://www.americanprogress.org/issues/education-k-12/news/2020/07/08/487386/fighting-systemic-racism-k-12-education-helping-allies-move-keyboard-school-board/.

37 George Lakoff and Mark Johnson, *Metaphors We Live By* (Chicago, IL: University of Chicago Press, 2003).

38 Beth Thomas, "Traditional Futures: Prospective Art Teachers' Possible Future Selves," *Art Education* 73, no. 5 (2020): 32–37.

39 Laura J. Hetrick, "Exploring Art Student Teachers' Fictions of Teaching: Strategies for Teacher Educators," *Journal of Social Theory in Art Education* 37 (2017): 38–48.

40 Nora E. Hyland, "Being a Good Teacher of Black Students? White Teachers and Unintentional Racism," *Curriculum Inquiry* 35, no. 4 (2005): 429–459.

41 Beth A. Thomas, "Traditional Futures: Prospective Art Teachers' Possible Future Selves," *Art Education* 73, no. 5 (2020): 32–37.

42 Arthur D. Efland, *A History of Art Education: Intellectual and Social Currents in Teaching the Visual Arts* (New York, NY: Teachers College Press, 1990): 255.

43 Rubén A. Gaztambide-Fernández, Adam Saifer, and Chandni Desai, "'Talent' and the Misrecognition of Social Advantage in Specialized Arts Education," *The Roeper Review* 35, no. 2 (2013): 124–135.

44 Joni B. Acuff and Amelia M. Kraehe, "Visuality of Race in Popular Culture: Teaching Racial Histories and Iconography in Media," *Dialogue: The International Journal of Popular Culture and Pedagogy* 7, no. 3 (2020).

45 Angela Valenzuela, *Subtractive Schooling: U.S.-Mexican Youth and the Politics of Caring* (Albany: State University of New York Press, 1999).

46 Amelia M. Kraehe, "Arts Equity: A Praxis-Oriented Tale," *Studies in Art Education* 58, no. 4 (2017): 267–278.

47 Alexandre Frenette and Timothy J. Dowd, "Careers in the Arts: Who Stays and Who Leaves?" Special report, Strategic National Arts Alumni Project, 2020, http://snaap.indiana.edu/pdf/SNAAP_Special%20Report_Spring2020.pdf.

48 Nora E. Hyland, "Being a Good Teacher of Black Students? White Teachers and Unintentional Racism," *Curriculum Inquiry* 35, no. 4 (2005): 429–459.

49 Anthony L. Brown, Mary E. Dilworth, and Keffrelyn D. Brown, "Understanding the Black Teacher through Metaphor," *The Urban Review* 50 (2018): 284–299.

50 Bettina Love, *We Want to Do More Than Survive: Abolitionist Teaching and the Pursuit of Educational Freedom* (Boston, MA: Beacon Press, 2019): 99.

51 Loney Abrams, "'We're All Brothers and Sisters': Artist Gio Black Peter on Uncensoring Queer Lifestyles," *ArtSpace*, May 10, 2019, para. 10, https://www.artspace.com/magazine/interviews_features/qa/were-all-brothers-and-sisters-artist-gio-black-peter-on-uncensoring-queer-lifestyles-56064.

52 Mat Smith, "A Q&A with Ghada Amer: 'Being a Woman Artist Closes All Doors for Solo Museum Shows,'" *ArtSpace*, October 25, 2019, para. 5, https://www.artspace.com/magazine/interviews_features/qa/a-qa-with-ghada-amer-being-a-woman-artist-closes-all-doors-for-solo-museum-shows-56300.

53 Courtnie N. Wolfgang, "The White Supremacy of Art Education in the United States: My Complicity and Path Toward Reparation Pedagogy," *Journal of Cultural Research in Art Education* 36, no. 1 (2019): 14–28.

Chapter 6

Anti-Racist Art Pedagogy

Activating Visual Racial Literacy with Students

"Art is important only to the extent that it helps in the liberation of our people."

—Elizabeth Catlett

I n this final chapter, we focus on anti-racist art pedagogy. Organized around four unifying principles, our model of anti-racist art pedagogy is grounded in decades of research, our own teaching experiences, and the spirit of abolition (see Chapter 5). We also share a sampling of learning activities that may be used and adapted to help students develop a critical understanding of race and creative skillsets to confront racism. Finally, we offer some tips to encourage and support art teachers as they bring anti-racism into their own practice.

In this chapter, we focus on these key concepts:
- Political clarity
- Protective care
- Deep connection
- Courageous witnessing

Guiding Principles for Anti-Racist Art Pedagogy

Four principles guide our anti-racist art pedagogy: political clarity, protective care, deep connection, and courageous witnessing. Each one reinforces the others and is an inextricable part of a holistic teaching practice. We draw from them when considering what artists and artworks to feature in the curriculum, what big ideas and enduring questions to use, how to engage students in interpreting works of art, and how to recognize and assess student learning. A coherent set of guiding principles orients an art teacher's advanced planning and on-the-spot decision-making. There is so much that could be covered within an art curriculum, for instance, that a guide is helpful in making choices about what to include, how to sequence lessons, and how simple or complex to make art activities and projects.

Perhaps more important than their curricular function is how the principles for anti-racist art pedagogy serve as a guide for developing positive and respectful relationships with students, families, and even colleagues. Without it, the application of anti-racist methods is likely to be piecemeal in its organization, unclear in its purpose, and potentially counterproductive or harmful in its effects on students. Indeed, highly skilled art teachers do not think about teaching in a haphazard way. They make decisions with an awareness of their beliefs about the purpose of art education, values regarding subject matter, and perceptions of actual learners and what learning looks like.[1] We urge readers to spend some time listing the beliefs that guide their teaching. After reading this chapter, it may be fruitful to revisit that list and consider if and how it aligns with the principles for anti-racist art pedagogy. That reflective process, which should be ongoing throughout a teacher's career, goes hand-in-hand with practice and leads to refinement of teaching methods and their efficacy over time.

What follows are the four guiding principles for anti-racist art pedagogy, explained.

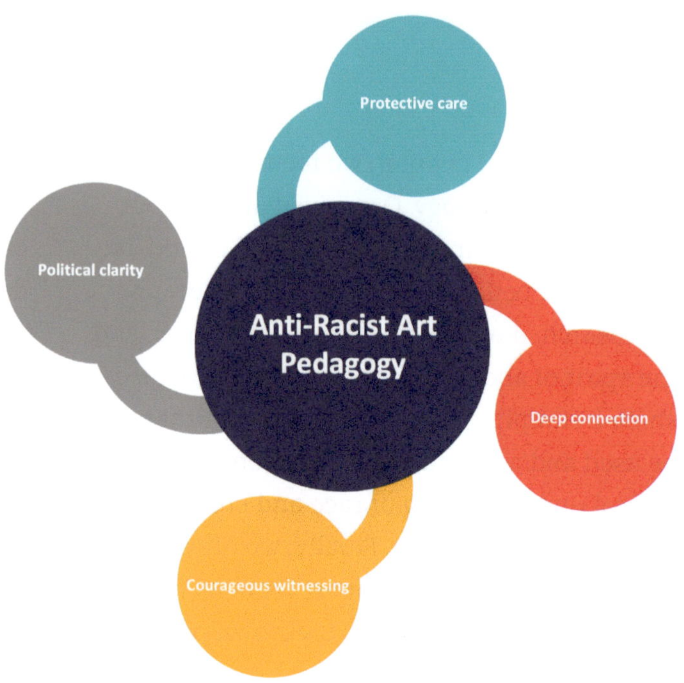

1. Political Clarity

Anti-racist art pedagogy is grounded in political clarity.[2] Political is a scary word for some teachers who associate it with government, elections, and ideological parties. However, here, political simply refers to power relations. We are all political actors whenever we make decisions within a group, use our influence to shape outcomes, and create systems that allocate resources in ways that express our values. To be apolitical is itself a political choice to be indifferent to uneven power relations in the classroom and society. If we consider who among us can afford such indifference, it becomes clear that an apolitical stance reflects a position of privilege, as many of our students and colleagues cannot afford to be unconcerned or apathetic about matters that affect their quality of life and life chances. Political clarity, on the other hand, is when teachers are aware of the political aspects of education and the ways schools reproduce social inequality.

Teachers who practice anti-racist art pedagogy understand their teaching in the context of a K–20 art education system that is uneven and inequitable on the basis of race, class, and gender. Political clarity enables art teachers to see themselves and their teaching as part of a larger historical struggle for racial and social justice in the arts and through arts education.[3] They reflect on the ways whiteness and racial hierarchies conditioned their own education and influence their current teaching practice. Whether teaching directly about racism or making other pedagogical decisions, they support students in becoming actively and critically engaged in their own learning and knowledge construction rather than passive repositories of knowledge already made.[4]

2. Protective Care

Racism is systemic and pervasive. Students are almost certain to be the targets, observers, or perpetrators of racial discrimination and violence in and out of the art classroom. So, although art teachers cannot end all of racism, they can intervene by bringing their political clarity to bear in protecting students. The principle of protective care is integral to anti-racist art pedagogy. It is not about creating a colorblind bubble in which discussions of race are avoided. That is neither caring or protective in a world structured by systemic racial inequality. Nor is protective care about saving students. On the contrary, practicing protective care is to safeguard students' potential because all young people need someone to look out for them and "have their backs."[5] Anti-racist art pedagogy prepares students to protect themselves as well by supporting students' capacity to resist racism and help-

ing them to achieve at a high level even while navigating an inequitable educational system.[6]

3. Deep Connection

Cultural and social connection to students, their families, and their communities is fundamental to practicing protective care. Although racial identity does not determine connectedness, often connections form organically because of common experiences, kinship, or shared history. We distinguish these kinds of connections from individual teacher-student connections where, for instance, a teacher might survey students at the start of the school year to glean their likes and dislikes, their hobbies, and basic facts. Surveys like these are not an adequate basis for connected teaching because they give a view of the student with little or no context. This is akin to viewing a work of art out of context. There is a strong likelihood we will misinterpret what we see or miss what is most significant in their lives.

Anti-racist art pedagogy considers students not simply as individuals but also as beings with social histories and cultural lifeways that shape their sense of self, feelings of belonging, and linguistic and behavioral expression.[7] Art teachers whose practice is anti-racist understand how colorblind ideology and racial inequality shape the contemporary world that they and their students inhabit. Moreover, they appreciate that these social and cultural contexts influence students differently and much of that difference can be attributed to the ways in which people and places are racialized. They are attentive to this larger context and, therefore, have a greater capacity to recognize the full, complex humanity of their students. For teaching in economically isolated and racially marginalized communities, this is essential since art teachers who strive for connection are better able to value, build upon, and sustain the social networks, lived experiences, and worldviews of their students.[8] With deep connection, art teachers can "explore, honor, extend, and, at times, problematize [students'] cultural practices and investments."[9]

4. Courageous Witnessing

Anti-racist art pedagogy is a practice of courageous witnessing. To witness is to remember rather than hide from history and inherited racial traumas of displacement, enslavement, genocide, police brutality, and other contemporary horrors.[10] At the same time, we bear witness when we emphasize the desires and strivings of those individuals and communities who experience racism.[11] Indeed, creative cultural practices are testimonies to the various

Creating Connections

Marit Dewhurst, White American art education scholar and author of *Teachers Bridging Difference: Exploring Identity with Art*, suggests meaningful ways art teachers can create deeper connections with students, families, and communities with whom they have little prior experience.

- Go to public events and talk with community insiders.

- Create a community map and keep adding to it over time.

- Read works of fiction written by a cultural insider of the heritage group.

- Identify artists and public artworks within the community.

- Visit spaces that are considered significant by members of the community.

- Create a historical time line of the community.[12]

When undertaking these activities, it can be easy to stereotype. Therefore, it is imperative that art teachers continually reflect on their own biased assumptions, any emotional responses they have to new situations, and the ways status, power, and privilege shape their encounters.

ways marginalized people create joy, goodness, and healing even in the midst of pain and struggle. Witnessing through art can inspire feeling, which can incite learning. It does not end there, however. Courageous witnessing is a professional obligation and a course of action that extends beyond the four walls of the classroom. It calls for art teachers to acknowledge the truth of students' experiences with racism in and out of schools, and it means being present, side-by-side with non-White students and communities, in larger social movements for racial and educational justice.[13]

All Together Now

These four Cs—clarity, care, connectedness, and the courage to witness—come together when implementing anti-racist art pedagogy. The first step in developing a practice guided by these principles is self-education. Reading this book, for example, and other resources noted throughout is key to becoming knowledgeable about racism, how it affects your life, and what teaching art as a form of racial justice entails.

Education is more than acquiring new knowledge and self-awareness, though. It is enacted in daily practices and habits. One way to make anti-racism a habit is to consider the instructional resources in the art classroom. What do students see and have access to? Is it a color-blind environment that shows little in the way of racial awareness or does it invite students into dialogue about race, representation, discrimination, and fairness? Fill the walls and shelves with reproductions and books with artworks by non-White artists. Include photographs of the artists, as well as short biographies and a map for context.

In addition to the physical surroundings, consider the social environment. Is there space in classroom interactions for students to share their lived realities and ask hard questions? Can they feel confident that their experiences and curiosities will be honored? How might the curriculum become that space? Art teachers can document how the arts are activated in social movements past and present and turn that into curriculum. There are examples in this chapter of how to do this.

A critical next step toward an anti-racist art pedagogy is to understand that teaching is not a solitary undertaking. Many art teachers experience isolation as the only art teacher at their school. If they are part of an art department, it might be that their colleagues do not yet see the importance of grappling with race and racism. This, too, can feel isolating for someone who values racial equity. Racial awakening is a journey with unexpected ups and downs. Sustaining oneself through the journey requires a collective approach to professional development, self-care, and advocacy.

A collective approach can take many forms. The website Anti-Racist Art Teachers was created by a small network of full-time art educators from across the U.S. It contains professional resources, artist interviews, and sample lesson plans the members have assembled. Together they are "working towards removing biases, stereotypes, and false narratives in art education" (antiracistartteachers.org). Finding or creating a group like this enables busy art teachers to pool their resources and find affirmation and support.

Creative advocacy and activism are two more ways anti-racist art pedagogy is expressed and nourished through collective action. In the midst of the COVID-19 pandemic, Joseph, one of Amy's former students and an early career elementary art teacher, wrote to her about the racial inequities he was seeing for the first time. Take a moment to read an excerpt of his letter in Voices from the Field on page 157. There are elements of each of the four Cs. With newborn political clarity, Joseph recog-

nized that his students' potential was being systematically eroded by inequities. He drew upon the networks and know-how within the community to care for and protect non-White students from the disproportionately negative effects of the pandemic. With the help of the community, he was able to crowd-source the funds needed to create art instructional kits that would supply materials and lessons to students whose access to art education had been cut off. When advocacy and activism are infused with a spirit of abolition, they are courageous acts of witnessing.

In short, anti-racist art pedagogy reimagines art teachers as agents of change both in and out of the classroom. As Joseph's story illustrates, it is not enough to see there is a systemic problem. We also must act. This means giving voice to immediate harms caused by racial inequity, but also getting involved with local and national organizations that are engaged in long-term projects and movements aimed at dismantling and replacing systems that produce racial disparities. Racial justice organizations are rich yet frequently overlooked resources. Perhaps this is the next step for Joseph. Art teachers stand to gain a lot by getting involved. When we participate—whether artistically, intellectually,

"I wasn't receiving anything from my diverse students, especially those whose families were immediately impacted by the shutdown. From what I gathered, the biggest barrier was the access to supplies. I remember getting a sweet message from one elementary student in my email: 'I have no paper. Please send paper to my house through mail.' There was something resonating in that. I want to bridge the access.

I created a GoFundMe totally rogue from the school district …. I'm so grateful the community saw what was happening. The chaos was shedding light on barriers that have always been there in the community.

We were totally funded and actually received more than what I asked for in less than 24 hours! …. My plan is to create quality art kits for kids in the city. I want to give them out through shelters (one of which serves many LGBT children escaping family shaming) and also by giving them out in libraries and apartment complexes. I learned that in order to give these communities access, I can't just ask them to meet me online, I have to meet them in person."

—Joseph, a White American art teacher in his third year of teaching

emotionally, or physically—in organizations that are working collectively to create a more equitable future, joy and rejuvenation is often an unexpected outcome.[14] Moreover, getting involved is an excellent way to increase racial awareness, build interracial relationships, and acquire practical strategies that can be used to create a culture of anti-racism in our classrooms and schools, all while helping to advance justice in the community.

Learning Activities for Visual Racial Literacy

It is vital to develop our own racial awareness so we can act on it, but it is equally important that we develop teaching methods that help activate students' visual racial literacy. The following section presents learning activities to inspire lessons and curriculum units. They are appropriate for K-12 students, however, we leave it to art teachers to determine what appropriateness means in their own context, keeping in mind that age is often used as the justification for avoiding discussions of race and racism, particularly in groups that benefit from racial privilege and rarely, if ever, are the targets of racial violence and hate speech. Judgments about developmentally appropriate content for students should be determined by their experiential readiness, which is based on the sociocultural context and prior knowledge as much as it is on numeric age.

Goals

- Understand the difference between skin color and racial categories.

- Recognize white supremacist ideology in everyday visual and material culture.

- Decenter whiteness as a neutral, invisible norm in art and society.

- Think critically about meanings encoded within language and materials of artmaking.

Materials

- Images of "flesh-colored" items such as bandages, hosiery and ballet tights, creams and cosmetics.

- Images of Crayola's "flesh" crayon.

- "Crayola Monologues," a film by artist Nathan Gibbs available on YouTube.[15]

What Color Is Flesh?

Background Information

What color is flesh? The crayon color the Crayola company named "flesh" in 1949 was changed to "peach" in 1962 after the company received letters of protest. The letter writers objected to a color resembling Caucasian skin tones being given the title "flesh," as though that color represented the range of human skin colors.

On its website, Crayola states: "Although flesh was included in the original box of 64 Crayola Crayons, we felt it would be insensitive to include it in the [1958] commemorative box. Since the crayon color remains unchanged, we felt we were remaining true to history."[16] It was not until 30 years later that the company issued a "multicultural" series of colors reflective of the wide spectrum of human skin color.

Guided Practice

1 Display assorted "flesh-colored" items similar to those shown here. Many can be found on the internet. Ask students:
   - What do all these materials have in common?
   - What are they used for?
   - How are they meant to work?

2 Scaffold the discussion to focus on the function and application of the objects.
   - What makes skin the color that it is? (Here you might introduce words like *pigment* and *melanin*.)

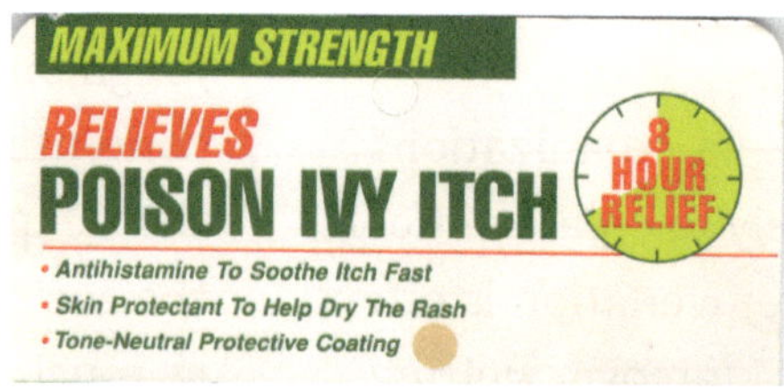

6.1 "Tone-Neutral Itch Cream" by nathangibbs. CC BY-NC-SA 2.0.

- What is "Tone-Neutral Itch Cream"? What is a neutral tone designed to do?
- What does that imply about skin that is not "neutral"?
- The Band-Aid plastic strips are described as "flesh colored." What color is flesh? What is a flesh coloring designed to do?

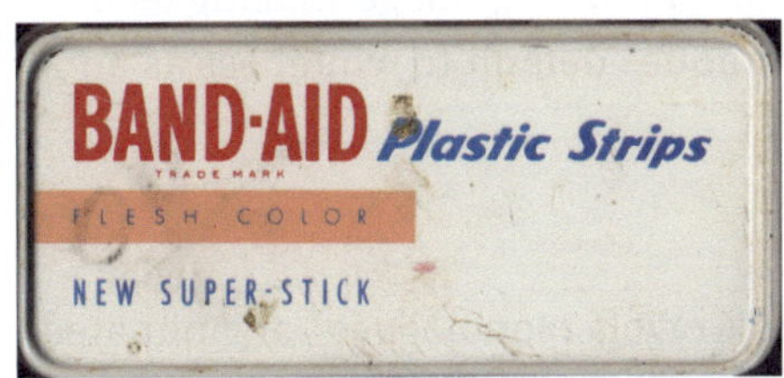

6.2 "Flesh Band-Aids" by nathan-gibbs. CC BY-NC-SA 2.0.

3 Show image 6.3 or one similar to it (many can be found on the internet). You might start by showing only the "flesh" crayons. (In the image below, we would cover the bottom two crayons renamed "peach.")

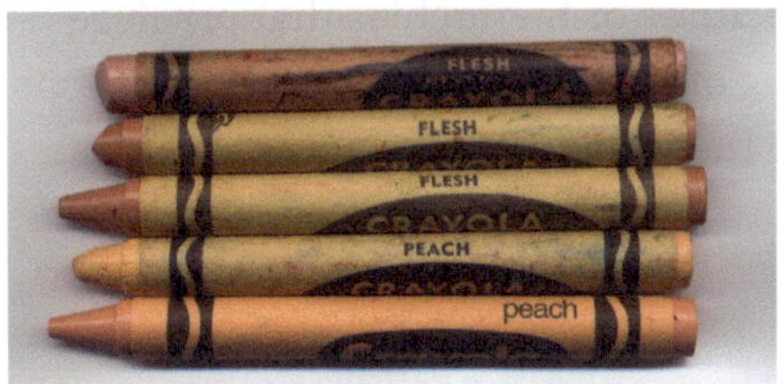

6.3 "Flesh Crayons" by nathan-gibbs. CC BY-NC-SA 2.0.

4 Lead a discussion:
- What do you notice?
- How does changing the name of a crayon matter in children's perceptions of themselves and the world they live in? How might this be different for lighter-skinned children and darker-skinned children?
- In what ways does renaming a crayon address racism and in what ways does it not?

Pedagogical Principles

Political clarity

Protective care

Chapter Connections

Social construction (2)

Racism (2)

White racial privilege (2)

The Conscious Kid booklist: Children's literature to support conversations about race, racism, anti-racism, and healthy racial identity development in children and youth[17]

Commercial advertisements promoting flesh-colored products, such as Band-Aid brand's 1955 television ad for "Neat, flesh-colored[18]

Art supply makers Faber-Castell, Tombow, and Winsor & Newton grapple with how to undo the emphasis on whiteness in their products and practice. Read *ArtNews* reporting in "Art Supply Companies Contend with Racism as 'Flesh Tones' Come Under Scrutiny."[19]

- Why do you think it took Crayola so long to offer a "multicultural" crayon set?
- What is meant by multicultural? Is culture intended to replace race?
- In what ways does the multicultural label challenge or reinforce racism?
- What other ordinary cultural products, image-making technologies, and artistic techniques default to whiteness as an invisible, universal norm?

Extensions

For artistic inspiration, watch "Crayola Monologues," an animated video by artist Nathan Gibbs that shows crayons articulating how their lives have been influenced by hierarchies. It is a metaphor for racism.

After discussing the film, create an artwork or series of artworks that comment on overt or implicit cultural associations between color and racial categories. Advance to more critical thinking by creating artwork or a series that explores the relationship between color and racial structures or hierarchies that privilege some groups while oppressing others. Incorporate Crayola crayons or objects of material culture that treat White people's skin as a universal norm or standard.

Color Codes

Background Information

Color theory is widely considered at all levels of artistic production, from creation to editing to marketing and display. The color scale is commonly used to train artists' visual perception. Like all scales, it is an organizing device or schema that overlays a theory or system for explaining a phenomenon. Color theory is an overlay for visual perception. Its premise is that colors can be understood as though they exist on a graded, linear scale—gradations of value from white on one end of the spectrum to black on the other. The bipolar logic of a color scale is that white is the lightest of light and black is the darkest of dark. White and black are made to appear naturally distant and opposite each other. As increasingly subtle differences in value are perceived, these differences are codified in relation to each other through culturally encoded symbolism. This activity takes something as seemingly obvious as color and helps students understand that visual perception, even of something as obvious as color, is conditioned by cultural logic inherited from previous generations. In the modern world, racial hierarchy and prejudice are encoded through valuations linked to (skin) color.

Guided Practice

1 On a piece of paper, students write two side-by-side lists. On one side, they list everything they can think of associated with the idea of *light*. On the other side, they do the same for *dark*. Typical associations:
   - *light:* purity, beauty, radiance, goodness, safety, knowledge, celebration, life
   - *dark:* absence, nothingness, unknown, immorality, danger, ignorance, misery, death

Goals

- See the social construction of race.
- Link past images to present thinking.
- Recognize how racism and racial logic is encoded in Western color theory.
- Understand social and cultural conditioning of visual perception.
- Make implicit knowledge and bias explicit for the purposes of critical reflection.

Materials

- Pencil and paper.
- Reproductions of a castas painting. Chapter 3 has an example and many reproductions can be found with a simple internet search.

These associations are pervasive in Western European languages and literature. They are commonly used in everyday speech, popular culture, and art.

2 Ask:

- What do you notice about the items in the first list? What do they have in common?
- What do you notice about the items in the second list? What do they have in common?
- What is the relationship between the items in the two lists?
- Where did the associations come from? Where have you seen or heard them?

3 As a group, view a castas painting. Use visual thinking strategies to guide your looking, noticing, and discovering[20]:

- What is going on in the picture?
- What do you see that made you say that?
- What more can we find?

This questioning strategy builds skills in careful observation, talking about visual perceptions, interpretation of images and the ideas they convey using evidence, listening to and considering the perspectives of others, and discussion of various interpretations. The instructor adopts the role of facilitator. Allow everyone to respond to the three questions so that new responses may be added beyond what has already been offered and agreements and disagreements may be worked out. This discussion may last 15 minutes depending on the size of the group.

Through this looking activity, students are often able to identify for themselves that, in addition to dividing humans into types, castas paintings were organized as a progression from lighter- to darker-skinned figures. Figures were commonly arranged in a grid with compartments numbered one to sixteen. What they see are human beings placed on a value scale where skin color determines human social value. They quickly grasp that lighter skin is meant to represent higher social status, power, and privilege through its placement on the visual plane. The color scale imposes this logic and valuation schema on differently hued bodies, none of which are actually white or black.

4 In order to prompt students to think and wonder aloud about the context of castas paintings, ask:
   - Why do you think someone might have created a painting like this, depicting people in boxes organized from lighter to darker skin?
   - How do you think people at the time might have responded to the ideas expressed in the painting?
   - What would you like to ask the person who created the painting?

5 After the looking activity, provide social and historical context for the castas paintings (see Chapter 3). The *systema de castas*, or caste system, was both a cultural and legal invention aimed at bringing order to the interracial unions between Indigenous, African, and Spanish peoples in the Americas during the colonial period. There is no evidence that the castas reflect the reality that existed in the 18th and 19th centuries. Instead, they were images that projected the desires of the powerful colonial elites at the time. Castas paintings invite the viewer to adopt a colonial gaze, a particular worldview in which whiteness is the purest form of humanity and blackness is its opposite. Human skin color was assigned social value in the caste system. This meant skin color determined ideas about beauty and desirability, as well as rights and restrictions of daily life. For example, only Peninsulars were permitted to hold public office, and they held the vast majority of the wealth. The lower castes were expected to contribute more taxes to the state and tributes to the Catholic Church. To be lighter was to be better off, and to be darker was to be worse off.

Suggested Encounters

"Color Lines: A Chicago Art Class Challenges the Racist Assumptions Behind the Color Wheel," an article on classroom practice by Olivia Gude[21]

"How Skin Color Became a Racial Marker: Art Historical Perspectives on Race," a scholarly article by Anne Lafont[22]

Shades of Black: A Celebration of Our Children, a children's picture book by Sandra Pinkney[23]

6 Go back to students' side-by-side lists of associations with *light* and *dark*. Ask:

- Connect your side-by-side list with the castas painting. How do they both represent light and dark?
- What are the similarities and differences between the associations of light and dark?
- How do cultural meanings of light and dark change over time and from one place to another?

7 Make artworks responding to the challenge of creating new (skin) color associations that do away with hierarchical valuations anchored in a black-white binary. An example can be found in the children's book *Shades of Black: A Celebration of Our Children*. The various tints and shades that compose the spectrum of colors in Black people's skin are positively associated with delicious foods like chocolate, popcorn, and ginger cookies. The artwork of Byron Kim's painting *Synecdoche* takes a more abstract, non-figural approach (see Chapter 3).

Trope Bingo

Background Information

For consumers of media, visual racial literacy is imperative. An intentional and nuanced examination of racial tropes in the media can develop and nurture racial consciousness and help us become critical observers of content. The discussion of racial tropes and stereotypes in Chapter 3 should be revisited before and during this activity.

Guided Practice

1 Lead a class discussion about racial tropes and their historical origins, purpose, and impact as it relates to the development of racial hierarchies. (Revisit Chapter 3 content for support.)

2 Offer examples of racial tropes that span from early 1900s popular culture to present-day popular culture.

3 Pass out the laminated trope bingo cards and bingo chips.

4 Most movies, and even cartoons, activate some type of trope script. So, choose any G-rated movies that feature human characters from diverse backgrounds and your students are sure to identify at least one or more trope scripts being used. Ask your students to place a bingo chip on the racial tropes that they identify as they watch the clips. Continue playing movie clips until a student calls "BINGO!"

5 Have the student who called "BINGO!" share which tropes they identified in which movie clips.

6 Lead a class discussion about the tropes the student named. Discussion prompts include:
   - How might these images and characterizations impact the racial identity development of those represented?
   - What impact did these racial tropes have on how we perceived each other in real time?

Goals

- Identify and reflect on how beliefs about groups of people are conceived.

- Identify and reflect on how beliefs about people and the world are mediated by imagery.

- Make connections between what is represented in media and popular culture and what becomes belief and ideology.

Materials

- Pencil and paper

- Create a printable bingo card and enter various racial tropes listed in the trope characterization table in Chapter 3 (page 57). Print out and laminate enough bingo cards for each student to use.

- Bingo chips or any small objects that can be placed on a bingo card.

- Previewed movie clips that present very distinct racial tropes.

Pedagogical Principles

Protective care

Courageous witnessing

Chapter Connections

Social construction (2)

Visual racial literacy (3)

Racial iconography (3)

Whitestream media (3)

Racial tropes (3)

Identity (4)

Stereotypes (4)

Implicit biases (5)

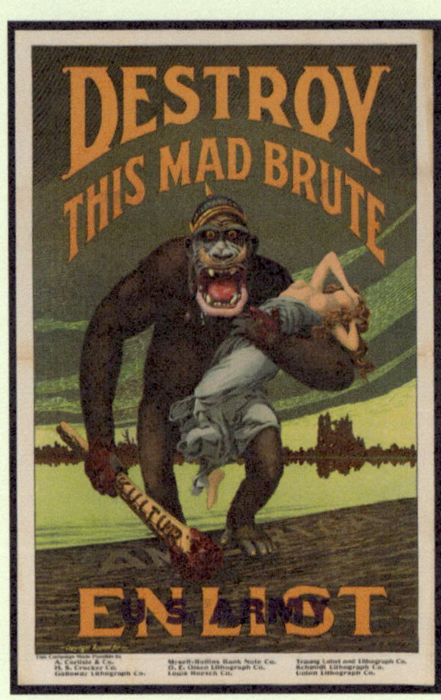

6.4 U.S. Army poster. Library of Congress.

7 Guide students through a brainstorming activity in which they list movies or television shows that present characters as multidimensional and intersectional. Have students describe how characters in the same racial or ethnic group demonstrate different behaviors in the movie/show over a sustained time. Further, ask students to describe the character traits that are outside of a trope narrative that they have seen before.

8 Ask students to write a reflection paper about a time when they applied a trope script to other people in real time. Have students reflect on how their tacit acceptance of certain tropes impacted their interactions with people from different racial backgrounds. Invite students to identify specific moments in time that have impacted how they make sense of their own differences and the differences of others. This final activity helps students conjure up flashpoints, which refers to "a heightened occasion arising from the activation of power that disturbs a seemingly fixed relationship."[24]

Extension

The 2008 cover of *Vogue*, which featured Black American professional basketball superstar and race activist Lebron James and Brazilian supermodel, actress, and activist Giselle Bündchen, received tremendous criticism of its imagery and conceptualization. National and international commentaries claimed racism and insensitivity to the historical association of Black people with monkeys.[25] Particularly, when juxtaposed with a vintage King Kong poster, the justification of the critique becomes stronger. The continuity of stereotyping and trope scripts are visually clear when these images are side-by-side, thus leaving readers to question the *Vogue* design team's explicit racism or their complete ignorance of historical iconography. Revisit racial tropes in Chapter 3, paying close attention to the research cited on page 64 that describes how the majority of U.S. American citizens still associate Black people with apes.

Assist students in generating interpretations of the *Vogue* cover. Using Stuart Hall's framework of preferred, negotiated, and oppositional "reading," students learn three strategies for identifying and articulating the way racial tropes are a part of the contemporary cultural milieu.

Ask, What is the **preferred reading** of this image? Explain that a preferred reading is when the viewer interprets the visual artifact in the way the producers of the artifact intended. In mainstream media, the dominant racial ideology (whiteness) usually frames the producer's preferred reading.

Ask, What is the **negotiated reading** of this image? A negotiated reading is when the viewer agrees with some aspects of the visual artifact's preferred reading but not all aspects. The emphasis in this reading is in negotiating contradictory interpretations that reflect, on one hand, preferred authoritative meanings and, on the other, meanings that represent a non-mainstream worldview.

Ask, What is the **oppositional reading** of this image? An oppositional reading is when the viewer formulates meaning that is in complete disagreement with the product's message or setting.

After completing preferred, negotiated, and oppositional readings of the *Vogue* cover, share the World War I propaganda poster "Destroy This Mad Brute: Enlist"[26] (image 6.4).

Alongside students, engage in a compare and contrast discussion of the two images. Explicitly identify the trope scripts that were used to orchestrate the imagery on the *Vogue* cover. Then pose the following questions to students:

- What questions do you have for the producers and designers of the *Vogue* cover?
- Who should take responsibility for the *Vogue* cover, the magazine's editor, the photographer, or the models in the photo?

Suggested Encounters

Disclosure, a film about the longstanding absence of transgender representation in media and film.[27]

Miss Representation, a film that exposes the ways that mainstream media contributes to the narrative that women should not be in positions of power or influence.[28]

Stuart Hall's "Encoding/Decoding" chapter in *Media Studies: A Reader* offers a comprehensive explanation on preferred, negotiated, and oppositional readings of texts (written and visual) and their complexities.[29]

Goals

- Interpret visualizations of race in the media.

- Make connections between what is represented in media and popular culture and what becomes social values and ideologies.

- Identify how stereotypes can be developed and sustained.

- Recognize the ways repetitive imagery in media impact understandings of self and others.

Materials

- Pencil and paper

- Pre-screened news clips of crime reports on different television stations

- Mixed media for collage making (e.g., magazines, construction paper, textiles and fabric, acrylic paint)

- Heavyweight mixed media paper for each student

- Printmaking materials (e.g., stamps, rollers, ink, stencil options, etc.)

Critical Race Scavenger Hunt

Background Information

Even news stories that are supposed to objectively detail criminal acts exhibit white privilege by using linguistic maneuvers that present White criminals in a more flattering, empathetic light than non-White criminals. Are you paying attention to the tools of the news media?

Refer to the discussion of implicit bias and deficit ideology in Chapter 5 before and during this activity.

Guided Practice

1 Lead a class discussion about implicit bias and deficit ideology, their origins, consequences, and impact as they relate to the development of racial equity. (Revisit Chapter 5 content for support.)

2 Play multiple news clips in which reporters present crime stories about people from different perceived racial identities. Try to find news clips for at least three different racial identities. Make sure that one of the clips presents a crime committed by a person with a perceived White racial identity.

3 Ask students to search for ways that the news media report on crimes differently depending on the perceived racial identity of the people involved. Be on the lookout for these common media maneuvers. How many examples can you find of each?
   - Prioritize White people's accomplishments, as opposed to non-White people's alleged crimes.
   - Present charming photos of White victims but incriminating photos of non-White victims.
   - Empathize with the motivation of White people who are "sheltered," "depressed," or a "loner."
   - Emphasize that the "hateful" White person acted alone, while casting non-White people as stereotypes of their race.

- Humanize the troubled lives of white supremacists, calling them mentally ill instead of examining other factors.
- Discredit justice movements for non-White people and give rioting White people a pass.
- Position non-White victims as at fault and White suspects as in self-defense mode.

4 Lead a discussion with students about their findings. Ask:
- How did you feel as you were doing the critical race scavenger hunt?
- What was most challenging or troubling, and what made it so?

5 Ask students to complete a seven-minute quick write in which they consider:
- What is the role and function of the media's skewed racial representations and communications?
- Is there a double-standard applied by the media when they pursue "truth," report on "reality," and present "evidence" in support of a particular story? Why might this be?

Extension

Have students engage in an art inquiry. Instruct them to use the news media examples from the scavenger hunt to create a critical race artifact.

Inquiry 1: How do white supremacist beliefs and assumptions that were once openly embraced by the public still exist in the forms of storytelling used by news media today? Employ mixed-media collage techniques to make visible the connections between past racial imagery and narratives and contemporary news images and narratives from the scavenger hunt. Present students with various media to use to create their artifact. Give each student a piece of heavyweight mixed media paper to work on.

-or-

Inquiry 2: How can the images and narratives circulated in the news media be re-encoded to challenge racial bias and

Pedagogical Principles

Political clarity

Protective care

Courageous witnessing

Chapter Connections

Social construction (2)

White racial privilege (2)

Racial prejudice (2)

Visual racial literacy (3)

Gaze (3)

Whitestream media (3)

Stereotypes (4)

Critical consciousness (5)

Deficit ideology (5)

Implicit bias (5)

supremacist ideologies? Artist Glenn Ligon works with historical texts and typography to create artworks that contest dehumanizing meanings ascribed to non-White people. Using Ligon's work as inspiration, employ digital scanners and editing tools to reappropriate the text or text-image combinations from the scavenger hunt into a printable work that speaks to racial injustice. Digital tools may also be used in combination with traditional printmaking techniques.

Gazing Back

Background Information

When teaching students to critically discern racist imagery, we connect historical examples with contemporary popular culture. The Hottentot Venus (see Chapter 3) is a prevalent racial trope that students will likely encounter in movies, television shows, and advertisements. The trope refers to 16-year-old Sarah Baartman, who was removed from her home in South Africa, enslaved, and transported to Europe around 1810. Baartman was dressed in feathers and beads and put on display to be viewed as a part of so-called "freak" shows. She was promoted as the "Hottentot Venus" for the entertainment of European onlookers, who took particular interest in her buttocks. Art historian and artist Deborah Willis notes, "We have only to look at contemporary culture to see the way in which Sarah Baartman's image continues to be recycled as fashion in the works of some contemporary photographers. . . . [I]t is this plethora of visual representation that makes her so significant, so enduring. What she represented visually—even exaggerated and distorted—had a much greater audience and extended life and impact than her physical self ever could have."[32]

The music video from singer Taylor Swift's hit single "Shake It Off" traffics in the trope by appropriating aspects of Black culture and Black women's bodies, or body parts rather. It offers a clear illustration of objectifying stereotypes that are formed at the intersection of a white gaze and a male gaze. The video stars Swift, a young, blonde, White American woman. Many students are already familiar with the catchy song, as many encounter the song as young children when watching the G-rated movie *Sing* (Universal Pictures). They often move their bodies to the beat while listening to and watching the music video. This aesthetic pleasure is part of how stereotypes are encoded to maintain currency in a new era.

Goals

- Recognize contemporary racial stereotypes in relation to historical tropes.

- Consider the relationship between racial stereotype and cultural appropriation.

- Critically "read" images for racial meanings.

- Distinguish between dominant practices of looking that appeal to a White (male) gaze and oppositional practices of looking that disrupt racial tropes.

Materials

- Pop singer Taylor Swift's music video for the single "Shake It Off" (available on YouTube)

- Historical reproductions of Hottentot Venus iconography (see Chapter 3)

- Tracey Rose's photographic artwork, *Venus Baartman*, 2001

- Senzeni Marasela's fiber artwork, *Covering Sarah*, 2009–2010

Materials, cont.

- Elizabeth Alexander's poem, *The Venus Hottentot (1825)*, with a recorded reading by the poet[33]
- Information about #SayHerName campaign[34]

Pedagogical Principles

Protective care

Courageous witnessing

Chapter Connections

Racial tropes (3)

Popular culture (3)

Cultural appropriation (3)

Identity (4)

Stereotype (4)

Guided Practice

1 Locate the frames in the "Shake It Off" video where Swift is dressed like the women dancing behind her, in thigh-revealing cut-off shorts with high top sneakers, a cheetah print cropped top, and large gold chains and hoop earrings. Looking toward us, the viewer, with eyes wide and mouth open, Swift gawks at the diversely hued women twerking behind her. Their rear ends are a spectacle, punctuated by a camera closeup of a Black dancer's derriere.

2 A number of concepts can be discussed in this video. However, we usually focus on stereotypes and instances of cultural appropriation that connect to racial tropes. Therefore, ask students what they know about stereotypes and generate a shared definition. Then, ask students to watch the video and look for evidence of stereotypes.

3 Compare the still frames from the "Shake It Off" music video with historical posters depicting the Hottentot Venus, a racist gender trope based on Sarah Baartman's likeness.

4 Introduce the concept of cultural appropriation (see Chapter 3). Ask students to look for and discuss evidence of appropriation in the historical images of the Hottentot Venus and the "Shake It Off" video. Practice using vocabulary when discussing these questions:
   - How is cultural appropriation related to racial stereotypes?
   - What audiences are these images meant to appeal to?
   - Who benefits from cultural appropriation?
   - What harm is done by appropriation?
   - Why do racial tropes persist?
   - Who has the power to intervene in cultural appropriation?
   - What is an appropriate response to appropriation?

5 Contrast the posters and video with these works that incorporate oppositional practices of looking to humanize Sarah Baartman and reappropriate the Venus Hottentot trope:

- Tracey Rose's photographic artwork, *Venus Baartman* (2001)
- Senzeni Marasela's fiber artwork, *Covering Sarah* (2009–2010)
- Elizabeth Alexander's poem, *The Venus Hottentot* (1825), with a recorded reading by the poet.

Return to some of the same questions:

- What audiences are these images meant to appeal to?
- What are the effects of reappropriation?
- What might these artists say about why this racial trope persists?
- Who has the power to intervene in cultural appropriation?
- What is an appropriate response to appropriation?

Extension

Go further by learning about #SayHerName, a present-day racial and gender justice campaign to re-humanize Black women by remembering individual Black women and girls who have been victimized by police violence. The campaign resists the white racial frame that renders Black women's bodies simultaneously hypervisible and highly consumable, yet invisible and, therefore, disposable. Artists have contributed to this movement through artmaking, posters and street art, auctions, and collective work within community organizations. Artists who have explored the humanity of Sarah Baartman and the power of Black and Brown women refusing the white gaze include Lorna Simpson, Deborah Willis, Hank Willis Thomas, and Simone Leigh.

Goals

- Learn the difference between cultural appropriation and cultural appreciation.

- Learn practices of critical questioning skills that embolden students to be curious about information and imagery.

- Understand the many ways blackface can show up in contemporary imagery.

- Identify the responsibilities of artists as producers of imagery.

Materials

- Pencil and paper

- Access to technology for internet research

"Trying On" Identity

Background Information

The practice of cultural appropriation impacts the lives and the futures of those whose culture is taken and altered, which are generally marginalized groups. When we consider who gets to appropriate culture, we should note the economic and social power that is aligned with that particular group of people and the longevity of that power. Artists have long debated the idea and validity of cultural appropriation, especially as it relates to artists being "inspired by" other artists and their practices of cultural production.

Nikki S. Lee, a Korean-born artist based in New York, is well known for her series titled *Projects*. In the series, Nikki immerses herself in different racial and cultural groups, eventually "trying on" the identity of the specific group. To transform, she experiments with her physical attributes (darkening her skin color, changing hair, applying stage makeup) in an effort to align her phenotype with those in the group in which she is immersed. Lee's series includes *The Hispanic Project*, *The Hip Hop Project*, *The Lesbian Project*, *The Schoolgirls Project*, *The Exotic Dancer Project*, *The Seniors Project*, and more. Lee has been heavily critiqued for her method of assimilation into racial and cultural groups for the purposes of her artwork. Refer to the discussion of cultural appropriation in Chapter 3 and racial identity development in Chapter 4 before and during this activity.

Guided Practice

1 Lead a class discussion about cultural appropriation, its historical origins, purpose, and impact as it relates to the development of racial hierarchies. (Revisit Chapters 3 and 4 for support.)

2 Conduct an internet search using the phrase "Nikki S. Lee Projects."

3 Alongside students, preview the images generated in the search. Together list the identities that you think Lee "tries on" in her photographs. It is important to make the list based on imagery alone; *do not look at the titles of the images.*

4 After you have compiled a list, refer to the image captions to find out whether the identities on your list align with Lee's representation.

5 Lead a class discussion with students that is attentive to Lee's choices around the characteristics she decided to adopt during her immersion experiences. Discussion prompts include:
  - Is Lee's performance of racial identity convincing?
  - In what ways does her art reduce race, ethnicity, culture and gender to particular clothes, posture, cosmetic adornment, and body type?
  - In what ways does Lee's work play into trope characterizations?
  - Did you find yourself referring to trope scripts to help you identify certain identities?

6 In her preliminary research of the groups that she would enter, Lee had a choice regarding which characteristics to adopt during her immersion. For example, in *The Hip Hop Project*, Lee surrounds herself with a particular "type" of hip-hop artist— those who fit inside her understanding of what hip hop looks like. Based on the images she constructed, Lee identified hip hop artists as bandana- and gold chain–wearing Black men who entertain an abundance of oversexualized Black women. Lee herself transformed into one of those women, darkening her skin with makeup, donning revealing clothes, and posing in ways that evoke sensuality. However, there are subcultures within hip hop that do not look and perform like those Lee chose to portray. So, the way that hip hop identity was fashioned is reflective of Lee's perceptions and decisions concerning the use of ethno-racial codes. This point can be made for any of

Pedagogical Principles

Protective care

Deep connection

Courageous witnessing

Chapter Connections

Essentialism (2)

White racial privilege (2)

Cultural appropriation (3)

Blackface (3)

Gaze (3)

Racial identity (4)

Lee's ethnographical "projects." Ask students to get into groups of three and attend to the following questions together:

- How do Lee's representations of certain identities affirm the white imagination?
- How do Lee's choices speak to her power to validate essentialized characterizations of certain people?
- Issues of cultural appropriation are forefront in critiques of Lee's work, and some critics even call her work modern-day blackface and brownface. Do you agree? Why or why not?
- Who gets to "try on" racial, cultural, and gender identity?

7 Lastly, ask students to complete a self-reflection writing in which they ask themselves:

- Have I engaged in cultural appropriation, thinking it was cultural appreciation? How would I know?
- What was the context in which I adopted another's culture?
- Was it for entertainment?
- In what ways did I honor the cultural item's (dress, hairstyle, practice) original intent if I wore it as an accessory (or practiced it for pleasure)?
- Is it respectful to alter its cultural meaning?
- Am I interested in understanding how and where the dress, hairstyle, practice, etc. originated?
- In what ways am I committed to supporting this culture in ways that do not benefit me?

Counter-Visual Strategies

Background Information

Cultural reappropriation is the process of recovering cultural texts (art, artifacts, ideas, rituals, language, imagery) that have been taken by those from the dominant culture for their own social, political, cultural, or economic gain. Reappropriation also happens when an oppressed group reclaims once pejorative texts that were meant to disparage their cultural community and shifts their connotation to be empowering.

Contemporary visual artists assume counter-visual strategies as a means for cultural reappropriation. To do this, artists use strategies such as:

- Recontextualization: the practice of taking items, colors, or ideas from their original, usual context and resituating them in an unfamiliar context.
- Juxtaposition: the practice of placing two or more items, colors, or ideas together that seemingly contrast, thus disrupting the original meaning of each and making a new meaning together.
- Abstraction: the practice of using a nonrepresentational set of styles to make reality external to the work.
- Repurposing: the practice of using items, colors, or ideas outside of their original, intended use.
- Reconfiguration of imagery: the practice of shifting or rearranging items, colors, or ideas to make something new.

Guided Practice

1 Lead a class discussion about daguerreotypes, their historical origins, purpose, and impact as it relates to the development of racial hierarchies. (Refer to Chapter 3 content for support.)

2 Present students with the original daguerreotypes of Delia and Renty (from Chapter 3) and ask them to describe what they see.

Goals

- Explore how artists use their practice to claim agency in the ways that certain bodies are represented.
- Identify how cultural meaning evolves through different interpretations, engagements, and negotiations.

Materials

- Pencil and paper
- Laminated copies of Carrie Mae Weems's *From Here I Saw What Happened and I Cried*, 1995
- Sticky notes (multiple pads)
- Push pins or tape for hanging work on the wall
- Vocabulary list of counter-visual strategies presented in the Background Information

3 Introduce the concept of counter-visual strategies and the tactics artists use to destabilize the power intentionally embedded in some images. Define the vocabulary terms presented in the Background Information. Utilize varying artists and their artworks to illustrate each counter-visual strategy.
Tip: Suggested artists for this task are listed in Step 7.

4 Put students in groups of two to three. Present them with laminated copies of Carrie Mae Weems's *From Here I Saw What Happened and I Cried*.

Weems used the aforementioned counter-visual strategies to resist dominant racialized meanings that are attached to Black bodies. Her work demonstrates the fluidity with which culture is constantly remade.

Give students sticky notes and ask them to identify the counter-visual strategies Weems used and how she used them. Have them place their sticky notes on the laminated copies of her work. Offer 8-10 minutes of work time.

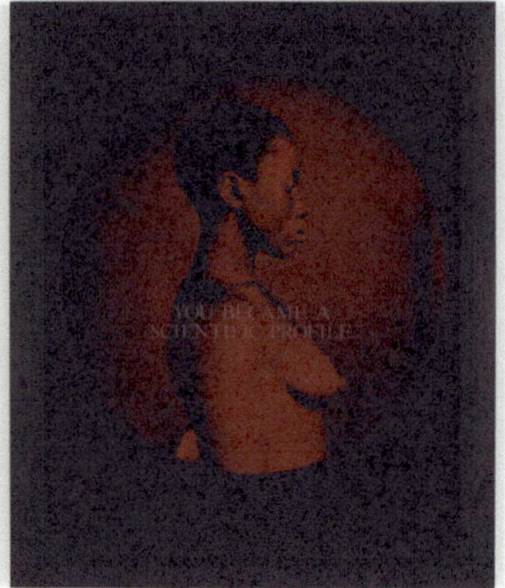
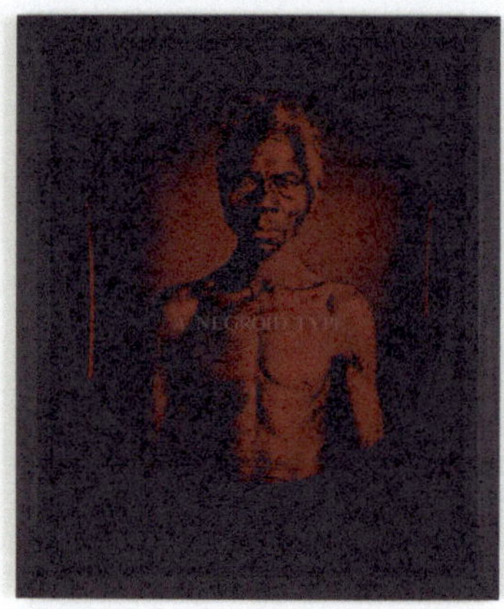

6.5 Carrie Mae Weems, *From Here I Saw What Happened and I Cried*, 1995. Chromogenic color prints with sand-blasted text on glass, 70.97.1 and .34: 42" x 31" (106.7 x 78.7 cm); 70.97.2-33: 26 5/8" x 22 3/4" (67.6 x 57.8 cm). Gift on behalf of The Friends of Education of The Museum of Modern Art. © Carrie Mae Weems. Courtesy of the artist and Jack Shainman Gallery, NY. Digital image © The Museum of Modern Art/Licensed by SCALA / Art Resource, NY.

5 Ask the students to hang their laminated copy of Weems's work with sticky notes in the room so other groups can walk around and view them. Have students pay attention to the similarities and differences amongst each groups' identification of counter-visual strategies.

6 Lead a discussion with students about the process of identifying counter-visual strategies and their impact on the original cultural artifact. Discussion prompts include:

- How did the meaning and/or purpose of the daguerreotypes shift with Weems's work?
- What questions might Weems be beckoning you to ask with her work?
- What makes you curious about Weems's use of counter-visual strategies?

7 What other artworks could be unpacked for their use of counter-visual strategies? Explore works by Byron Kim, Yong Soon Min, Hank Willis, Thomas Nicholas Galanin, and Michael Ray Charles. What do these artists have in common (artistically, socially, culturally)? How are they using counter-visual strategies similarly? How are they using counter-visual strategies differently? Can you identify a possible intention each of these artists may have had for their artwork? How does their work inspire you to be intentional in the goal creation and the decision-making process for your own artistic practice?

Goals

- Identify the role of art in renegotiating the distribution of oppressive visual imagery.

- Identify the function of counter-visual strategies.

- Identify the ways historical racial iconography shows up in contemporary popular culture.

- Identify how images in an environment can be racial microaggressions.

Materials

- Pencil and paper

- Digital versions of Betye Saar's *The Liberation of Aunt Jemima* and the 1935 Aunt Jemima Pancake Flour ad

- Multiple 8.5" x 11" printouts of *The Liberation of Aunt Jemima* and the 1935 Aunt Jemima Pancake Flour ad (enough for each group of students to have both)

Reclaiming Visual Representations

Background Information

Chris Rutt, the founder of the ready-made pancake mix "Aunt Jemima," came up with the product name and visual concept after watching a minstrel performance in which a White female actress wearing blackface sang a song titled "Old Aunt Jemima." "The song features a mammy, a racial stereotype of the Black female care-taker figure devoted to her White family. This image of supposed Southern hospitality inspired the hopeful entrepreneur."[37] Rutt and his business partner Charles Underwood filed a trademark for "Aunt Jemima" and attempted to sell the product nationally. After failing to get the product off the ground successfully, Rutt and Underwood sold the company and their recipe to R.T. Davis, owner of R.T. Davis Milling Co. Davis hired Nancy Green, a Black woman, to be a model for his newly acquired products. In line with minstrel iconography, Green was presented as a mammy trope on the original products. Over its 120-year lifespan, the product logo evolved from Green's face to a fictional Black woman who is presented as more contemporary, donning pearl earrings and a lace collar. However, the name and concept behind "Aunt Jemima" has remained.

Betye Saar, a Black American artist best known for her collage and assemblage work, uses found relics and ordinary objects to comment on the past while simultaneously considering the future. In her work *The Liberation of Aunt Jemima*, Saar recoups the mammy trope and replaces it with a multidimensional narrative about Black female existence. Saar's work counters the mammy trope by adding artifacts that compel her audience to accept a different story.

Guided Practice

1 Search the internet for Betye Saar's 1972 mixed-media collage *The Liberation of Aunt Jemima* (see image 6.7).

2 Alongside students, compare and contrast Saar's work with the 1935 reference image 6.6. This image can be found online by searching for "Aunt Jemima Pancake Flour, 1935." Note the similarities and differences between the two representations of Aunt Jemima. Be attentive to the 37-year time span between the original advertisement and Saar's work. Consider the evolution (or lack thereof) of the representation of Aunt Jemima.

3 Organize students into groups of three and pass out the 8.5" x 11" printouts of both the 1935 advertisement and the reproduction of Saar's artwork.

4 Ask groups to complete a three-step analysis.
  - First, identify and describe the *components* or parts of each image. No detail is too small. Descriptions may be written

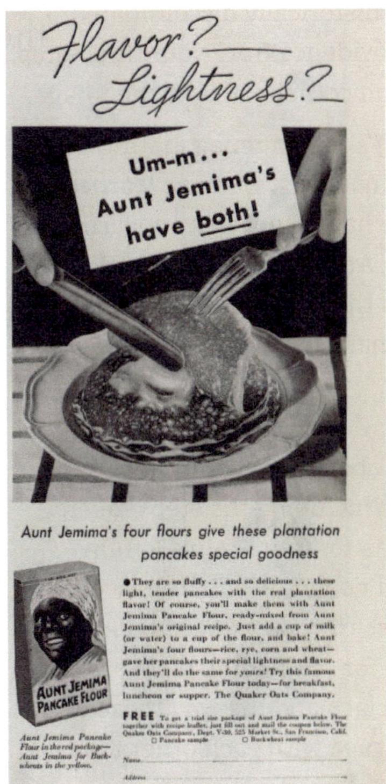

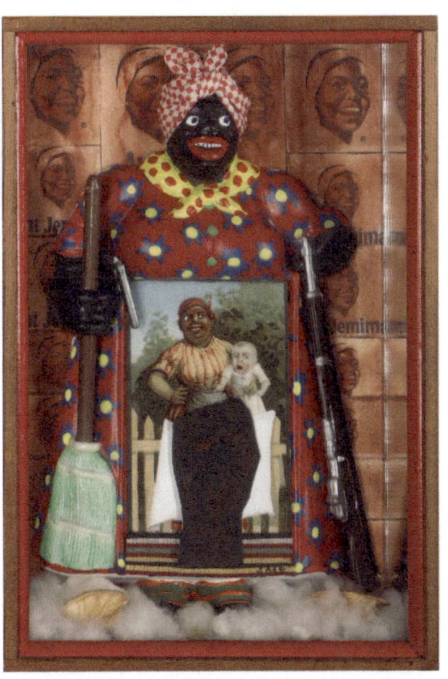

6.6 1935 advertisement of Aunt Jemima pancake flour. **Public Domain.**

6.7 Betye Saar, *Liberation of Aunt Jemima*, 1972. **Mixed media assemblage, 11 3/4" x 8" x 2 3/4" (29.85 x 20.32 x 7 cm). Collection of Berkeley Art Museum and Pacific Film Archive, Berkeley, California; purchased with the aid of funds from the National Endowment for the Arts (selected by The Committee for the Acquisition of Afro-American Art). Courtesy of the artist and Roberts Projects, Los Angeles, California. Photo Benjamin Blackwell.**

directly on the image reproductions either by marking or labeling the parts. Provide plenty of time for this step.

- Then, discuss how each part identified in the images *functions* as a cultural code that references particular associations, feelings, and connotations.
- Finally, identify the complex *relationships* between the parts that compose the images. How do the parts work together harmoniously or not? What meanings, messages or sensibilities are registered by the image? Point out and draw connecting lines between specific evidence to support your point of view.

5 To reflect on their analysis, ask students to complete a two-minute "quick write" in which they craft a response to the prompt:

In her attempt to reappropriate Aunt Jemima through her art, does Saar's work perpetuate the oppressive message that Aunt Jemima's stereotypical image has historically disseminated? Explain your answer using visual evidence from your three-step analysis of the parts, functions, and complexities of the image.

This activity emphasizes the artist's role in renegotiating the distribution of oppressive visual imagery. If we have learned about race and racism by what we have seen, we can learn about anti-racism by what we see. Artists are leaders in disseminating counter-visual images that help the world conceive new and more multidimensional narratives.

Extension

Lead students through a discussion about the evolution of Aunt Jemima's appearance over the years, including the steps taken in 2020 by food company Quaker Oats to "retire" Aunt Jemima as their logo. Does the evolution and now removal of the iconic image negate its racist visual origins? How do we reconcile this tension? This discussion is effective for scaffolding dialogue around tropes, minstrelsy, and blackface and the way these visual tools continue to impact how we engage with each other today.

Manipulating Media

Background Information

As discussed in Chapter 3, in 1850 Louis Agassiz hired artist Joseph Zealy to create daguerreotype photographs of enslaved non-White people to demonstrate that they were a separate species inferior to White people. He believed the images would provide scientific proof that different races of humans existed. Agassiz's photographs employed techniques of portraiture photography. His use of scientific methods alongside photographic techniques worked to dehumanize certain groups of people, globalize the white colonial gaze, and justify the practice of slavery.

A century later, Mamie Elizabeth Till-Mobley used photography in a different way. In 1955, her 14-year-old son, Emmett Till, traveled from Chicago, Illinois, to visit family members in Money, Mississippi. During the visit, Emmett, who was Black, was falsely accused of whistling at a White woman as she passed him to enter a store. This allegation prompted two White men to kidnap Emmett. They beat and shot the child before throwing him into the Tallahatchie River. The White assailants used barbed wire to tie a gin mill to his neck so his body would submerge in the river. When Emmett's body was found he was unrecognizable, having been brutalized and bloated from river water.

Till-Mobley recognized the power of the image of her dead child. Understanding the power of the gaze, she exploited it. She showed the world the violence that had been inflicted upon Emmett by insisting on an open casket funeral so photographs could be taken of her son's body. The images were widely circulated by individuals who attended the funeral. However, most notably, an image of Emmett's body was published in *Jet* magazine, a mass-produced publication described as "the weekly source of African American political and entertainment news."

In contrast to Agassiz's use of photographic images of naked enslaved people to dehumanize the subjects, Till-Mobley refused

Goals

- Understand the social construction of racial categories and the struggle over their meanings.

- Develop an awareness of the power of photographs to shape perceptions of reality.

- Center ethical problems in the representation of subjects.

- Learn about iconic photographs that have catalyzed racial justice movements throughout the 20th and 21st centuries.

Materials

- Venn diagram

- Photographs:

  - Joseph Zealy's photographs of Renty and Delia commissioned by Louis Agassiz in 1850s

  - Photographs Mamie Elizabeth Till-Mobley decided to publish of her son, Emmett Till, in 1955

  - The iconic photograph of Ieshia Evans taken by Jonathan Bachman in 2016

Materials, cont.

- Biographical resources such as:

  · *A Wreath for Emmett Till* by Marilyn Nelson[39]

  · *The Murder of Emmett Till: A Graphic History* by Karlos Hill and Dave Dodson[40]

  · *The Murder of Emmett Till* by WGBH/Firelight Media[41]

- Roll of paper, markers, rulers, glue, scissors, computer and printer access for creation of photographic timeline

Pedagogical Principles

Political clarity

Deep connection

Courageous witnessing

Chapter Connections

Technologies of looking (3)

Gaze (3)

Racial iconography (3)

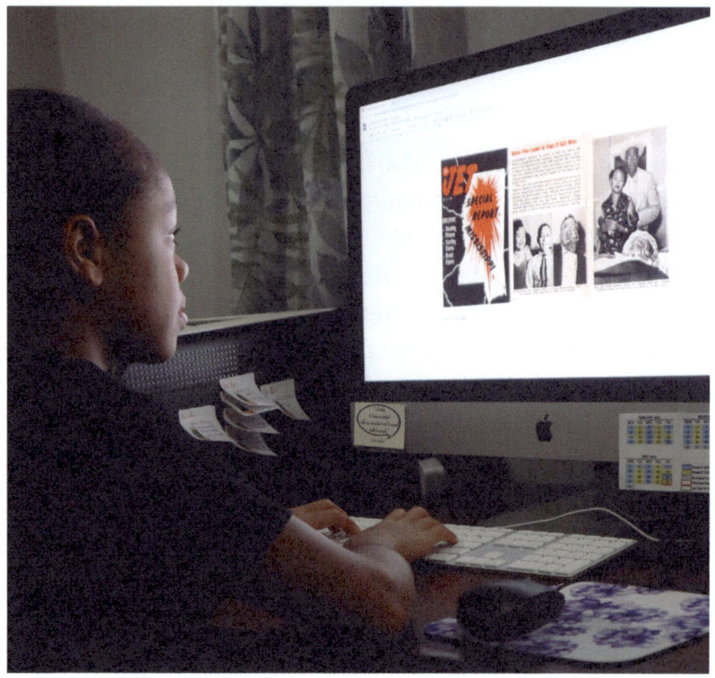

6.8 *Jet* magazine, September 15, 1955 issue, layout of Emmett Till story and images

to cover over the murder of her child, instead using photography to affirm the humanity of Emmett and, by extension, all Black and Brown people. In doing so, she helped catalyze the Civil Rights Movement, and the photographs have become iconic. This activity invites students to learn this important history and link race photography of the past to contemporary concerns driving global protests and social movements for racial justice and an end to anti-Black racism.

Guided Practice

1 Introduce students to the story of Emmett Till and Mamie Elizabeth Till-Mobley. Begin with a biographical sketch (such as the article "Who was Emmett Till?" by the WGBH Educational Foundation). Focus on his early years, the neighborhood he grew up in, his friends and personality before talking about the fateful trip that would end his life. Use respected resources that sensitively and accurately depict the traumatic racial events and the historical context in which they occurred. Excellent resources to use, in part or whole, include:

- *A Wreath for Emmett Till*, an illustrated children's book by Marilyn Nelson written as a series of 14 sonnets
- The graphic novel *The Murder of Emmett Till: A Graphic History*, a joint venture by scholar Karlos Hill and artist Dave Dodson
- "The Murder of Emmett Till," an episode in the television documentary series *American Experience* produced by WGBH/Firelight Media

Help students process their feelings about the story. If using Nelson's sonnets, ask students to draw the scene as you read aloud. If using Hill and Dodson's graphic novel or documentary, the "world of the work" technique can be used with one or more frames to focus on a moment within a racial event. This technique supports students in processing their feelings through imaginative use of their senses (touch, smell, taste, sights, hearing) and descriptive language.[42]

2 Compare and contrast racial photographs taken in different historical contexts so students can understand the concept of the gaze. A Venn diagram may be a useful tool for this.

The gaze is about the power of looking and representing a subject (see Chapter 3). Photographs offer a good entry point for learning about this power and how it is deployed across time through racialized looking and representation. As visual culture scholar W. J. T. Mitchell says, "The 'taking' of human subjects by a photographer (or a writer) is a concrete social encounter … [with] a relatively privileged observer, often acting as the 'eye of power.'"[43]

Racial photographs are an enduring feature of the modern world. From daguerreotype portraiture of the mid-19th century to print news media of the mid-20th century to mobile device

Suggested Encounters

I AM A MAN: Photographs of the Civil Rights Movement, 1960-1970 by William R. Ferris and Lonnie G. Bunch, III[44]

Seeing through Race: A Reinterpretation of Civil Rights Photography by Martin A. Berger[45]

Picturing Resistance: Moments and Movements of Social Change from the 1950s to Today by Melanie Light and Ken Light[46]

"33 Powerful Black Lives Matter Murals," a visual essay by Amelia Holowaty Krales and Vjeran Pavic showing the role of the arts in the racial justice movement for Black life[47]

digital images and video footage in the early 21st century, there are numerous options for comparing and contrasting racial photographs. We recommend selecting photographs from different time periods since the characteristics of a racial gaze can change from one era to the next. We also find it is generally easier for students to understand the concept of the gaze when analyzing photographs taken in a time or place that differs from their own. We suggest the following options:

Option 1: Invite students to analyze the gaze by comparing and contrasting Louis Zealy's photographs of Renty and Delia commissioned by Louis Agassiz in the 1850s (from Chapter 3) with the photographs Mamie Elizabeth Till-Mobley decided to publish of her son, Emmett Till. Note: Use your judgment as to the appropriateness of these photographs for your students.

Option 2: Invite students to analyze the gaze by comparing and contrasting the photographs of Emmett Till with the iconic photograph of Ieshia Evans, a mother from New York City who in 2016 traveled to Baton Rouge, Louisiana, to join protests against the extrajudicial killings of Black people. She stands stoically face-to-face with armed police in riot gear. The photograph is an iconic symbol of Black Lives Matter and other global movements for Black life.

Ask questions to support comparative analysis and race dialogue:

- What audience is intended or assumed in each instance?
- To whom would the photograph appeal?
- How are the subjects of the photographs perceived—by the photographer, the intended viewers, by us?
- Are there similarities or differences in those perceptions?
- What racial meanings help shape those perceptions?
- How is power being exercised and who is exercising it?
- How are photographic media manipulated?

3 Create a collaborative classroom timeline of iconic photographs that have helped catalyze racial justice movements. Begin by

asking students to recall any instances in which photographic imagery, including video, sparked a collective protest. Consider the evolution of social media like Twitter, Instagram, and Facebook. In what ways has the capturing and distribution of images impacted the larger society and movements toward racial justice? Name specific events and/or people who have been captured, shared with the public, and ignited collective action.

Contextual information is essential. If wall space is limited, this information can be treated as a flip-up element on the back of the photographs featured. Be creative in your approach. Display the timeline on the classroom wall as a tool to continue discussions about race and anti-racism.

You may not know where to begin. We suggest Gordon Parks's photographs are "must see" images; however, the work of lesser-known photojournalists and documentarians are important resources for understanding the changing styles, strategies, and uses of photography as well. Please see "Suggested Encounters" for great starting points.

Goals

- Connect past and present patterns of anti-Asian racism.

- Understand the role of portraiture in resisting racist narratives and raising awareness.

- Experience joy in the struggle for racial justice.

Materials

- News stories that document anti-Asian racism

- Jeff Wall's artwork *Mimic*

- Selections from primary sources: The Chinese Immigration Act, 1882, U.S. Library of Congress and Canada's Chinese Exclusion Act of 1885[48]

- The film *The Chinese Exclusion Act* from WGBH/PBS[49]

- Chinese exclusion posters

- Instagram portraits by artist Red Hong Yi

Anti-Racism Resistance Portraits

Background Information

In 2020, incidences of anti-Asian racism increased in the U.S.[50] The news media reported that a young family from Myanmar was stabbed, including children ages 2 and 6 years old, because the perpetrator believed they were Chinese and would spread the so-called "China virus," a racialized term used and promoted by President Donald Trump and fringe media to erroneously refer to COVID-19.[51] This is just one example of a broad pattern of racial events across the world perpetrated against children and adults who "look Asian."

It is part of a much longer history of xenophobia, exploitation, and violence against people of Asian descent. Alienation and demonization of Asian people is motivated by global white supremacy and nativist sentiment that casts White people as belonging and people of Asian descent as foreign, unhealthy, and dangerous.

Guided Practice

1 Resistance portraits have a long history among marginalized groups. Perhaps this is because they allow an artist to reframe how a person or group is seen. In essence, portraits are as much about the gaze as they are about the sitting subject.

Begin with a discussion of portraits: What is a portrait? Where have you encountered portraits? How are they made and what forms do they take? What is the purpose and significance of portraiture? What is the relationship between a portrait and reality? How do portraits influence perceptions of identity?

2 Share age-appropriate news stories of slurs or other forms of attack against people who "look Asian." Stories may be recent, as with COVID-19 pandemic-related violence and hate speech toward people who "look Asian," or they may be more historic, as in the murder of Vincent Chin in 1982 in Detroit, Michigan, by auto workers Ronald Ebens and Michael Nitz who, believing

Chin to be Japanese, attacked him for the success of Japanese automotive imports at a time when U.S. domestic car industry was in decline.[52] In the aftermath of Chin's death, artist Jeff Wall created *Mimic*, a cinematic photograph staged to depict a racial incident he witnessed in which a gesture of anti-Asian hatred was used.

Animosity toward people of Asian descent goes back even further in history.[53] Watch PBS's *The Chinese Exclusion Act*. Older learners may read excerpts from primary texts. Examples include the 1882 passage of The Chinese Exclusion Act in the U.S. and selections from Canadian officials in 1898 who falsely blamed Chinese communities for smallpox epidemics. Posters from that period also reflect the dominant anti-Asian narrative in which "the White man is on top." A mixture of these sources is preferred as it offers a richer context in which to view the systemic and protracted nature of white supremacy and xenophobia (racialization based on intolerance of people from other countries).

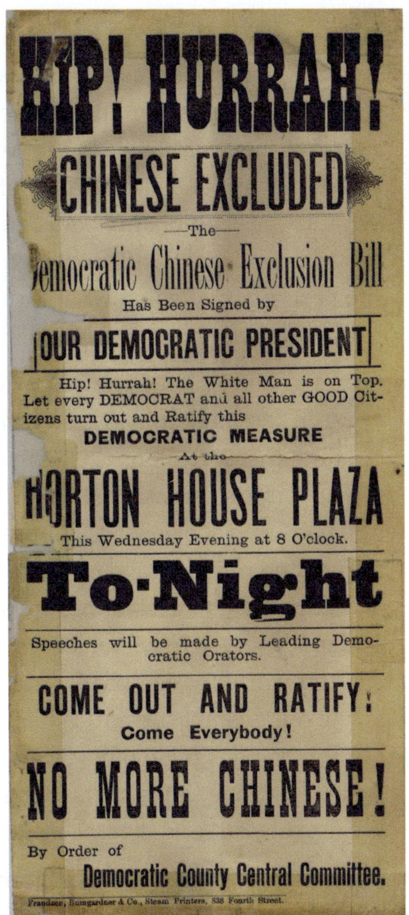

6.9 Poster in support of Chinese Exclusion Act. Image courtesy of the Royal BC Museum.

3 Against the backdrop of news stories, show artist Red Hong Yi's series of anti-racist resistance portraits in its social media context and lead an open-ended discussion. Revisit the questions raised earlier in relation to the series: What is a portrait? What is the purpose and significance of Red Hong Yi's portraiture? What is the relationship between the portraits and reality? How might the portraits influence perceptions of identity? How are the portraits made and what forms do they take? Why did Yi exhibit her work on social media?

4 Listen to Red Hong Yi's words to learn how she only recently became activated to resist racism: "Honestly, I was very hesitant creating this series on racism. Speaking about race makes me uncomfortable. Also, the world is now hurting, scared and confused. However, the more I hear about things like this happening the more I want to take a stance to fight this horrible 'disease' that is racism. I recognise that racism exists in every country, every skin colour. We must squash it so we can build a better world for everyone. I'm making this 10 piece series to speak out against the anti-Asian that is happening right now, but this applies to all of us (even Asians can be racist to fellow Asians!). I hope these posts inspire you to stand up for a more loving, tolerant and diverse world."[58]

5 Build connections to other contemporary or historic racial events by creating anti-racist resistance portraits that humanize people who historically have been racially stigmatized, demonized, excluded, displaced, or made the target of racist speech and physical violence. Portraits may be inspired by Red Hong Yi's artwork. Here are some things to think about and discuss along the way:

- Consider the location and audience for the work and how to bring viewers' attention to data and information about real-world racial injustices.
- Consider the materials. Each of Yi's portraits is composed of a different material she had in her home. She uses kitchen staples such as matcha leaves, fennel seed, candies, and rice

to create "paintings" that humanize her subject. The materials are
relevant to her personally and
culturally. When selecting materials,
avoid ethnic and racial stereotypes.

- Consider the format. Yi's choice of
how to apply the materials—tiny
granular specks accumulate until
they become fuller renderings—
exemplifies the cumulative effects
of everyday racism. The artist chose
to create a series of portraits in a
compositional format that echoes
the style of popular protest posters.
What does the stylistic connection
to protest posters suggest about the
power of art in collective movements
to resist racism?

- Consider the effect. What do you
want the artwork to do? Will it call
that viewer's attention to a specific
racist practice or marginalized
community? Will it humanize a
marginalized group and challenge
stereotypes? Will it inspire self-
reflection or solidarity?

Extension

What other artworks could be consid-
ered anti-racist resistance portraits?
Explore works created by W.E.B. Du Bois,
Harmonia Rosales, Roger Shimomura,
Nina Chanel Abney, Titus Kaphar, Wendy
Red Star, Jordan Casteel, Njideka Akunyili
Crosby, Kehinde Wiley, and many others.

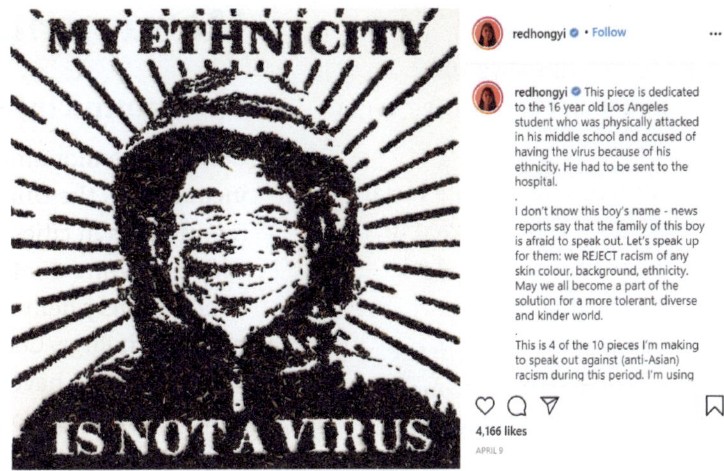

6.10 Red Hong Yi, From the series *#Iamnotavirus*, 2020. Black/purple rice. Courtesy of the artist.

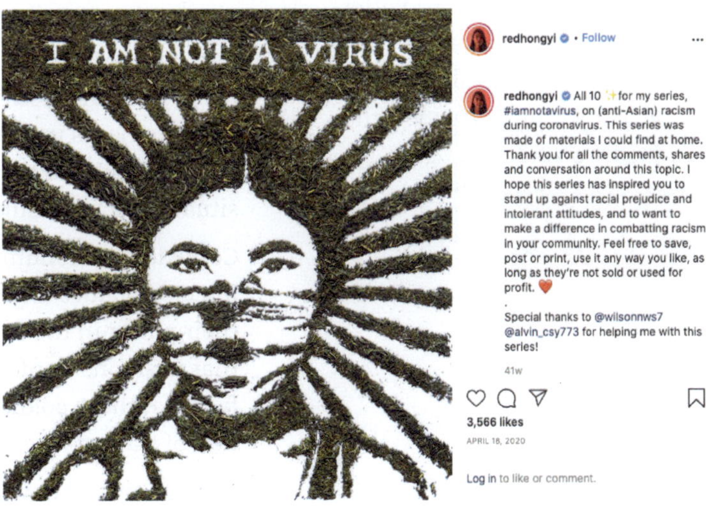

6.11 Red Hong Yi, From the series *#Iamnotavirus*, 2020. Matcha leaves. Courtesy of the artist.

Goals

- Identify the ways white supremacy is pervasive in our visual milieu.

- Recognize how white racial privilege is normalized in the seemingly universal American ideals.

- Understand how artists can renegotiate racial iconography through their work.

Materials

- Pencil and paper

- Printed copies of artists' work from "Building a Better Monument" or if any of the artists work digitally, have a way for students to view the media on a device

Monumental Art Problems

Background Information

Confederate monuments provide information about racial inequality in the United States. Specifically, erecting confederate monuments in cities all over the U.S. makes clear that the glorification of White Confederate soldiers supersedes the recognition of how slavery dehumanized and inflicted violence upon Black people writ large. Confederate monuments are representative of both those who have violently secured their economic and social power, as well as those stripped of their power. Thus, there is an ongoing debate about the continued development and public display of Confederate monuments throughout the United States. Confederate monuments were not built during the Confederacy (1861–1865) but were actually built during the 1900s. Even more, Confederate monuments and even the naming of public schools after Confederate soldiers increased dramatically during the Civil Right Movement in the 1960s. These actions are, in essence, racial microaggressions, as the timing of them directly aligns with advancements in black-white equality such as *Brown vs. Board of Education* and the development of educational frameworks situated around multiculturalism and ethnic studies.

Confederate monuments support collective memories that "reinforce the values and beliefs of those in power and help to project their power in the future."[59] These monuments embolden rhetoric that positions Confederate soldiers as heroes, which negates the fact that these soldiers' primary goal was to uphold the institution of slavery.

Artists can and have worked to change these skewed narratives. For example, artists like those in the exhibition "Building a Better Monument," curated by Seph Rodney, create artwork to memorialize the fallen and present anti-racist imagery that aims to "invigorate [non-White] futures."[60]

Guided Practice

1 Lead a class discussion about Confederate monuments. Use the following two articles as a guide for organizing the content:
  - "Monuments Outlive History: Confederate Monuments, the Legacy of Slavery, and Black-White Inequality" by Heather A. O'Connell[61]
  - "Confronting Hate: Ideas for Art Educators to Address Confederate Monuments" by Melanie Buffington[62]

Be sure to discuss the ongoing debate about the ways monuments "preserve history" and "represent heritage" rather than being symbols of white supremacy.

2 Introduce "Paper Monuments" as a collective artist intervention that honors the erased histories of people, places, and events. Emphasize the origins, values, and goal of the "public art and public history project."[63]

3 Organize students into groups of three. However many groups your class size makes, choose an identical number of artists from the "Building a Better Monument" project: Kenseth Armstead, Yelaine Rodriguez, Didier William, Yvette Molina, Tsedaye Makonnen, Jesse Krimes, Dominique Duroseau, Alexandria Smith, Jori Minaya.

4 Place each artist's name and a printout of their artwork on a separate table in the classroom. If there is a video, leave the URL and ask students to watch it on a device.

Ask students to complete a round robin in which each group gets to explore each artist for seven minutes. Ask them to answer the questions below. Each of the artists uses different strategies to tackle the concept of "monuments," so the diversity in answers will create a dynamic follow-up discussion.
  - Based on the artist's work, how do you think the artist defines "monument?"
  - Based on the artist's work, how do you think the artist identifies the function of a monument?

Pedagogical Principles

Political clarity

Courageous witnessing

Chapter Connections

Institutionalized racism (2)

White supremacy (2)

White racial privilege (2)

Racial iconography (3)

Willful ignorance (5)

Deracializing (5)

- In what ways does a monument's location and social context impact an audience's reading of it?
- In what ways does a monument's lifespan (permanent versus ephemeral) impact its ability to speak to or memorialize a person, idea, event, etc.?

5 After students complete the round robin, ask each group to summarize their observations, paying attention to major similarities and differences among artists' approaches.

6 Ask students to come up with some possibilities for creating a monument. Have them consider contemporary people, issues, moments, and movements that they believe need to be archived through a monument. Have students make a concept map to unpack content and context surrounding the person, issue, moment, or movement that they want to memorialize. Then, ask students to flesh out how they would create a monument that communicates the people, issues, moments, or movements to future audiences, even those who see the work a century from now. Ask them to consider what materials they would use and if sustainability is a goal for their work. How might the temporality impact the message?

Extension

Other historical objects that have been deemed sacred, like the American flag and the U.S. Constitution, hold similar lopsided collective memories. Black contemporary artist Mark Bradford's work *We The People* (2017) attends to the absence of Black humanity in the language of the U.S. Constitution. Learn about Bradford's *We The People* project in a video on the U.S. Department of State website.[66] In his large scale installation piece, Bradford is attentive to the preamble of the U.S. Constitution and investigates the language used to proclaim that "We," Americans, are rightfully due justice, tranquility, liberty, and prosperity. Bradford grapples with this historical proclamation and its (mis)alignment with the historical and contemporary treatment of Black people, as

Black people were deemed only three-fifths human when the Constitution was written in the late 1700s. Simply put, those with Black bodies were and arguably still are not included in the "We" of this sacred document. In addition, to date, neither explicit revisions to the document nor implicit acknowledgments have ever been spoken to include Black bodies in the "We," even though slavery and the establishment of Black bodies as property was abolished over a century ago.

To this end, Bradford justifiably asks, "Where do I fit into this document that was made when they weren't thinking about black bodies? They were thinking about black bodies, but not as humans with rights."[67]

How do Bradford's artwork and his postulations impact the presumed sanctity of the U.S. Constitution? Distorting excerpts and full articles from the U.S. Constitution, how does Bradford's artwork function to dismantle the symbolic power of such a "sacred" document?

Alongside your students, develop a list of additional artifacts, documents, ceremonies, and practices that we engage in in the U.S. that may uphold collective memories that are harmful to certain bodies and racial identities.

Withstanding the Journey

Now that you have engaged with a few learning activities aimed at activating visual racial literacy with students, we offer you some critical tips for sustaining the work. We hope these "tips for success" will guide and support you through your anti-racism journey.

Don't Fail to Begin

The easiest way to fail is to never begin. So, start where you are. Yes, it will be hard, but anti-racism is a lifelong process, one that begins with humbling ourselves around what we think we know about teaching and learning and what we believe to be "foundational" content for art education. At the beginning, it may feel like you are starting from ground zero, which is understandably quite daunting. But, with an ever-changing ecosystem, we all are starting over every day with new social and cultural contexts. So, get started by setting some short-term and long-term goals. However, make sure your goals are realistic and measurable. Make a one-year plan, a three-year plan, and then a five-year plan. This will give you some flexibility and time to grow, make mistakes, reflect, and start over again. And finally, find a place of comfort in never getting to "expert status."

Practice Makes ~~Perfect~~ Practice

Spanish surrealist painter Salvador Dalí famously said, "Have no fear of perfection—you'll never reach it."[68] Dalí was most certainly onto something. Find a home in practice, not perfection. Mistakes are a part of the process. If you attempt a lesson once and you are overcome by challenges the first time, plan to teach it again to the same students—but with revisions based on the first attempt. Or, if the first day of a lesson crashes and burns, start day one over the very next day. If you do feel the urge to stop, ask yourself, "Am I in a privileged position to be able to stop or pause my attempts at anti-racist teaching?" No one should be in such a position. In addition, you can find or create a practice circle in which art teachers gather to support one another by co-authoring and workshopping lessons, enacting them in their classrooms, and reflecting on the practice with one another. In discussion with Dan Harris, author of the book and podcast *10 Percent Happier*, meditation leader Turera Sala cites an ancient proverb, "If you want to go fast, go alone. If you want to go far, go with others."[69] This idea is simple. Share the weight of the practice with other teachers with similar excitement and goals for anti-racist teaching. Practicing together will help you sustain the work and forget about perfection.

Fall in Love with the Content

Review, review, review. Being comfortable with the material in this book will build the confidence needed to present information with clarity and assuredness and answer student questions, no matter how difficult. In Chapter 1, we named "complacency" as a pitfall to avoid while engaging with this book because anti-racist art pedagogy requires ongoing practice and tenacity. Our suggested activities are not linear and static. They connect with multiple and varying ideas and concepts throughout the book, so review the chapter connections included with each activity before engaging students in guided practice. Get lost in the materials and resources that are listed. Make the connections by knowing the connections. Reading, then reading again, is key.

Racist Events Are Teachable Moments

Anti-racist art pedagogy goes beyond the common practice of teaching the art lessons that have been planned for the day. Daily there are events that occur in our world that our students see, experience, consume, and can feel in their bodies as they watch them on television and through social media platforms. These opportunities for educating are even more important as they relate to race and racism because they function as a kind of public pedagogy. Watching racism play out in real time through state-sanctioned violence communicates that the structures that have been created to keep everyone safe regardless of color are faulty. Racist events, in society and in the classroom, that are left unaddressed will teach students that racial hierarchy and access to power is non-negotiable.

There Are No Make-and-Takes

Art teachers are often under pressure by administrators and parents to provide school hallway art, or refrigerator art that makes them feel warm and fuzzy. While there is a time and a place for one-day lessons that foster isolated technical skills or support carefree creative exploration, these activities are not those. Each activity in this chapter can span for days if not weeks. When being attentive to race in the art classroom, it is necessary to build time and care into all conversations and art practices that explore the topic. Building lessons that extend for long periods of time communicates that a topic is complex and important.

Also, falling into the same category of the make-and-take, is the trusty, go-to lesson "the replica." We caution teachers to not fall into the trap of copying media or subject matter of contemporary artists. This often happens when teachers and students rush to make something. Teaching in the spirit of abolition requires scaffolding that moves beyond imitating the surface features of an artist's work. Be inspired by artists' work but go beyond it by providing students plenty of time and structure to conduct their own research into racial events, share what they are learning with their peers, and develop their own responses to their learnings and conversations. This will help guard against superficial treatment of an artist's work and its subject matter.

Keep Going

Each activity in this chapter has an ending, but that should not indicate the learning is over. Developing and practicing anti-racist art pedagogy takes time; so does activating visual racial literacy with students. Therefore, the anticipated gains may be slow to appear. Track and field Olympic gold medalist Usain Bolt is quoted as saying, "I trained four years to run only nine seconds. There are people who do not see results in two months, give up, and quit. Sometimes failure is sought by oneself."[70] Like Bolt, art educators should always be in training mode, continuing to learn. This likely means putting in a lot of hours just to provide a quality 45- or 60-minute art lesson. This is to be expected because anti-racism is a long

game. Big impact cannot be achieved if you have made yourself a finish line. Racial justice has no finish line, no final state of completion. It is achieved in the act of running the race, in the transformations that occur along the way. So keep going. Keep believing in yourself. Have faith in your students' capacities. Above all, keep dreaming of a more just future and imagining the ways it is possible.

Notes

1   Paul E. Bolin and Kaela Hoskings, "Reflecting on Our Beliefs and Actions: Purposeful Practice in Art Education," *Art Education* 68, no. 4 (2015): 40–47; Mary Hafeli, "Knowing When to Step In and When to Step Back: 'Reading' Students as Developing Painters," in Judith M. Burton and Mary Hafeli's (eds.) *Conversations in Art: The Dialectics of Teaching and Learning* (Reston, VA: National Art Education Association, 2012): 51–68.

2   Lilia Bartolomé, "Beyond the Methods Fetish: Toward a Humanizing Pedagogy," *Harvard Educational Review* 64, no. 2 (1994): 173–194.

3   Tamara Beauboeuf-Lafontant, "A Movement Against and Beyond Boundaries: Politically Relevant Teaching among African American Teachers," *Teachers College Record* 100 (1999): 702–723.

4   bell hooks, *Teaching to Transgress: Education as the Practice of Freedom* (New York, NY: Routledge, 1994).

5   Bettina Love, *We Want to Do More Than Survive: Abolitionist Teaching and the Pursuit of Educational Freedom* (Boston, MA: Beacon Press, 2019).

6   Gloria Ladson-Billings, *The Dreamkeepers: Successful Teachers of African American Children* (San Francisco: Jossey-Bass, 1994).

7   Geneva Gay, *Culturally Responsive Teaching: Theory, Research and Practice* (New York: Teachers College Press, 2000).

8   Tara J. Yosso, "Whose Culture Has Capital? A Critical Race Theory Discussion of Community Cultural Wealth," *Race Ethnicity and Education* 8, no. 1 (2005): 69–91.

9   Django Paris and H. Samy Alim (eds.), *Culturally Sustaining Pedagogies: Teaching and Learning for Justice in a Changing World* (Teachers College Press, 2017): 3.

10 Roger I. Simon, *The Touch of the Past: Remembrance, Learning and Ethics* (New York: Palgrave Macmillan, 2005).

11 Eve Tuck, "Suspending Damage: A Letter to Communities," *Harvard Educational Review* 79, no. 3 (2009): 409–427.

12 Marit Dewhurst, *Teachers Bridging Difference: Exploring Identity with Art* (Harvard Education Press, 2018).

13 Sofia A. Villenas, "Pedagogies of Being with: Witnessing, *Testimonio*, and Critical Love in Everyday Social Movement," *International Journal of Qualitative Studies in Education* 32, no. 2 (2019): 151–166.

14 Kim Cosier, "What Can Art and Art Education Do in the Perilous Present?" *Studies in Art Education* 60, no. 3 (2019): 260–268.

15 Nathan Gibbs, "Crayola Monologues," animated video, 2003, https://youtu.be/dE2Iy0jCZwM.

16 Crayola, "Why Does the Color 'Flesh' Not Appear in the 1958 Limited Edition Box of 64?" online FAQ, https://www.crayola.com/faq/.

17 The Conscious Kid booklist, https://www.theconsciouskid.org/antiracist-childrens-books.

18 Band-Aid brand's 1955 television ad for "Neat, flesh-colored, almost invisible" bandages, https://youtu.be/MX8aK0ZsQHo.

19 "Art Supply Companies Contend with Racism as 'Flesh Tones' Come Under Scrutiny," *ArtNews*, August 27, 2020, https://www.artnews.com/art-news/news/art-supplies-racism-flesh-tones-1202697759/.

20 Philip Yenawine, *Visual Thinking Strategies: Using Art to Deepen Learning Across School Disciplines* (Harvard Education Press, 2013).

21 Olivia Gude, "Color lines: A Chicago Art Class Challenges the Racist Assumptions Behind the Color Wheel," *Teaching Tolerance* 19 (2001) https://www.tolerance.org/magazine/spring-2001/color-lines.

22 Anne LaFont, "How Skin Color Became a Racial Marker: Art Historical Perspectives on Race," *Eighteenth-Century Studies* 51, no. 1 (2017): 89–113.

23 Sandra L. Pinkney, *Shades of Black: A Celebration of Our Children* (Scholastic, 2006).

24 Amelia M. Kraehe and Tyson E. Lewis, "Introduction: Flashpoints—The Breakthrough of Sociocultural Difference," in Travis, S., Kraehe, A.M., Hood, E.J., Lewis, T.E.'s (eds.) *Pedagogies in the Flesh: Case Studies on the Embodiment of Sociocultural Differences in Education* (Palgrave McMillan, 2018): 1–14.

25 Harry Allen, "Monkey See, Monkey Doo-Doo: How VOGUE 'Honoured' LeBron James by Smearing Black People with White Supremacy & Gorilla Feces," Media Assassin, March 31st, 2008, harryallen.info/?p=363.

26 U.S. Army, "Destroy this mad brute: Enlist," Library of Congress, www.loc.gov/pictures/item/2010652057/.

27 Sam Feder (director), *Disclosure*, 2020, film, Field of Vision.

28 Jennifer Siebel Newsom, Kimberlee Acquaro (directors), *Miss Representation*, 2011, documentary film.

29 Stuart Hall, "Encoding/Decoding," in Stuart Hall, Dorothy Hobson, Andrew Lowe, and Paul Willis's (eds.), *Culture, Media, Language* (London: Hutchinson, 1980).

30 Media Matters for America, "Video: What Happens When Local News Over-Represents African-Americans As Criminals," https://www.mediamatters.org/legacy/video-what-happens-when-local-news-over-represents-african-americans-criminals.

31 The Heinz Endowments, "Portrayal and Perception: Two Audits of News Media Reporting on African American Men and Boys," 2011, https://www.heinz.org/UserFiles/Library/AAMB-MediaReport.pdf.

32 Deborah Willis, "Introduction: The notion of Venus," in Deborah Willis's (ed.), *Black Venus 2010: They Called Her "Hottentot"* (Temple University Press, 2010): 6.

33 Elizabeth Alexander, "The Venus Hottentot (1825)," https://vimeo.com/217929036.

34 #SayHerName campaign, https://aapf.org/sayhername.

35 Olivia Gude, "Postmodern Principles: In Search of a 21st-Century Art Education," *Art Education* 57, no. 1 (2004): 6–14.

36 Julia Marshall, "Five Ways to Integrate: Using Strategies from Contemporary Art," *Art Education* 63, no. 3 (2010): 13–19.

37 Miriam Fauzia, "Fact Check: Aunt Jemima Model Nancy Green Didn't Create the Brand," *USA Today*, June 30, 2020, https://www.usatoday.com/story/news/factcheck/2020/06/30/fact-check-aunt-jemima-model-didnt-create-brand-wasnt-millionaire/3241656001/.

38 Jim Edwards, "20 Ads That Changed How We Think About Race In America," *Business Insider*, February 11, 2013, https://www.businessinsider.com/20-ads-that-changed-how-we-think-about-race-in-america-2013-2?utm_source=copy-link&utm_medium=referral&utm_content=topbar.

39 Marilyn Nelson, *A Wreath for Emmett Till* (Boston: Houghton Mifflin, 2005).

40 Karlos Hill and Dave Dodson, *The Murder of Emmett Till: A Graphic History* (Oxford University Press, 2021).

41 Marcia A. Smith (writer) and Stanley Nelson (director), "The Murder of Emmett Till," in M. Drain (exec. producer), *American Experience*, Season 15, Episode 6, January 20, 2003, TV series episode, WGBH; Firelight Media.

42 George Geahigan, "Teaching Preservice Art Education Majors: 'The World of the Work,'" *Art Education* 52, no. 5 (1999): 12–17.

43 W. J. T. Mitchell, *Picture Theory: Essays on Verbal and Visual Representation* (University of Chicago Press, 1994): 288.

44 William R. Ferris, *I AM A MAN: Photographs of the Civil Rights Movement, 1960–1970* (University Press of Mississippi, 2021).

45 Martin A. Berger, *Seeing through Race: A Reinterpretation of Civil Rights Photography* (Yale University Press, 2011).

46 Melanie Light and Ken Light, *Picturing Resistance: Moments and Movements of Social Change from the 1950s to Today* (Ten Speed Press, 2020).

47 Amelia Holowaty Krales and Vjeran Pavic, "33 Powerful Black Lives Matter Murals," The Verge, July 5, 2020, https://www.theverge.com/2020/7/5/21304985/black-lives-matter-murals-round-up-artists.

48 "Chinese Exclusion Act: Primary Documents in American History," U.S. Library of Congress Research Guides, https://guides.loc.gov/chinese-exclusion-act; Canada's Chinese Exclusion Act of 1885, https://www.ourdocuments.gov/doc.php?flash=false&doc=47.

49 *The Chinese Exclusion Act*, WGBH/PBS, www.pbs.org/wgbh/americanexperience/films/chinese-exclusion-act/.

50 Angela R. Gover, Shannon B. Harper, and Lynn Langton, "Anti-Asian Hate Crime During the COVID-19 Pandemic: Exploring the Reproduction of Inequality," *American Journal of Criminal Justice* 45 (2020): 647–667.

51 Marc Ramirez, "FBI Says Texas Stabbing that Targeted Asian-American Family Was Hate Crime Fueled by Coronavirus Fears," *The Dallas Morning News*, March 31, 2020.

52 Curtis Chin and Tony Lam (directors), *Vincent Who? The Murder of a Chinese-American Man*, 2009 film, Asian Pacific Americans for Progress and Tony Lam Films.

53 Roger Daniels, *Asian America: Chinese and Japanese in the United States since 1850* (Seattle: University of Washington Press, 1990); Peter S. Li, *The Chinese in Canada* (New York, NY: Oxford University Press, 1998).

54 "Masked Kids," https://soundcloud.com/karin-patterson-148776835/masked-kids.

55 Asian Pacific Policy and Planning Council's "Stop AAPI Hate" campaign, https://stopaapihate.org/.

56 Center for Asian American Media, https://caamedia.org/films-and-projects/projects/asian-americans/.

57 Mae Yen Yap, "This Artist Is Creating a Series of Portraits Titled 'I Am Not A Virus' to Criticize Anti-Asian Racism," Mashable SE Asia, 2020, https://sea.mashable.com/culture/9997/red-hong-yi-criticizes-anti-asian-racism-through-series-of-art-portraits-titled-i-am-not-a-virus.

58 Red Hong Yi's Instagram, https://www.instagram.com/p/B-uGvTHj3xE/?utm_source=ig_embed.

59 Melanie L. Buffington, "Confronting Hate: Ideas for Art Educators to Address Confederate Monuments," *Art Education* 72, no. 1 (2019): 15.

60 "Building a Better Monument," curated by Seph Rodney, artintimeslikethis.com/building-a-better-monument.

61 Heather A. O'Connell, "Monuments Outlive History: Confederate Monuments, the Legacy of Slavery, and Black-White Inequality," *Ethnic and Racial Studies* 43, no. 3 (2020).

62 Melanie L. Buffington, "Confronting Hate: Ideas for Art Educators to Address Confederate Monuments," *Art Education* 72, no. 1 (2019): 15.

63 Loney Abrams, "'Racists Will Always Find Racist Ways to Be Racist': How Art Organization 'Paper Monuments' Is Creatively Replacing New Orleans' Confederate Monuments," *ArtSpace*, November 30, 2018, https://www.artspace.com/magazine/interviews_features/qa/racists-will-always-find-racist-ways-to-be-racist-how-art-organization-paper-monuments-is-55792.

64 Nikkole Hannah-Jones, *The 1619 Project*, audio series, *New York Times*, August 23, 2019, https://www.nytimes.com/2019/08/23/podcasts/1619-slavery-anniversary.html.

65 Caroline Randall Williams, "You Want a Confederate Monument? My Body Is a Confederate Monument," *New York Times*, June 26, 2020, www.nytimes.com/2020/06/26/opinion/confederate-monuments-racism.html.

66 Mark Bradford, *We the People*, U.S. Embassy London, art.state.gov/portfolio/we-the-people-mark-bradford/.

67 Anita Hill, "Interview: Mark Bradford: 'Everybody Should Have a Little Protection, a Little Cover, a Little Bit of a Net and Society Should Give It to Us,'" *ArtSpace*, August 12, 2020, https://www.artspace.com/magazine/interviews_features/qa/interview-mark-bradford-everybody-should-have-a-little-protection-a-little-cover-a-little-bit-56626.

68 Michael Elsohn Ross, *Salvador Dalí and the Surrealists: Their Lives and Ideas, 21 Activities* (Chicago Review Press, 2003): 22.

69 Dan Harris, "The 2021 New Year's Challenge," *Ten Percent Happier*, podcast, Session 17 with Teure Sala, January 20, 2021, https://www.tenpercent.com/challenge.

70 Dr. Crystal Laura, "Teaching with Tenderness: A Virtual Workshop," City Neighbors Progressive Education Summit, January 23, 2021.

Racial Literacy Glossary

ALLYSHIP when a person who is not the target of racism willingly stands with those who are and proactively takes on the problems borne of racial injustice as their own. It is more than caring about or wanting to help out a cause. Genuine allies are accomplices who co-conspire to end racism and repair the damage it has caused. (See Chapter 5.)

ANTI-RACIST a stance that refuses to accept and actively disrupts the societal norms that privilege the ways of whiteness. (See Chapter 5.)

ANTI-RACIST PEDAGOGY a commitment to understanding and grappling with racism in classrooms and in one's own life as teacher. It is a clear-eyed stance against racism that aims to tear down educational systems that maintain racial inequality and replace them with new ways of teaching and learning that support an egalitarian society, thriving communities, and education as a practice in freedom. (See Chapter 5.)

ASSETS-BASED APPROACH an intentional focus on the strengths of not only the child but the child's cultural community. Teachers should ask "What is present in this child that can be built upon?" instead of "What is missing in this child that needs to be fixed or attended to?" An assets-based approach perceives diversity in thought and culture as positive assets, not challenges. Teachers can use student assets as starting points for curriculum and instruction. The explicit shift in a teacher's focus to hope instead of despair can affirm students' humanity and support their potential in the classroom. (See Chapter 5.)

BLACK/WHITE BINARY a way of thinking and talking about race that assumes Black and White are the only racial categories that matter. (See Chapter 4.)

COLORBLIND IDEOLOGY argues that all people are the same, regardless of race, and thus should all be treated the same. While colorblind ideology attempts to support equality, in actuality, it suppresses equity and attention to difference. Failing to acknowledge the race, and thus the racialized lived experiences, of students in the classroom means there is no attention given to students' individual needs. Students from different racial backgrounds have different lived experiences and different circumstances that impact their educational experience. Not recognizing the unique needs of students, based on their racialized lived experiences, is negligent. If you don't see color, you fail to see discrimination on the basis of race. People who subscribe to colorblind ideology often engage in forms of colorblind racism. (See Chapter 4.)

COLORBLIND RACISM the practice of denying racism based on the belief that racism no longer exists, yet continuing to behave in ways that support racialized structures. The concept of "non-racial" denies that race is at the crux of the systemic inequalities experienced by non-White people. Rhetorical maneuvers, such as using words like "culture" and "ethnicity" instead of race, are used to deny that race has a central place in discussions of equality. These tools of whiteness actually confirm racism's place in the world. The deracialization of bodies is most often done by those in privileged racial positions (i.e., White Northern Europeans). Groups of people who are systemically impacted by their race do not have the opportunity to "not see color," as race mediates every aspect of their lives, all day, every day. (See Chapter 4.)

CRITICAL CONSCIOUSNESS an awareness of structural causes of social problems that is awakened every time we pose questions that get at root causes of everyday living conditions. An uncritical awareness of social problems leads to the acceptance of dominant ideas as truth. Recognizing, naming, and interrogating white supremacy are ways of practicing more critical consciousness. (See Chapter 5.)

CULTURAL APPROPRIATION the practice of using, borrowing, or "taking" another culture's intellectual property, cultural expressions, artifacts, history, and ways of knowledge. Cultural appropriation becomes problematic when the group being "taken" from has been marginalized and even oppressed for having specific cultural habits and ways of being, but once these cultural habits and ways of being have been adopted by the dominant group, then these traits are accepted and even desired. (See Chapter 3.)

DEFICIT IDEOLOGY the belief that achievement gaps and other inequalities result from individuals' intellectual, cultural, familial, or moral deficiencies, not from social inequalities such as institutional racism or economic injustice. (See Chapter 5.)

DERACIALIZING ignoring race when race was implicated in situations. (See Chapter 5.)

DISIDENTIFICATION a process of distancing and dissociating the self from a social position or cultural type as it has been defined, practiced, and valued in the dominant discourse. (See Chapter 4.)

ECOLOGICAL APPROACH viewing art learning not in isolation but instead as a reciprocal interaction between what happens with learners in art classrooms and the dynamics taking place in the broader physical, ideological, and economic environment. This enables art teachers to understand how they and the students they teach are part of a larger network or web-like system of relationships that produces racial inequalities. (See Chapter 4.)

ESSENTIALISM the idea that objects have stable intrinsic qualities or an "essence" that make them what they are. (See Chapter 3.)

GAZE the dynamic or relationship (of power) in which looking and being looked at takes place. It is a social understanding through which individuals' thoughts, emotions, and behaviors are filtered. A shared gaze enables members of a group to make sense of the world and to derive meaning in roughly similar ways. (See Chapter 3.)

IDENTITY an ongoing and dynamic psycho-social process in which individuals fashion themselves and form a sense of belonging (or non-belonging) on the basis of visible traits and behaviors that mark the body and the culturally meaningful representations and narratives that frame reality and give certain bodies power, status, and privilege. Identity is not a one-time process. It must be articulated and performed repeatedly over time. That repetition, if reinforced by others through recognition of me as the kind of person I imagine myself to be, can calcify into a durable and stabilizing identity. Identity is, therefore, not who we are but rather a process of becoming that we participate in each day through social interactions and cultural associations with others. (See Chapter 4.)

IMPLICIT BIASES deep-seated, pervasive beliefs, mental images, and assumptions that combine to form stereotypes that impact thinking and guide behavior on an unconscious level. While unconscious in nature, implicit biases cause humans to pay more attention to things that confirm and justify their beliefs, regardless of whether they are situated in fact or reality. Implicit biases are essentially mental shortcuts that we take to save time and make quick decisions. Unfortunately, at times, these shortcuts are based on race. (See Chapter 5.)

INSTITUTIONALIZED RACISM the ways in which racism manifests in the day-to-day operations and outcomes of institutions and laws. Examples include redlining, gerrymandering, convict-lease system, and vagrancy laws. (See Chapter 2.)

MERITOCRACY the belief that social and economic power is earned by individuals who work hardest, develop their innate talents, and excel based on personal achievements alone. (See Chapter 4.)

NEGATIVE STEREOTYPE THREAT a phenomenon in which stereotypes are internalized and become an impediment to student learning and engagement. Research shows that when a person identifies with a group that is the target of a negative stereotype, the stereotype can actually undermine that person's performance in measurable ways. When a negative stereotype is connected to the racial group a person identifies with, their desire to ward off that stereotype may impact their ability to self-define, engage with people, and perform tasks in ways

that are authentic to them. Unfortunately, negative stereotype threat can result in people trying to distance themselves from central aspects of their identity or even their racial group. (See Chapter 4.)

NON-RACIST a complacent stance that is satisfied with and uncritical of the way things are. It gives a wink and a pass to racial injustice. (See Chapter 5.)

ONLINE RACIAL DISCRIMINATION denigrating or excluding individuals or groups on the basis of race through the use of symbols, voice, video, images, text, and graphic representations. (See Chapter 3.)

RACE an idea that was invented by influential thinkers in Europe in the 17th century that identified, described, and classified human beings according to a hierarchy of distinct types or species based on visible traits, such as skin color, hair texture, skull size, facial features, and other bodily characteristics. Race is often called a social construction because it is based not on nature or biology, but rather finds its origins in European and Euro-American beliefs in the superiority of so-called White people and a racial hierarchy that places lighter-skinned people at the top, as fully human, and darker-skinned people at the bottom, as less than human. As part of Western European conquests in Africa, Asia, and the Americas, the idea of race was imposed on colonized peoples. Although it has been debunked by genetic science, the myth of race nonetheless persists as a global phenomenon. (See Chapter 2.)

RACE TALK an explicit discussion about race and racism that aims to introduce children to and inform them about physical and symbolic racial violence. (See Chapter 4.)

RACIAL BATTLE FATIGUE the cumulative stress caused by racism. Usually experienced by non-White people, racial battle fatigue can cause individuals to lose confidence in themselves and question their life's work and even, tragically, their life's worth. It is not uncommon for non-White people to experience race-based trauma so often that it induces racial battle fatigue. (See Chapter 5.)

RACIAL ICONOGRAPHY a visually encoded system of images that communicates dominant racial ideas and narratives of racial hierarchy. (See Chapter 3.)

RACIAL LITERACY the capacity to recognize, decode, and critically interpret the various forms and methods by which racism is communicated, from overtly vicious to polite expressions (See Chapter 3.)

RACIAL MICROAGGRESSIONS the subtle slights, put-downs, and questions of competence that reflect implicit biases of individuals and institutional norms. (See Chapter 5.)

RACIAL PREJUDICE preconceptions and biases about people on the basis of their perceived racial identity. (See Chapter 2.)

RACIAL TROPES an overused rhetorical device or visual image that is created for the audience to easily recognize a concept or character. More specifically, racial tropes are stereotypical representations of people that contribute to the durability of race over time. Racial tropes in media, especially film and television, can be persuasive, as they produce cultural memory and implicit knowledge. They consist of characters and storylines that are static and recurring. Historically, the racial characterizations of non-Whites are generally disparaging. Racial tropes fuel cultural stereotypes with sociocultural consequences for those group members in real time. (See Chapter 3.)

RACISM a system of inclusion and exclusion, privilege and disadvantage, domination and subordination based on racial categories. Racism is a relational system; its forms and targets can shift, depending on relationships or hierarchies of power in a given context, to create and reinforce unequal economic, political, and social power. Racism results in the systematic oppression of groups and individuals who find themselves on the downside of the power relationship. (See Chapter 2.)

SCHOOL-TO-PRISON PIPELINE a system in which Black, Indigenous, and other non-White students are treated more harshly than White students, creating a funnel for them from the classroom to the juvenile and criminal justice system. In this case, a prison sentence does not begin when a person commits a crime as an adult; it begins when a child is profiled in the preschool classroom by a teacher, principal, or school counselor. (See Chapter 5.)

SOCIAL CONSTRUCTION a set of beliefs, ideas, and assumptions people share about reality. (See Chapter 2.)

STEREOTYPES fixed, overgeneralized beliefs constructed by persistent stories, images, or ideas about people's personality, ability, and dispositions. While stereotypes can be connected to some aspects of truth, they are most often erroneous in that they can become blanket expectations for whole groups of people, leaving little room for them to be anything outside of that stereotype. (See Chapter 4.)

TECHNOLOGIES OF LOOKING the modes and processes by which ideas and social relations are made visible. (See Chapter 3.)

VISUAL RACIAL LITERACY knowledge and skills that enable a person to recognize, critically interpret, and respond to visual codes, conventions, representations, and technologies used to prop up the myth of race and racial hierarchy. (See Chapter 3.)

WHITE FRAGILITY when those who perceive themselves to be White become defensive, angry, withdrawn, or consumed with guilt in peer-to-peer discussions about racial privilege. This emotional response is triggered by discomfort and stress. White fragility is often accompanied by tears that can indicate a need for more practice and stamina in difficult conversations about race. (See Chapter 5.)

WHITE RACIAL PRIVILEGE the unearned and often invisible economic and psychological advantage that attaches to people who are perceived as White and, to some degree, people who engage in cultural practices that are associated with whiteness. White racial privilege is not something that an individual necessarily asks for or is even aware of. It is the complex of economic, social, and symbolic resources owing to race ideology that are embedded within laws, social institutions, and culture more broadly. A person does not need to espouse racist views or hurl racist insults to benefit from the unearned advantages of racial privilege or for others to be harmed by it. (See Chapter 2.)

WHITE SUPREMACY a system of human hierarchy based on: (1) a belief in an innate moral, intellectual, and cultural superiority of persons perceived to be White, and (2) a set of tacit norms and explicit rules that prove mostly beneficial for White-identified people. (See Chapter 2.)

WHITESTREAM MEDIA a concept that properly recognizes that White men have held nearly exclusive rights over the production, distribution, and even cultural criticism of media. This has resulted in the creation of certain aesthetic preferences and value judgements that show the viewing public who and what is normal, desirable, loathsome, and worth looking at. White men who hold media power have been able to place their own subjective views of the world at the forefront. They have created a visual environment within which others must operate. (See Chapter 3.)

WHITEWASHED describes renderings that are reductive and limited in scope. Ideas and images are considered whitewashed when they are conceptualized without the consideration of non-White people or the narratives that derive from their experiences and perspectives. (See Chapter 3.)

WILLFUL IGNORANCE is a non-racist tactic. It is used to absolve oneself of responsibility for dealing with racism. When people avoid learning about the construction of race and racism's detrimental impact on non-White communities, they are engaging in an act of willful ignorance by choosing to be uninformed. (See Chapter 5.)

Index